Michael Matthews was a police o[fficer for] twenty years. He spent fourteen w[orking] including eight years at Scotland Y[ard]. He has [worked] across the US, spending time w[ith a large number of police] departments and law enforce[ment agencies, and has vast] experience with many different aspects of policing. He is considered an expert on US and UK policing, and has appeared on television and radio around the world.

American Ruin is Michael's third book. His first, *We Are the Cops*, is a collection of stories gathered from American police officers. His second, *The Riots*, is a fast-paced narrative on the devastating 2011 English riots, told from the point of view of frontline police officers.

Michael now lives in Canada but continues to spend time in the US and UK.

AMERICAN RUIN

RUIN

Life and Death on the Streets of Detroit –
America's Deadliest City

Michael Matthews

SILVERTAIL BOOKS • *London*

For Lisa

Some details have been changed for legal or privacy reasons. Some dates, times and order of events have also been changed, for readability and flow. The incidents that I have described, however, happened exactly the way that I have told them.

'Out beyond ideas of wrong-doing and right-doing, there is a field. I'll meet you there.'

Rumi (13th-century Persian poet)

Contents

Author's Note

Over the 15 years that I have been visiting the Detroit Police Department, I have accompanied uniformed officers on patrol, chased after stolen vehicles, been on multiple narcotics raids and attended numerous homicide scenes. I have also seen many changes: chiefs have come and gone, some officers have been promoted, some have retired, some have been fired and some have been imprisoned.

Most recently, I was granted unrestricted access to the department so that I could write this book. No one else, I was told, has ever been afforded that level of access before. Part of the reason for this was because I myself had been a police officer, but it was also down to the number of years that I had been visiting the city and the department. The people here knew me – and there was a level of trust that might not have existed for somebody else. They knew I had no kind of agenda, and they also knew I would be writing the truth. It has been a great privilege to be able to get to know a group of police officers far more intimately than I ever could through a single ride-along or a short interview; this unique opportunity has helped me to understand and to present Detroit in an equally unique way.

Over the years, I have also come to know local people who, despite their challenging circumstances, have been welcoming, inquisitive and friendly. Most fascinating of all for me was getting to know gang members. It took some time, but eventually I could drive to a gang neighbourhood on my own to meet up with former members, who would then introduce me to others. Before long, I developed many great connections and gained a number of good, and sometimes unexpected, friends.

Detroit is a place I have come to know intimately and which I have grown to love. My relationship with the city hasn't been fleeting or random; it is a solid, emotional, and genuine bond.

This city, with all of its problems, is the place that I came back to time and again – and not just in person but also in my thoughts and dreams, for there have been times over the years when I have thought about little else.

In this book, I want to introduce the Detroiters – good people trying to get by in the most desperate and dangerous of places. I shall write about the men and women of the Detroit Police Department – an underpaid, under-funded and under-equipped force – who are some of the best cops I have ever met, and who step out every day to protect those same good citizens. Their dedication is inspiring and their sacrifice can be heart-breaking.

This book does not mark the end of my relationship with Detroit but is instead the culmination of all the years that I have been coming here. 'The D', as Detroit is sometimes known, will always be part of my life – and I wouldn't want it any other way.

Why, then, call the book *American Ruin*? The word 'ruin' may seem obvious, unsubtle and even unfair to the people working hard to revitalise Detroit, as well as to locals who live in hope of great improvements to their city. Possibly even offensive, too. In fact, I was warned that the title would draw criticism because some people would feel that by using that word I would be kicking the city in the teeth just as it was trying to get back on its feet.

So let me explain why I chose it. I fully expected some people to believe the title was a reference the city's blight but I can tell you that it is not. The 'ruin' I am talking about is the generations of Detroiters – in particular, the children – who have been killed, abused, neglected and who suffered and continue to suffer through no fault of their own.

The kids here say, 'The struggle is real,' and for them it is. The issues they face are not just a Detroit problem – nor just an American problem, for that matter – but they are bigger in Detroit than in any other place I have visited, and I have visited dozens and dozens of cities across America. The stories I heard from Detroit kids, the wrongs committed against them (criminal as well as political), the desperate conditions I have witnessed in their decaying neighbourhoods, their homes, within their families and in their schools, are truly heart-breaking. That is the ruin that I am talking about.

As I mentioned, I love Detroit. I believe that to care about a place means speaking about what is wrong with it as well as what is right, in the hope that those wrongs can be fixed. Furthermore, highlighting the negatives is, I would argue, more important than shouting about the positives. This book is not a cheap shot at the City of Detroit. It is a truthful portrait of a certain time and place in the extraordinary history of this great city.

Michael Matthews, 2019

1

'Welcome to Detroit, America's Comeback City!'

These were the words I read as I arrived at Detroit International airport. The claim – 'America's Comeback City' – interested me a great deal, since the day after I had booked my flight to Detroit, a friend had sent me an online link to an article listing the 20 most deadly places in America. I scrolled through them, starting at Number 20 (Miami, Florida) then past others that could have been guessed at (Washington DC and Baltimore) and others that were more surprising (New Haven, Connecticut) until I reached the Number 1 most deadly place in America: *Detroit, Michigan.*

Detroit has been close to the top of these types of lists for decades. So, 'Comeback City'? This was a vastly different message from times gone by, when locals had taken to putting up 'welcome' signs of their own at the city's borders: *Warning! This city is infested by crackheads. Secure your belongings and pray for your life. Your legislators won't protect you!* And: *Welcome to Detroit. Do you feel lucky?* with the image of a gun barrel pointing towards the viewer.

I thought about a spoof tourism video I had once seen, purporting to be from Cleveland, Ohio, another city with big problems: *Cleveland! At least we're not Detroit!*

*

Recent statistics reveal that in Detroit there are 2,052 violent crimes per 100,000 of the population – over five times the US national average. 'Violent crimes' are classed as murders, rapes, robberies and assaults; in America, one violent crime is said to occur approximately every 30 seconds, with a murder every 30 to 40 minutes. In 2015 the murder rate in Detroit was almost nine times higher than the US as a whole. Back in 2012, when population size was taken into account, Detroit was recording a murder rate more than *ten times higher* than New York City.

These figures are shocking. However, the tide is beginning to turn. Detroit has recently experienced some of its lowest crime rates for decades. Detroit Chief of Police James Craig chose to be realistic about the drop; he didn't call it a 'success' but he did call it 'progress'. In 2009, mayoral candidate Stanley Christmas put it another way when he said, 'I don't mean to be sarcastic, but there just isn't anyone left to kill.'

*

American policing has long fascinated me. As a teenager in the genteel suburbs of north-west London, I spent my spare time watching American movies and TV shows, most of which seemed to have some crime and police element, and soon convinced myself that a future in American law enforcement was the life for me. My dad had been a policeman in London and in turn I became a police cadet, but the British police just didn't compare to what I had seen onscreen. Policing in America looked like the most exciting, crazy, fun job there could possibly be. The American cops (even the word 'cop' seemed fantastically cool) with their guns, sunglasses, squad cars, chewing tobacco and attitude, were everything that the mundane British bobbies, with their buttoned-up tunics, awkward-looking helmets, wooden truncheons and Panda cars, emphatically were not.

So, as I neared the required age, I picked up the phone and called the American Embassy in London to enquire about becoming a cop with the NYPD. It was a short conversation. When the baffled woman on the other end of the line asked me if I was an American citizen, I told her I wasn't. She hung up.

Time passed and I joined the London Metropolitan Police and put the funny-looking helmet on my head. But I never forgot about my American cop dreams.

*

Some years into my career with the Met, I became a firearms officer at Heathrow

Airport; we carried Heckler & Koch MP5 submachine guns and Glock handguns. One evening, at the start of a nightshift, I was sent to Terminal 4, where two drunk Australians had assaulted a member of British Airways staff after they had been refused permission to board a flight. I was trying to arrest one of the men when he resisted. We ended up on the floor and began to fight. Concerned that he would try to take my Glock, which I carried in a holster on my hip, I did my best to fend him off as he set about assaulting me. He tried to gouge out my eye. He tried to rip off one of my ears. He tried to bite off one of my nipples. The right side of my face has never felt the same since, and to this day I carry his teeth-marks in my chest.

Afterwards, I asked a superior what would have happened, had I drawn my gun and shot my attacker. I would have gone to prison, was the brisk reply. At that point I remember thinking – rightly or wrongly – that an American cop would not have got the same response.

A court awarded me a small amount of compensation for my injuries, and I used the money to fly to the United States. I had always wanted to see the small towns and white-painted picket fences of Cape Cod as well as the island of Martha's Vineyard, where the movie *Jaws* had been filmed; the police chief, Brody, played by Roy Scheider, was one of my movie heroes. On Martha's Vineyard I met a local cop. We exchanged police patches and kept in touch – and are still good friends to this day. I then returned to the island a few months later and went for a 'ride-along' with his department (where members of the public accompany police officers on patrol). That experience opened up a whole new world to me – the world of American policing, but for real this time, not just onscreen.

I then went to other cities and set up more ride-alongs. Eventually I took three months off work for the ultimate busman's holiday and toured the nation from Alaska to Maine, Los Angeles to New York City, riding with officers at each and every stop. I rode in police helicopters, went on SWAT raids in Las Vegas, accompanied homicide detectives in Chicago, spent a lonely night in a remote police station in Alaska, blew up beaver dams in Mississippi (it's a long story) and was once trapped between three tornadoes on an Indian reservation in South Dakota. I saw wealthy neighbourhoods and poor neighbourhoods. I patrolled big cities and tiny hamlets. There were quiet days and there were busy days. There were moments of utter bliss and moments of sheer terror.

The American cops were everything I'd hoped they would be. The attitude was there, the chewing tobacco was there – I tried it and it made me sick – the adventure and drama were there.

One of the stops I made on that three-month odyssey was in Detroit, and my experience there would have a profound effect on me. On that first visit, Detroit was like nowhere else that I had ever seen in my life, and that statement is still true today, even after all the other places I have been to across America.

In the lead-up to my first visit, no one had a good word to say about the place. One cop I knew, after hearing that I was planning to visit Detroit, described it as being 'America's third world

4

project'. On being given the same news another cop friend simply quoted Colonal Kurtz from Conrad's *Heart of Darkness*, or perhaps *Apocalypse Now*, which was based on Conrad's work, yelling, 'The horror! The horror!'

When I first arrived in Detroit, I could see his point. The city looked as though an atomic bomb had been dropped on it. The downtown area was deserted, with dirty, trash-strewn streets and filthy, boarded-up buildings on the verge of collapse. There were few businesses that were still open, and those that were open didn't look particularly inviting. If I left my hotel, I would be the only person walking in the streets. The city felt – and looked – abandoned.

On my first evening with the Detroit police, I was sent out with Inspector Steve Dolunt, who was taking his turn as the late-shift duty officer which meant working from 7p.m. until 3a.m., an eight-hour shift. It was a freezing, wet night and he could easily have stayed in his office out of the cold. But that wasn't Dolunt's style. He was as keen as a rookie and wasted no time in getting out onto the streets, which were a patchwork of messy plots of wild grass and weeds, or else just a scattering of houses, many of which were nothing more than ruins that had collapsed under their own weight, piles of rubble, or burnt-out wrecks.

Within minutes of setting out we were called to a homicide, where a nineteen-year-old black man had been shot in the back. We were met in a dark residential street by a homicide detective. A few yards away, the victim's father was being spoken to by a cop in uniform. The father stood silently in the rain as he listened to the officer. The expression on his face was one of pain but also acceptance, as if this day had been inevitable.

The detective led us down a narrow passage between two large abandoned houses, to the back yard where the murder had taken place. A pair of uniform officers stood nearby, with their faces pressed into the top of their jackets as they tried to stay warm.

The yard was small, tight, pitch-black and secluded – a good place to murder someone, I thought. The body had already been taken away, leaving only a few drops of blood on the ground as evidence of the killing.

The detective told us that the victim had been shot in the spine. His neck had also been broken in three places. The victim had dirt on his hands, and the detective reasoned that he had been trying to crawl away from his killers before they had murdered him. We stayed there until Dolunt was on top of the situation, and then it was time to go elsewhere.

No sooner had we left the scene of the shooting than a call came over the radio to an armed robbery in Warren, a small city bordering Detroit.

Over the radio, we were told that the robber had held up a gas station with a butcher's knife, and Warren officers now had the suspect surrounded in a nearby Detroit house. We arrived a few minutes later to find that Warren officers had already entered the building. The robber had locked himself in the basement, and two Warren officers were thumping their fists against the door which opened onto the stairs leading down there, ordering the robber to open up. A K-9 officer stood close by, his black Alsatian barking aggressively. You couldn't exactly blame the guy for not opening it. In his position I wouldn't have come out either.

We were behind the officers, when suddenly the basement door went in with a loud crash and the officers charged down the stairs.

'GET DOWN! DOWN!' they ordered the suspect. 'ON THE FLOOR!'

I followed Dolunt down the stairs. A black man in his twenties was on his knees in the middle of a cluttered, filthy basement with his hands in the air. He looked shocked and was trying to lean away from the fierce police dog, which was snapping its jaws at him. A butcher's knife – the robbery weapon – was found hidden under a mattress which was crawling with cockroaches.

Shortly after we had left that scene, Dolunt got another call on his cellphone: there had been a double shooting on the east side of the city. One victim, a young woman, had only been grazed, but the second victim, a man, had been shot in the mouth. The shooting had happened after a man had driven into the back of their car. After they pulled over, the guy drew a gun and shot them both. No one knew the motive but it was believed to be one of three possibilities: gang-related, a robbery or a case of mistaken identity.

When Dolunt called an officer on the radio to find out what was happening, he was told that it was 'a bunch of ya-ya' and that he didn't need to attend.

'The girl who got grazed didn't even want treatment,' the officer told him.

'What about the guy who got shot in the mouth?' Dolunt asked.

'He didn't want to say anything.'

I snorted in laughter but the irony of this comment passed everyone else by.

During a rare quiet moment on the shift, Dolunt took me to Highland Park, a small, independent city within Detroit. He told me that Highland Park was in an even worse state than Detroit, and had become so poor that the city's police department had literally been disbanded. One day the cops were there and then the next day they weren't. The police building had been attacked and vandalised. Several abandoned police cars had also been set upon; the tyres slashed, the emergency lights broken off the roofs and the windscreens kicked in. It was a shocking vision – a failed city taken over by lawlessness and anarchy. People posted signs in their gardens warning drug dealers not to sell in front of their homes, and a small and brave band of county sheriffs patrolled the streets with shotguns.

As we returned to Detroit, Dolunt took a call on his phone. There had been another shooting. The victim was known as 'John

Doe 312' because he was the 312th person killed that year who could not be identified. John Doe 312 had been shot in the spine and in the back of the head. No one knew why he had been killed, although two women had earlier been seen dragging his corpse through the streets.

A detective – Inspector Plummer – met us at the scene. He was a broad, older-looking black man, wearing a long, dark coat and a black beret. As we stepped into the cold street, he greeted us with a warm smile and a firm handshake.

As with the murder scene we visited earlier in the night, the body had already been removed. The victim had been found lying on a small plot of waste ground between two dilapidated houses. We crossed over the yellow crime-scene tape and Inspector Plummer led us towards the rear of the plot and shone his flashlight at a large circle of damp, brown leaves, where there appeared to have been a fight or struggle. Amongst the leaves was a brand-new pair of Nike shoes and a partially-concealed revolver.

'We don't know yet whether it's the murder weapon or the victim's own gun,' Plumber said.

After another firm handshake, we left the beret-wearing inspector to his bleak murder scene.

Dolunt and I were hungry (as cops always seem to be after dealing with death) and we stopped in a deserted parking lot to eat a sandwich. As soon as we settled down, the radio came to life again. Officers were chasing a van, the driver of which had stolen $40 of gas and was now heading towards the city airport. Dolunt threw his sandwich at me and put his foot on the accelerator.

Vehicle pursuits usually ended up in one of two ways: either the bandit vehicle would get away or it would crash. Mostly they crashed. Sure enough, moments later, the excited voice of a chasing officer informed us that the van had done just that.

'He's gone through the airport fence! The van's tipping over! It's in a roll!'

A couple of minutes later we pulled up in a dark back road, outside a remote corner of the city airport. Half-a-dozen squad cars were abandoned with their doors open and emergency lights illuminating the scene in rapid flashes of red and blue. The cars were pointing like direction arrows to a large hole in the airport's perimeter fence. A little further beyond, on a patch of torn-up grass, just feet from the end of the runway, the van lay battered and motionless on its roof, wrapped in a low sliver of creeping mist. The driver, who was miraculously unharmed, was in handcuffs.

And there, the shift ended. All that happened in only eight hours, and it was just another normal night for Dolunt and his city. This had been my first time in Detroit, and it had been quite the introduction. No wonder I was hooked.

Since that night shift, in 2004, I have returned to Detroit whenever I could, year after year, and during that time I have seen some radical changes. Whilst many of the neighbourhoods are as bad as ever, the downtown is unrecognisable from my first visit. It's actually quite pleasant and inviting, thanks in part to the huge investment of a businessman named Dan Gilbert. The millions that he has invested into the city have led to a transformation which has been rapid and very much welcomed. It is now having one hell of a revival.

My own attitude towards the city has also changed. Whereas I was once drawn to Detroit because it was just so damn bad, now I am drawn to it through deep affection, for the city that refuses to give up, for its resourceful people, and for its courageous police officers. Despite everything – despite the economic horror it has suffered for decades – Detroit keeps going, and that tenacity may now be paying off. Having said that, the city still has huge problems to overcome.

*

The City of Detroit is 140 square miles in size, with a declining population of less than 700,000, from a high of nearly 2 million in the 1950s. It is the largest city in the Midwest state of Michigan. Settled on the banks of the Detroit River, the city faces towards Windsor, Ontario – a smaller, cleaner, *safer* city in Canada. The Ambassador Bridge, which links the two cities and the two countries, is the busiest international border crossing in North America. I have heard people joke that this is because everyone is desperate to escape Detroit.

The City of Detroit's Latin motto, seen on its seal, reads: *Speramus Meliora; Resurget Cineribus*, translated as: *We hope for better things; it shall rise from the ashes*. The motto had come about after a fire had destroyed the city in 1805 – but never have those words been so appropriate. Anyone there must spend an inordinate amount of time hoping for better things. And as for rising from the ashes, Detroit is once again literally doing just that. Here is a city that has been burning for decades, mostly due to thousands upon thousands of arson attacks.

Downtown Detroit has now, however, become a place worth spending time in. There are scatterings of cafes, casinos, restaurants and high-end stores. A new streetcar is being installed to run up and down the city's main thoroughfare, Woodward Avenue, and new condominiums, hotels and sports arenas are also springing up. A cop friend who lived outside Detroit in one of the affluent townships to the north is even considering moving into the city with his family – something that a few years ago would have been unthinkable.

Another change is that the population of downtown and midtown Detroit has finally been increasing, although as a US Population Rank city, Detroit now, incredibly, places lower than it did before the Civil War.

During my first ever visit to the city, the Detroit Police Department's public relations unit had arranged for a local TV news station to interview me about my trip. I was unaware of this, however, and after returning to a precinct following a raid on a crack house, I suddenly found a bright light, a television camera and a microphone shoved in my face. The reporter asked me what I thought about their city. Wanting to be polite, I told the reporter that I thought Detroit was 'a wonderful place'. The reporter squinted at me. 'Really?' she asked doubtfully. 'Sure,' I said. 'In fact, if I were to move to America, this is where I'd want to live.'

The interview was quickly wrapped up, with the reporter staring at me like I was an idiot. That news report would go on to be seen by many of the Detroit cops I met during my time with the department and they all looked at me in the same incredulous way.

Saying something like that now may still get you some looks but it wouldn't seem quite as crazy as it did back then.

However, outside of its small area of resurgence, old Detroit prevails. Venture into the forgotten neighbourhoods and you could very quickly find yourself in a whole world of trouble. There is little reason to go to these areas – unless, of course, you are looking to score some drugs, pick up a cheap, heroin-addicted prostitute or else are simply – and dangerously – lost.

Some people come to these neighbourhoods out of curiosity, and I guess I fall into that category, albeit with an added interest in the way the city is policed.

As I wrote earlier, Detroit captivated me from my very first visit and I am not alone in feeling this way. Many people are fascinated by Detroit – because of its motor industry, or its music scene. For many others it is the 'ruin porn' of devastated houses and neighbourhoods that is the attraction.

Hundreds of streets and entire neighbourhoods are lined with crumbling homes and burnt-out buildings, the result of arson, gang warfare and riots. These areas linger like an American version of Angkor Wat, and just like those ancient Cambodian temples, these modern-day ruins are mesmerising – even beautiful, in a way. To see former homes, some ornate, with turrets and gothic details, now lying empty, with their roofs collapsed into the body of the building, windows blown out, walls blackened with fire damage, wild vegetation growing around the abandoned structures … it is like something from a dark fairy tale.

It is hard to look away.

And then you will see a street that doesn't have *any* houses – not even ruined ones. The piles of broken bricks and stacks of scorched wood have been cleared away, and weeds, bushes, trees and tall grass have been left to run riot. Plot after plot, hidden beneath the rampant foliage, blend into each other to the point where you can believe that you have left the city altogether and are in a strange rural landscape, with evidence of a former life only occasionally appearing through the undergrowth – an old couch, a rusty car part, a stained mattress … a dead body.

There is a morbid appeal in seeing these things, but the 'ruin porn' sightseers are often viewed negatively in a similar way to 'dark tourists' – those who travel to warzones, or places that have suffered a disaster. They come in, take photos, and then return home to show them off and boast about the 'dangerous' places they have been to.

I myself truly believe that parts of Detroit should be left exactly as they are, as

ruins, much like the French village of Oradour-sur-Glane after World War Two, or the Atomic Bomb Dome in Hiroshima. Because, upsetting as they are, these places bear witness to what happens when things go badly wrong. They are both a memorial to those who lost their lives, and a warning. Detroit doesn't look the way it does because of a conventional war or a natural disaster; Detroit looks the way it does because of how people have worked, behaved, how they have treated one another – and how they have failed.

Of course, this isn't just Detroit's legacy; this is one that belongs to us all. It is part of the modern history of mankind. Look at it this way. Detroit is arguably the birthplace of the 20th century and all that came with it – the mass production of motor cars, pop music, modern industry, middle-class wealth and the 'American Dream' – not to mention different races working and living side by side. Detroit delivered all those things. And then it lost them all, going from American Dream to American Nightmare in just a few decades.

If it could happen to Detroit, it could happen anywhere. Detroit's story is *our* story. It is about what we have created – our society, the rights, the wrongs, our laws, our wealth and our poverty. It is a signpost of where we have come from and where, if we are not careful, we are going.

Detroiters themselves are rightly protective of their city. *Detroit vs. Everybody* is the slogan locals wear on their T-shirts. The place has been the butt of other people's jokes for so long, and many still look down on it, but Detroiters and those like me who know the city, are aware of what an astonishing, resilient and seductive place it is – one of the true, great American cities. Its history and its culture are, I believe, second to none in the USA. If you want to know about America, study Detroit.

*

So, what sort of place is this to police? Parts of it look, as I have described, like a warzone. The gunfire, the level of criminality, the violence, the desperate people, the corruption – this calls for *extreme policing*. Nowhere else in America have I seen cops working in such an alarming and punishing environment. The fact they turn up for work each day seems amazing to me – and some senior officers have said as much to me.

What difference can they make? Why do they even take the

risk? Why not just join another, better paid – not to mention safer – police department? When I put these questions to a Detroit cop, he told me, 'Because you join the police to be *police.*'

And that, right there, is the reason why I kept coming back to Detroit. This is as real as policing gets.

There are many other cities that I have visited in America where the streets and neighbourhoods felt just as risky – Chicago, Baltimore and Los Angeles, for example. In those cities too, the cops work a hazardous beat, but it is Detroit that, for me, has an extra edge. Cops will often tell you that policing is a game. I never heard that term being used in Detroit.

The Detroit police operate out of 12 precincts, situated around the city. They are kept busy. In just one small area – the area where I would end up spending most of my time – there was gunfire every four hours, and half of those incidents involved multiple shots. Over a 15-month period, where the number of shots fired was recorded using an electronic ShotSpotter system, there had been almost 9,000 shots – in just a three-mile-square area of East Detroit. Most of those shots went unreported, with no one bothering to call the police, since gunfire in the streets was so common. I imagine that for people living in these neighbourhoods, it must be like living near a busy main road or a rail line; after a while you stop hearing the noise.

On one of my first visits to the city, I stayed at the house of a police sergeant who lived in a Detroit neighbourhood – unusual in itself at that time. One evening, whilst we were in her kitchen preparing a salad for dinner, I heard gunfire in the street. I looked at her, concerned.

'Oh, you get used to that around here,' she said casually, and returned to tossing the salad.

*

Arson is, or used to be, another major feature of Detroit. Epidemic levels used to occur on what is known as 'Devil's Night' – the night before Halloween. At that time, the city burns. Every year, people go into the streets and set fire to abandoned houses. In former times it was mayhem, and only added to the image of a city out of control and beyond help.

At its peak in the 1980s, more than 800 fires were started on a single Devil's Night. Incredibly, even homes that were still occupied were targeted. Overwhelmed, the Fire Department was unable to cope, and properties were reduced to ash-covered rubble. The results can still be seen throughout the city today.

As word of the annual pyromania-fest spread around the world, news crews from as far away as Japan came to film, which did nothing for Detroit's reputation. In an effort to reverse the situation, Devil's Night was rebranded: it is known as Angel's Night now.

Along with the police and fire crews, local people – Angel's Night volunteers – organise themselves into groups and patrol the streets. Their numbers have now reached tens of thousands, and this, along with a curfew for under-18s, has made a real impact on the number of arson attacks.

In 2016 there were 'only' 59 fires on Angel's Night; in Detroit this was considered a major success. But it isn't just on Angel's Night when fires are started. In this city of fewer than 700,000 people, there have been as many as 9,000 'structural fires' in a single year – that's an average of around 24 house or building fires a day. And up to 6,000 of these can be classed as 'suspicious'.

With so many abandoned houses, arson attacks are common and easy. People will even set fire to their own buildings – or else pay others a few bucks to set the fire on their behalf, often as a way to claim insurance. With so many fire-damaged and structurally unsound buildings, firefighters are always in danger of being killed or seriously injured. As an arsonist, however, your chances of being caught are low. In Michigan in 2016, the clearance rate for arson was just 16%.

Sometimes fires are started for revenge – one gang attacking another. Some are started for entertainment. Setting fire to a house to watch it burn, and seeing the Detroit Fire Department coming out, can be just something to do to while away the evening.

Like so many other city departments in Detroit, the Fire Department has long been up against it financially. Firehouses have been shut down, and pay, conditions and equipment have been poor and inadequate. As recently as 2012, some Detroit firefighters were even forced to set up their own alarm systems. Whereas most fire departments will have loud bells ringing, in Detroit it has been known for empty soda cans to be placed on top of fax machines, so that the noise of the cans falling would alert the firefighters that there was an emergency to attend.

This would be funny if it weren't true.

Latterly, Detroit has increased the budget of the Fire Department and invested in new trucks and equipment. For a city that is so often in flames, it is not before time.

*

To return to the theme of abandoned buildings and empty homes, their number is believed to stand at around 80,000 to 100,000, with a further 90,000 empty plots. Foreclosures are frequent, and with many people struggling to pay their bills or rent, thousands are evicted each year. Properties that may once have cost $100,000 are sold at auction for less than $500. One man, desperate to unload a property, even offered to swap his 3-bedroom house for a new iPhone.

So, whilst things are improving downtown, the outlying neighbourhoods are continuing to decay. As well as arsonists, empty houses attract all sorts of unwelcome people – squatters, drug dealers, drug addicts, prostitutes and thieves. The latter strip out and steal anything of value, and the people left behind and still living in these streets can only watch as their communities are taken over by gangs and turned into urban swamps of murder and vice.

There is an important imbalance here: while residents are confronted by unaffordable rate hikes, business corporations in Michigan get tax breaks and effectively pay nothing to the state or to the city. The argument goes that by giving big business tax breaks you are encouraging them to set up shop in your town, which in turn generates jobs and wealth. Even so, it seems unfair that if you are a big business, you get a free ride – even a net refund – but if you are a poor family who have hit hard times and are unable to pay the rent or mortgage on your substandard housing, before long you will find yourselves out on the streets, with your home promptly claimed back by the bank or city and sold off.

Recently, the city was selling off some beautiful family homes in the East English Village neighbourhood for just $1,000. The only catch was that buyers needed to fix the house to a habitable standard within six months and then live in it themselves. Although some homes remained empty, it was clear on my last visit that people had taken Detroit up on the offer. Any enticement to get people to move back has to be a good thing.

However, allegations were made against city employees who, it was claimed, were purchasing foreclosed, abandoned or vacant houses direct from the Detroit Land Bank, at huge discounts. Then, instead of moving into the homes, it was alleged that they were re-selling the properties for large profits. The allegations have since fallen under the eye of federal investigators.

*

As I mentioned earlier, Detroit has long been infamous for its 'blight' – its deserted, collapsing homes. To deal with the problem, the federal government has allocated hundreds of millions of dollars to help the city tear them down. Once the drug dealers, gangs and other criminals had been flushed out, the idea was that neighbourhoods would become safer and more attractive, and property prices could rise. But here too, there have been problems.

Under the old mayor, Hall of Fame basketball player Dave Bing, each house cost the city around $9,000-$10,000 to tear down. Under the new mayor, Mayor Mike Duggan (Detroit's first white mayor for 40 years), the cost had spiralled to $20,000. It was later discovered that prices were discussed and agreed with certain contractors before other contractors were even consulted, with the contracts then being awarded to the preferred companies. There were further allegations that the contractors were not completing the work to the required standard, filling in the holes where the houses had once stood with rocks and concrete rather than topsoil and grass, as had been agreed. Even the earth to fill in the holes had caused a controversy when it was found that the city itself had been given some earth for free, from a site in Detroit. The city then gave this free dirt to the contractors, also for free. The contractors then *charged* the city thousands of dollars to move the dirt. Much of this information was uncovered thanks to the investigative work of local reporter Charlie LeDuff.

Mayor Duggan was on a mission to increase the rate of demolitions from 25 buildings a week (before he came to office) to between 100-300 a week under his Blight Elimination programme. This was understandable, since with a rough total of 40,000 houses to bring down, 25 a week would have taken 30 years. However, there were further allegations of mismanagement and wrongdoing, and after 10,000 houses had been torn down, federal investigators stepped in to explore how the costs had spiralled. Demolitions were suspended and eventually state employees were sent in to oversee the work.

Detroiters are no strangers to allegations of wrongdoing. Mayor Kwame Kilpatrick, who served between 2002-2008 whilst still in his thirties, is currently serving 28 years in prison for multiple crimes, including fraud, bribery, extortion and racketeering. At one point, a hand-painted sign was put up in the city that read: *Detroit's so bad even the mayor admits to being a criminal.*

Kilpatrick was found to be using city funds to pay for a lavish lifestyle. Despite the $230 million budget deficit, he enjoyed luxury vacations, yoga lessons, spa treatments, fine wines and dining. He spent thousands just to lease a car for his wife.

Then there were rumours and allegations (unproven) of a wild, drug-fuelled party at the mayor's city-owned Detroit mansion. A stripper who went by the name 'Strawberry' was allegedly badly beaten after Kilpatrick's wife had caught her giving him a lap-dance. Some months later, Strawberry was shot dead and a rumour circulated that the Detroit police had murdered her in an effort to keep her from testifying against Kilpatrick; this rumour is based on the fact that the type of gun used was the same one issued at the time to Detroit police officers. At the time of writing, the dead woman's case remains unsolved.

There were more allegations of corruption and criminal activity against Kilpatrick, including assault against a police officer. There was also a scandal involving Kilpatrick and his chief of staff, Christine Beatty. The pair, both married to other people, had exchanged graphic sexual messages and had used city money to fund romantic trips away. They also conspired to fire a police chief from the Detroit Police Department.

In 2008 Kilpatrick was finally forced to resign from office, after pleading guilty to a number of felony charges. He was initially jailed for four months. Then, just over a year later, he was jailed again, this time for violation of the terms of his probation, after he had failed to make court-ordered restitution payments to the city. Finally, in 2013 he was sentenced to 28 years imprisonment for further, multiple felonies.

The comedian Chris Rock had called Kilpatrick 'America's first hip-hop mayor'. *Time Magazine* was more direct, naming Kilpatrick 'one of the worst mayors in America's history'.

2

A Brief History of Detroit

Once upon a time, Detroit was one of America's most prosperous and progressive cities. Its story began in 1701, when a French officer named Antoine de la Mothe Cadillac created the settlement which would become the city. After landing on the riverbank, he built a fort, calling it Fort Pontchartrain du Detroit – 'Pontchartrain' after a French aristocrat, and 'Detroit', the French word for 'strait' – referring to the strait now known as the Detroit River which connected Lake Erie and Lake St Clair, and which the fort overlooked.

The area prospered on the back of the growing fur trade, and the settlement quickly grew. Within 70 years, the city was one of the largest in what was then the Province of Quebec. The city was destined to change hands numerous times: from the French to the British (during the Seven Years' War), from the British to the Americans (during the American Revolutionary War), from the Americans to the British (the War of 1812) and finally from the British back to the Americans (also the War of 1812). Detroit has never been so popular!

Throughout these decades, Detroit continued to expand, with wide avenues and boulevards being built across the city, and leading to it becoming known for a time as 'the Paris of the West'. It was around the mid-19th century, however, that Detroit started to show real signs of importance and ambition. Industry and shipping brought genuine wealth to the city. Fortunes were made, mansions were built, and Detroit's future looked rich and promising.

The city's first industrial revolution happened in the middle of the 19th century

when, following the discovery of iron-ore in northern Michigan, and employing new techniques recently created in Britain, the Eureka Iron and Steel Company began to produce steel.

The second industrial revolution – and a far more significant one for the city – began in 1896, when Henry Ford founded the Ford Motor Company. By 1913, having created a conveyor-belt system on the assembly line, cars were being produced at a rate of one every 93 minutes – not bad for something that was made from around 5,000 parts.

With his system of mass-production, Ford was able to drop prices significantly, thereby making his automobiles affordable to the middle classes. Demand exploded and Ford needed more workers. Lots more. To recruit them, he came up with a plan to pay his workers a generous five dollars a day – known as the Five Dollar Day plan. This inviting offer came with intrusive conditions, however, for workers had to meet Ford's own high standards and beliefs about how a person should live their life.

This wage, practically double the industry standard, was paid to all men regardless of their race. Immigrants were pouring into Detroit, including people from the Middle East who would eventually make nearby Dearborn the centre of Arab America, and many ended up working in the auto industry. Hearing about this pay equality, black workers from the South also headed to Detroit to work on the car manufacturer's assembly lines, although they were usually given tougher jobs with fewer opportunities for promotion.

There had long been a black community in Detroit. It was an important destination, forming part of the 'underground railroad' system used by escaped slaves from the South, many of whom headed across the river to Canada. When the car industry took off, their numbers increased significantly, growing ten-fold between 1900 and 1920, from around 4,000 to 40,000. By 1930 their number had increased to 120,000. The movement of African-Americans to Detroit formed part of the 'Great Migration' – in which millions of blacks from the South headed north and west. Before 1910, only 10% of the black population of the United States lived outside the South.

The black population of Detroit continued to grow right up until the 1990s, when it reached a peak of around 780,000. This is in contrast to the white population, which had peaked earlier, in the 1950s, following the war years, where hundreds of thousands of poor whites from Appalachia and the South headed north. The white population grew to around 1.5 million before it started to drop rapidly, especially following the race riots of the 1960s. That was when, in what became known as 'white flight', thousands of white families left Detroit for the suburbs. Their number now stands at around 70,000 – a population decline of 95%. At the time of writing, the black population is estimated to be around 500,000 and the Hispanic population, once equal to that of the whites, stands at around 50,000.

Interestingly, the number of whites in the city is slowly starting to increase, whereas the black population is now in decline.

The race riots of the 20th century proved to be the catalyst for extreme change in Detroit; their legacy still affects and shapes the city today. Yet in the past, Detroit was no stranger to large-scale, race-based violence, with the Civil War and the draft causing conflict between the black and white communities. The city's first documented riot, in 1863, had come about following the alleged rape of a white girl by a black man who, it was later said, wasn't black at all but part-Spanish and part-Native American, or some other mixed heritage.

The rioting resulted in dozens of buildings being damaged or destroyed; many people were injured and two killed. At the time, the *Detroit Free Press* reported the riot as being 'the bloodiest day that ever dawned upon Detroit'. Compared to what was to come though, it would seem minor. The 1863 riots were also significant in the history of the city's policing, as it was due to the unrest that, two years later, the Detroit Police Department was established (and as far back as 1910 it faced allegations of mistreatment of blacks).

Other riots followed those of 1863, but it wasn't until 1943 that another significant event occurred. Once again, racial tensions were already high, with blacks and whites competing for housing and jobs. There were allegations of police brutality against blacks and claims that the latter were being excluded from certain types of work. Then one summer day, groups of youths began to fight on Belle Isle – a 1.5 square-mile island in the Detroit River, and now a state park. As the fighting escalated, a false rumour circulated that whites had thrown a black mother and baby into the Detroit River. Blacks were enraged and began to attack white businesses and properties. Another false rumour claimed that blacks had raped and murdered a white woman. Further fighting erupted around the city. Ordinary citizens were attacked and beaten as they travelled to and from work, caught up in the melee; buildings burned and thousands of troops were put onto the streets. It was three days before order was restored, by which time 34 lives had been lost; 25 of them black.

It was the 1967 race riots, however, that were by far Detroit's worst. In a decade that saw hundreds of riots across the country, including those during the 'long, hot summer of 1967', none were as deadly as those in Detroit. The city had seen some rioting the year before, following an incident where a group of black men had refused the instructions of police to move from a street corner, and the city would see rioting again in 1968, as many cities did, following the assassination of Martin Luther King.

The 1967 rioting – some call it an uprising or rebellion, even a *war* – came about after the Detroit police shut down an illegal drinking den, or 'blind pig', on the corner of 12th Street, now renamed Rosa Parks Boulevard, and Clairmount. It was summer, and the men at the bar had been celebrating the return of two GI friends from the Vietnam War. When officers came to close the bar down, a doorman at the bar threw a bottle at them. From that single act, Detroit descended into some of the worst rioting in US history.

For five days there was utter chaos, with both whites and blacks taking part in the rioting and looting. Store-owners were forced to arm themselves, standing guard inside their premises, ready to protect their businesses.

The State Governor, George Romney, flew above Detroit in a helicopter and peered down at the burning city, describing what he saw as 'a battlefield'. Footage of the riot was later used in a *Star Trek* episode titled 'Let That Be Your Last Battlefield', which dramatised a war between two rival factions, both of whom were coloured half-white and half-black, and who went on to completely destroy one another. The Governor ordered thousands of National Guard onto the streets but realising that they, along with local and state police, would not be enough, he also called in paratroopers from the 82nd Airborne. Tanks then rolled down the wide Parisian-style boulevards and soldiers, armed with rifles and bayonets, patrolled the streets like an occupying force.

When the rioting ended, 43 people – 10 white and 33 black – lay dead. In one infamous incident, at the Algiers Motel, it was alleged that police officers and National Guardsmen had murdered 3 black men, after they had stormed the building, searching for snipers. Of the 10 whites who were killed, the number includes one Detroit police officer, shot dead by another police officer's gun during a struggle with a looter, and two firefighters, one of whom died after touching high-voltage wire, and a second shot in the head whilst pinned down by a sniper. A National Guardsman was accidentally killed by another Guardsman.

In all, close to 200 police officers were injured, along with almost 100 firefighters and 20 National Guardsmen and soldiers. As many as 500 civilians were also hurt and thousands were arrested – whites and blacks. It was reported that 2,500 stores were attacked, looted and burned, with more than 400 buildings so badly damaged that they had to be demolished. About 400 families were left homeless and displaced. Estimates put the damage and looting costs as high as $80 million.

But it was the after-effects that would really hurt the city and its people. Many thousands of stores in the city closed permanently or else their owners moved them to safer neighbourhoods, outside of Detroit. When the businesses left, so did the jobs, wages and tax dollars. Detroit had a large middle class – both white and black – and as well as the whites leaving the city, many of the successful black families also moved away. 'White flight' was already happening before the riots, but the events of 1967 accelerated that exodus and furthered the population decrease.

Tens of thousands of people headed out of the city, never to return, and Detroit, which had once been a mostly successful, multi-cultural place, faced a major decline, its fortunes rapidly unravelling. Those five fateful days of rioting in 1967 would come to haunt Detroit – and America – for the next fifty years.

I've already mentioned 'white flight', but what is rarely spoken of is 'black flight' – something that could be argued was far more devastating for the city. Black flight came about with the end of segregation, better earning potential for black workers and higher incomes. Black families wanted the same things that the white families wanted – better schools for their children, safer neighbourhoods in which to live and to bring up a family, smarter homes, improved services and a better quality of life.

With the black working- and middle-classes leaving the city, the people who were left behind were often poor, uneducated and unskilled. The result was the creation of ghettos that were soon riddled with crime and drugs and violence. Then, in the 1980s, came crack-cocaine. The half-abandoned neighbourhoods were ripe for criminal gangs to move into – and that was when a whole new horror descended upon the city, shrouding it in unimaginable misery. So much despair in a place that had once given the world so many significant advancements – and so much hope.

*

As well as the car industry, people associate Detroit with music. In 1959, local Detroiter Berry Gordy founded Motown Records. The name is a combination of 'Motor' and 'Town', which like 'the Motor City', has become a nickname for Detroit. The music of Motown Records is arguably the sound of the 1960s, when local singers such as Diana Ross, together with The Supremes, were belting out hit after classic hit. Although Gordy would eventually relocate Motown to LA, the house where he had started his record company still stands and is now a museum, located just a couple of blocks away from where the 1967 riots began.

Some would argue that the motor industry, which had done so much to make Detroit the prosperous city it had become, was also partly to blame for a drop in its fortunes. With so many middle- and working-class people now able to afford a car of their own, they no longer needed to live in the city. Thanks to the wide avenues leading to downtown from outlying townships, many workers were happy to move to the suburbs, leaving the inner city behind. And even before the race riots of the 1960s, the three major car manufacturers in Detroit – GM, Ford and Chrysler – had already started to move production of their automobiles outside of the city. Many workers, and many of the businesses that had catered to them, were left behind, resulting in fewer jobs, lower wages, less business, and a reduced tax income for the city.

Ironically, today the Motor City has the fastest-growing number of households in America without a car, although that is hardly surprising when the price of the average car in America, and the price of an average home in Detroit, are practically the same – around $30,000.

The American motor industry later faced its own problems, however, with high gasoline prices and competition from car manufacturers in Japan, Korea and Germany hitting it hard and forcing it to go cap-in-hand to the city and the government in Washington DC.

Both GM and Chrysler have previously filed for bankruptcy – and as if that wasn't bad enough, the City of Detroit itself has also filed. In 2013, during the term of Mayor Dave Bing, and with estimated debts of up to $20 billon, Detroit became the largest municipal bankruptcy in US history. With a critically declining population, smaller tax base, high pension costs and appalling corruption, the city was broke, with some city debts and pensions going unpaid.

Unlike with the motor industry, Washington refused to bail the city out. Instead, it was the State of Michigan that moved in, placing their own emergency manager – Kevyn Orr – to take over the city's financial affairs. At one point, serious consideration was given to selling off city assets such as the art collection from the Detroit Institute of Arts (DIA), easily one of the finest art museums in the entire country, to pay off some of the city's debts. The DIA eventually changed ownership from the City of Detroit to the Detroit Institute of Arts, Inc. – an independent non-profit organisation. The change of ownership ensured that the art collections remained where they were, but not before the DIA agreed to pay $100 million as one part of a much larger deal – something that became known as the 'grand bargain'.

The city finally managed to exit its bankruptcy about 18 months later.

Although the city's very public decline has been on an epic scale, some things are changing. Thanks to the transformation happening downtown, a fresh cycle of optimism has entered the city – part of it, anyway. I only hope that all those trendy newcomers and rich investors, who are opening up breweries and smart boutique stores, don't forget about the poor Detroiters struggling to survive in the outer neighbourhoods. Many businesses do employ local Detroiters, of course, and some are training them in valuable new skills.

There are positives to this wave of 'progress' and 'gentrification', but it can also lead to people being displaced. Established communities suddenly see their property and land values increase, and then quickly find themselves taxed out of their homes or evicted by landlords looking to sell or increase rents. Locally owned stores close and long-term residents move away.

This is one of the challenges that I see for Detroit at this relatively early stage of its revival – embracing the good aspects of revitalisation whilst not forgetting about those less fortunate who wish to remain in the city, so that they too can enjoy the progress.

Detroit has always been a city full of people willing to work hard; after all, many successful corporations were built by – and made rich by – their hands. The past cannot be changed, with all its turmoil and triumphs, but if companies invest in local workers, invest in the outer neighbourhoods, and invest in the city's kids, everyone will benefit – and Detroit's future will be bright indeed.

However, the state of some people's lives in the outer neighbourhoods can be utterly desperate. For many of these people, waiting for the positive waves of Detroit's latest renaissance to reach them isn't an option; some of these people literally won't live that long.

3

The Homicide

Saturday, 19 December 2015

Six days before Christmas there was a homicide on Detroit's west side. The city sees plenty of murders but this one stood out because the victim was a Detroit firefighter named David Madrigal.

Two days after the killing, Madrigal's body was discovered by his son, and a Detroit homicide detective was dispatched to the scene – a small house on Vaughan Street, in a relatively well-kept neighbourhood in the 6th Precinct. This was an area where lawns were cut, houses were looked after and people worked. They weren't rich, but they cared, and that was enough for a neighbourhood in Detroit to look how a neighbourhood should look.

The detective entered the house through an open door at the side of the two-storey building. He checked it for signs of a forced entry but there were none. Directly ahead of him, a set of steps led down to a basement. The basement had been converted into a decent little usable space. It contained a bedroom and a bathroom. There was a bar, with a shot glass and a bottle of whisky sitting on the top, next to an empty ashtray.

Back upstairs, the officer went into the kitchen and dining area. Everything appeared neat and well ordered. On the upper floor, an open door led into a second bedroom. Unlike the other rooms, this one had been turned upside down; someone had been desperately looking for something – or looking for something to take.

Back downstairs again, the officer walked through the small hallway and into a room that had been set up as a home gym, complete with Harley Davidson décor. Another room had been arranged as a home office, with a computer and printer, along with a collection of bills, mail and papers.

Then the officer entered the living room. Along one wall was a large black couch on which a white man lay slumped. He was in his late fifties and was well built – no doubt having made good use of the home gym. He wore white socks, blue shorts, a blue T-shirt, and had a blue New England Patriots cap on his head. Near him on the couch was a small, child-size Detroit Pistons cap. The officer was confused; the Pistons cap was far too small for the man, and there were no children living in the house.

The officer looked around the room. The TV was switched off. On a table in the centre of the room was a pair of large dumbbells – each 25lb weights. Next to the dumbbells was a large Bible, a fireman's tribute book and a fireman statue. Behind the couch, he found a small pool of blood.

The officer looked back at the body on the couch. Blood had run from under the New England Patriots cap, slowly creeping down the dead man's face from a wound to his head. Other officers had assumed it was a gunshot wound but they were wrong. Blood was also coming from his nose and ears. The man had been struck on the skull with a blunt object – a hammer, perhaps – or a dumbbell.

David Madrigal, the 59-year-old murdered fireman, had been just months away from retirement after giving 26 years of service to the city. A safe from his house, and his black Ford SUV had been stolen. The car was found ten miles away, burnt out. The safe was still missing. The investigation had begun.

Thursday, 7 January 2016

Winter can be brutal in Detroit and an icy greyness had penetrated deep into the city and deep into my bones. Even with my rental-car heaters blowing at full power, I could still feel the frozen air falling away from the windscreen and landing against my face and hands.

I turned into 3rd Avenue, in downtown Detroit. The streets were covered in ice and the roads were almost empty, with just a couple of other cars and no pedestrians at all. Ahead of me was the large, green and grey Detroit Police Department headquarters building. It was modern, bright and shiny – a consequence of its former life as a casino – and it contrasted greatly with the black slush outside.

The last time I went to Detroit Police headquarters, it was situated in a 1920s stone building on Beaubien Street in nearby Greektown: mention '1300 Beaubien' and people immediately knew you were talking about the Detroit PD. I had heard that the new headquarters building had been sold to the department for just $1. 'We could never have afforded it otherwise,' a cop later told me, making it sound as though $2 would have been too much. I parked the car against a pile of dirty snow in the parking lot and rushed towards the building entrance, desperate to escape the painful wind and sinking temperature.

After the expected security checks at reception, I was taken through to see my contact – Steve Dolunt, who I had ridden with on that very first evening in Detroit, all those years ago. He was no longer Inspector Dolunt, however. He was now the Assistant Chief of Police.

Dolunt's rank may have changed but the weather was the same. My first visit to Detroit was in winter, and it was just as savagely cold now as back then, with a dank dome of frozen misery fixed above the city like a scene of biblical punishment. Despite the weather, Detroit had enthralled me on that first visit and I had returned to the city year after year. And now here I was again.

I was taken into Dolunt's bright new office – a desk, a few chairs, a bookshelf. On a counter top, a collection of 'challenge coins' from various police departments were laid out, along with a handful of plaques and police department patches. On a rack along one wall hung a small collection of baseball bats.

'Ah, here's the British guy!' I heard from behind me.

It was Dolunt. I couldn't help but smile, every time I saw him or heard him speak. He was a short but highly animated man. Friendly, helpful, and as a natural comic, he was always looking for a bit of fun or searching for the chance to make an amusing comment. Over the years, I have watched Dolunt rise through the ranks, and I was extremely pleased to see him make Assistant Chief. Dolunt is a great man, well-liked by his officers and is himself an excellent cop. He cares about the city, its people and its baseball team – the Detroit Tigers – just as much as he cares about the men and women who work under his command. He's a true cops cop and a huge asset to the DPD as well as the people of Detroit.

Dolunt is also the officer who, whilst he was working in Internal Affairs, initiated the investigation into Mayor Kwame Kilpatrick. The investigation came about after Dolunt had been looking into matters to do with the mayor's security detail. Later, Dolunt told the *Detroit News*, 'Investigating the mayor didn't exactly help my career. I was transferred twelve times in two years.'

Steve Dolunt is nothing short of a legend.

We greeted each other warmly and I made a mental note that he wasn't sporting a moustache. Since I had first known him, Dolunt always went one year with a moustache and one year without. He liked the moustache, his wife didn't, hence the annual alternation in facial hair.

Standing in his office now, I had no idea what lay ahead of me.

33

Dolunt had promised that he would embed me with an active team but other than that, I didn't know where I would be spending my time. I wasn't concerned, though, as I figured this being Detroit, wherever I ended up would be interesting.

'Mick,' Dolunt told me, picking up one of his baseball bats (In the police world I'm always 'Mick', never Michael. Outside the police, the opposite is true). 'I'm putting you out with my Gang Intelligence Unit. They've been real busy and they should be a good group for you to work with. Their sergeant, Ed Brannock, can be a tough guy though. He'll either love you or hate you. If he hates you, you're screwed.' Dolunt swung the bat and hit an imaginary homerun.

Dolunt explained that the unit were working on something called the Operation Ceasefire programme. It was a joint initiative by a number of agencies: as well as the Detroit Police Department, it included the Michigan State Police, the FBI, the Mayor's Office, Wayne State University, and the Prosecutor's Office.

Ceasefire had been set up in 2011 under the Obama administration's National Focus on Youth Violence programme. Operating in a number of cities, including Chicago, Boston, Memphis and Detroit, and through the funding of millions of dollars from the federal government, the idea was to prevent youth and gang violence through a multi-agency approach, utilising data and intelligence. Rather than just responding, officers on the Ceasefire programme were targeting identified problem hotspots. Cities were reporting some success and Detroit too had managed to lower gun and gang violence, although it was an on-going process; the streets were full of guns and there was always someone ready to step up and fill the void left behind by a dismantled gang or imprisoned gangbanger.

Detroit had set up the Gang Intelligence Unit (GIU) specifically to handle Ceasefire matters. Any gang-related shootings and homicides would fall under their remit. The unit had been posted to the east side of the city, where the Ceasefire data had identified the biggest problems, and where funding had been provided to deal with those neighbourhoods. The GIU would engage with the local community, enter the schools, target and disrupt gang activity, carry out pro-active operations to get the guns and criminals off the streets. Their job was to take down the gangs and bring the gang members before a court.

'You'll be in the thick of it,' Dolunt assured me.

As we spoke, a tall, solid white guy in blue jeans, a black hoodie and a black baseball cap walked into the office. The hoodie and cap both had *Detroit Gang Intel* printed on them along with an image of a grinning skull – its skeletal hands gripping a pair of revolvers, with the barrels pointed outwards.

'I asked them to send me their best cop and they send me Joe!' Dolunt said, with a cheeky smile.

Joe didn't say anything, as though he was used to this kind of abuse from the Assistant Chief.

'I'm joking,' Dolunt continued. 'Joe is a great cop. And notice that I called him a cop and not a police officer.'

This was one of Dolunt's things that I remembered from before. The way he saw it, there were 'cops' and there were 'police officers'. He once told me that, 'Police officers do their eight hours and then go home to their TV dinners. Whereas cops are out there, finding stuff, digging shit up ... being *cops*.'

Joe's cell phone rang. I made a mental note of the ringtone; it was 'Soul Bossa Nova' – the Quincy Jones instrumental that had been used as the theme tune to the Austin Powers movies.

'Yeah, I'm here now,' Joe said to the person on the other end. 'What do you want me to do with him? Okay ... okay ...'

Five minutes later I was sat in the front passenger seat of Joe's car – a blacked-out Detroit Police Dodge Charger.

'Dolunt was telling me about your sergeant,' I said, fishing for information.

'Brannock? Yeah, he's quite the character,' Joe said. 'But he's okay.' Then he leant forward and turned the volume up on the radio.

I was starting to get a little nervous. The last thing I needed was to be placed with a unit whose sergeant didn't want me around. I prepared myself for a difficult few weeks.

We headed towards the Gang Intelligence Unit's base, driving north-east along Gratiot Avenue, which everyone pronounced as 'Gra-shit', without any intention of sounding unpleasant. Gratiot was one of a number of avenues that cut through Detroit, heading from downtown to the outer neighbourhoods and townships. 'An escape route', I once heard someone call it. It was wide – six lanes – but other than us, there were hardly any other people using it. Gratiot was mostly lined with one- and two-storey buildings, many of which were boarded-up and covered in graffiti. Empty plots of wasteland were scattered here and there, with only the occasional open business – a laundry, a car lot, a gas station.

'Are you from Detroit?' I asked Joe.

'I'm straight up from The D,' he said. 'I was born and raised here.'

'Is your house still standing?' I asked next.

'Yep. Shouldn't be but it is.'

My question had been a genuine one. In this city, it wouldn't have been surprising to hear that his childhood home had disappeared along with thousands of others.

'Up until the year 2000, we had "residency",' Joe continued. 'It effectively meant we had to live in the city. Once the governor got rid of that, all the city workers ended up leaving town. A lot of them didn't live in the city before that anyway, although they were supposed to. But I lived in the city right up until they changed the residency rule.'

The rule that Joe spoke of was a law which required city workers to live within the City of Detroit. This way, the city was able to keep tax dollars here as well as ensuring that there were neighbourhoods occupied by working people. Typically, those neighbourhoods were in better condition and had lower crime rates, especially as Detroit police officers and firefighters tended to stick close together in neighbourhoods that became known as 'Coppers' Canyons'.

'So, what do you think of the city now?' I asked Joe. 'Are you happy with the changes and the investments made by Dan Gilbert?'

'I was actually walking around downtown during the summer and I was thinking that it was pretty cool down there,' Joe said. 'There were bands playing, people sitting outside having lunch. Dan Gilbert is doing good things in this city. I expect he intends to make a shitload of money out of it, though. I don't know why else he'd be doing it.'

*

The unit's base was in a long, two-storey brick building in a mixed industrial/residential area of the 11th Precinct, in Detroit's north-east. We passed by a chain-link fence and pulled into a large pot-holed yard lined with a mix of marked Detroit police cars – new Dodge Chargers and the older Ford Crown Victoria Police Interceptors – and officers' personal vehicles, which seemed to mostly be pick-up trucks.

After entering the building through a secure door, we headed up a set of concrete steps. The Gang Intelligence Unit office was located at the end of a long, dimly lit corridor, by a toilet.

Sergeant Brannock wasn't there to meet us, so Joe called his cell phone. There was no answer.

'Just take a seat,' Joe told me. 'He'll show up eventually.'

The office held a collection of mismatched furniture that looked as though it had been salvaged from dank basements, other people's offices and yard sales. In the middle of the room were a pair of leather armchairs but I didn't want to look too comfortable too soon, so I sat at a large meeting table. The table was old and worn, with half a dozen seats around it and a bunch of folders and paperwork stacked up on top. From a radio in the corner of the room, I could hear Adele singing 'Hello'.

Joe took a seat at one of a half-dozen old metal desks that were scattered around the office, each with its own tatty swivel chair. He stared at the computer screen in front of him and began to type. Taped to the wall next to him was a sheet of paper with a photographic image that had been printed from a computer. The image was of Joe, sat in the same seat, at the same desk, staring at the same computer, whilst wearing almost identical clothing.

At the far end of the office was an older, black officer. He nodded his head and smiled at me in greeting. He was dressed in all-black clothing including a long-sleeved Gang Unit skull-holding-revolvers top. There was a large map of Detroit behind him, split into different-sized squares and triangles of various colours. *Detroit Gang Territory Map* was printed along the top.

I got up to take a closer look. Each coloured shape represented a different gang and the area they operated in. There were over a hundred gangs identified on the map and some were split into further, separate factions. I read some of the names: Rich Nigga Shit, True Savage Niggas, Bang Squad Mafia, Arab Thug Lords, Self Made Niggas, Cash Money Savages, A-1 Killers, Seven Mile Bloods. The list went on. I searched the map for the street that the base was on, where I was currently standing. A small yellow square covered the area, meaning it was a gang neighbourhood. I read the gang's name: Hell Zone.

Standing at the side of the office was a tall, muscular white officer. His arms were covered in tattoos and he was wearing a tight-fitting Gang Unit T-shirt with the same skull design. He was talking about up-coming superhero movies with another black officer, who was wearing a Gang Unit hoodie. He looked younger than the others and had short, shaved hair and a goatee beard. He was only half-listening to the muscular guy, and was sat at a computer, searching for Star Wars Lego on the internet. Behind them both, along the entire wall, were about a hundred print-outs of gang members. Written below each image was information about the person, such as 'related to ...'; 'brother of ...'; 'gang shooting'; and 'car wash shooting'. A significant number of images had *Deceased* written on them.

I returned to the meeting table and sat in silence, still taking in the office. A few minutes later a short, stocky white guy walked in. He looked to be about my age – early forties – and was wearing a pair of dark jeans and a black zip-up sports jacket with some kind of brightly coloured sports shirt underneath. He had short grey hair which was starting to thin at the front.

'Did they arrest that guy who killed the firefighter?' the older black officer asked the man.

'No. They're running a source now, down at the dope house,' the man said, and he walked into a small office, by the end of the meeting table I was sat at, without acknowledging me.

Joe stood up and followed the man into the office. A minute later they both walked out and Joe returned to his position at his desk.

'You the British guy?' the stocky man asked.

'Yes. Mick Matthews. AC Dolunt set me up to ...'

'Come in,' he said, cutting me off. He waved his hand and walked back into the office. I followed him in.

The small room had a large desk with an enormous TV screen on it. The TV was hooked-up to a keyboard and doubled as a computer screen. A sign on the wall read: *My cave, my rules – no exceptions.* Pinned to a board were a couple of police patches and a photograph of a murder victim, lying in a muddy field. Standing next to the corpse was this same officer, looking unemotional, with his hands in his pockets.

'Are you Sergeant Brannock?' I asked.

'Yeah. Dolunt told me that you're spending some time with us, is that correct?'

'If that's okay with you?'

Brannock looked at me for a moment in silence. 'Sure,' he said. But he didn't seem very happy about it.

'I'm writing a book,' I told him, cringing as soon as the words left my lips.

'A book? About what?'

'Well, about Detroit, you guys and the time I'm spending with you.'

Brannock looked at me some more, in silence, nodding his head slightly, taking in what I had said. I thought maybe I had made a mistake by telling him about the book, but then again how could I *not* tell him?

He sat down behind his desk on a large, comfortable-looking leather swivel chair. Next to me was a regular wooden chair (no swivel). It was empty. I wondered if I should sit down but decided not to; Brannock hadn't offered it to me and our encounter had now reached an awkward moment where suddenly deciding to just sit would seem strange.

Brannock started typing on his computer and as he did so – and without invitation – I began to tell him a bit about myself, including my own police history as well as my history with Detroit and its Police Department. Brannock didn't seem remotely interested. I couldn't tell whether he was listening to me whilst reading emails, or simply ignoring me altogether.

'You guys don't carry guns in England, right?' he asked.

'For the most part, no.'

He looked at me like I was an idiot. 'What the fuck is that all about?'

'Well …' and that's as far as I got. One of the officers called out Brannock's name and he got up and left the room.

It was an interesting start.

I remained in Brannock's office, wondering if I should call Dolunt and ask for a transfer. Then Brannock walked back in.

'Have you met everyone yet?' he asked.

'No, not really.'

He waved me back out.

'Joe picked you up from headquarters, right?' Brannock asked.

'Yes.'

'Did he bore you with all his retirement talk?'

'Five months and two weeks,' Joe said cheerfully.

'You must be counting the days,' I said.

'I've been counting the days for three years. It's been a bit of a joke but now that the date is getting closer I'm starting to shit myself a little. I just have this fear of going to a regular nine-to-five job, where they can say, "We don't like you, you're fired." Or "You're laid off." Because I know that won't happen here, in the Police Department.'

'Aren't you applying for Berkley PD though?' Star Wars Lego asked.

'Yep.'

'Berkley PD!' Brannock scoffed. 'Talk about retirement! Besides, you have to pass the fitness test first and your body looks like bubble-gum.'

Joe looked over at Brannock. 'You talk about my body, when yours looks like that?'

'Your body looks like bubble-wrap,' Brannock said.

'We call him "Spanky",' Joe told me, pointing at Brannock.

'Spanky?'

'Yeah, from *The Little Rascals*; the naughty fat kid that was always getting into trouble.'

'We mostly use nicknames here,' Brannock told me. 'We deal

41

with a lot of gang members and we don't need them knowing who we are.'

The older black guy, I learned, went by 'AJ'. Joe was simply known as 'Joe'. Star Wars Lego was 'Whispers' because he always spoke so quietly. The muscular guy with the tattoos was 'Hollywood'.

As Brannock was introducing me, two more officers walked into the room. One, a stocky, olive-skinned man with a dark goatee beard, was Scrappy. The other, also stocky, wearing a black Gang Unit baseball cap and a couple of days' growth on his face, was Cooter. They both shook my hand and welcomed me to the unit.

A couple of Brannock's gang officers were away at the moment. One, 'Hype', was on vacation in Jamaica. And there was another, 'Reef', who was also off, although it took a while for me to find out why.

'Is Robo here?' Brannock asked.

'YES!' came a female voice from another side office. We walked in and Brannock introduced me to the female officer, 'Robo', which was a shortening of her Polish surname. She was in her late thirties and had long blonde hair hanging loose around her shoulders. She reminded me of the actress, Kate Hudson.

'This is the British guy that Dolunt's put with us,' Brannock told her.

'Well, yeah, I figured that out,' she said. Robo stood up from her desk and stepped forward to shake my hand. She gave me a broad, friendly grin, looked me directly in the eyes and welcomed me to the unit.

'Is this your first time to Detroit?' she asked.

'Actually, no, I've been coming here for a few years.'

'Oh? Doing what?'

'Going out with the Detroit Police, learning about the department and the city.'

'So you're a Detroit veteran?'

I grinned. 'Something like that,' I told her.

Of all the units and departments that I had toured with, it was the DPD and in particular, the Narcotics Unit – the Narcs – that I had worked with the most. My tours with them had practically become routine. I would show up, get posted with one of the teams, and away we would go, driving off in some beaten-up black *A-Team*-style van. We would then roll up outside some decrepit-looking house in a gang neighbourhood, the sliding door at the side of the van would be pulled open and we would all charge out towards the house. Incidentally, this usually took place in the middle of the day, in broad daylight, not in some dark, quiet, early-morning raid. The Narcs would run towards the front door with their guns aimed at the building, and then quickly smash their way in. The whole time I would be with them, snapping away with my camera and making hastily written notes.

I told all this to Robo and Brannock.

'The Narcs got disbanded,' Brannock said.

I turned my head and gave him a look, inviting more information.

'There was a big shake-up and Internal Affairs had to come in. They threw everybody out,' he told me.

I was surprised. I had heard that there had been some issues with the Narcs, but for the department to disband the entire unit, the issues must have been pretty serious. And as I found out, they were. With reports of mismanagement and allegations of serious corruption, including robbery and drug dealing, Chief Craig had made the only possible decision.

'So that's it? No more Narcs?' I asked.

'They disbanded the unit but then they kind of reopened it because they realised almost everything in this city revolves around dope,' Brannock told me.

The new unit was named Major Violators, and Brannock

explained that the department had tried to bring back the old Narc officers who they had identified as being 'good', not 'dirty'.

Brannock himself had worked narcotics for a time. 'Two raids a day,' he informed me. 'We'd run the source on Monday, get the warrants up, and boom, boom, boom. And if you didn't get anything, you had to do a street deal – street enforcement. You had to get something. God, I remember we used to have a crew for each precinct and then we had a couple of crews for conspiracy – big dope. We used to have twelve fucking raid crews at one time. Now we have four crews for the whole city.' He fell silent for a moment, thinking. 'That job is just too close to the edge,' he said. 'It's hard; you're seeing motherfuckers with hundreds of thousands of dollars and you ain't got shit! And the officers coming on now are making fourteen dollars an hour.'

It was an old argument – pay cops well and the level of corruption drops. Pay them badly and it goes up. For some, seeing and being around so much money, observing criminals doing better than they were themselves, could hurt. Most cops could deal with it but some struggled. Then there were the cops who were bad regardless, no matter how much they earned. The truth is, this type of officer is very rare.

Brannock walked me over to the large whiteboard in the main office and pointed to one of the pictures on the wall – a mug shot of a black man in his late twenties or early thirties, staring dispassionately towards the camera.

'He was a DPD officer,' Brannock said, tapping his finger on the image. 'And then he started to run drugs for the gangs. The gangs are selling weed, heroin, a little bit of crack and a *lot* of prescription pills. They call it "shooting trips", where they get these prescription pills and then they go down to West Virginia or Ohio or Kentucky to sell them. That's where the gangs are getting most of their money. And they're all doing it – all of them.'

'What sort of pills?' I asked.

'Oxys.'

OxyContin is a painkiller with similar effects to heroin; in fact, it is sometimes called 'hillbilly heroin' or 'synthetic heroin'. Although it has been used to treat cancer patients and people suffering from severe, chronic pain, Oxys are widely abused in the United States, and the gangs were able to make big money from them.

'How do the gangs get the pills?' I asked.

'They'll have girlfriends who work in pharmacies and nursing homes, who'll steal them. Or they buy them directly from elderly people who've been prescribed them. Sometimes they will break in somewhere to get them. We had a spate of pharmacy burglaries where they smashed their way in with sledgehammers in the middle of the night. We had around seventy pharmacies that were hit in the suburbs and in Detroit.'

'And how much do they sell the pills for in West Virginia?'

'Forty to sixty bucks apiece. Whereas in Michigan they'd only get about ten to twenty dollars.'

It was a hell of a mark-up. 'Why such a difference in price?' I wanted to know.

'Because it's a lot more restrictive down there than it is in other states. It's just harder for people to get them.'

A few years previously, a cop in Washington State had told me how people always assumed that gangs – of which there are more than 30,000 in America, with around 1.5 million members – only operated in the inner cities. But this wasn't true, he said. Even in rural Washington, where he worked, he had come in contact with them.

Knowing that many metropolitan departments have the funds and resources to take them on, gangs had branched out to small, isolated, poorer communities – some of which rarely see any policing from one day to the next. These are places where they can operate more freely or where they outnumber and outgun local law enforcement. As a result, some small towns have seen gang crime rise by more than 300%. Even so, the cities are still where much of the gangs' business – and their killing – is focused.

Robo had been listening to our conversation and walked over, joining us at the wall of images.

'The gangs will have a group of them just doing the pills,' she said. 'Like this

guy …' She tapped a photograph of a white man in his late twenties or early thirties. 'They pick a group of them and they will become the gang's trip runners. They probably picked the white guys because they wouldn't be noticed as much. Or they'll pick somebody that has a cleaner record, something like that. And then they take trips, do the pill stop, come back and exchange the money.'

'And then they start to set things up even further,' Brannock said. 'They get these girls down there – girls that are addicted to this shit – and then they fuck 'em and get them pregnant. So now they have a *straight connect*, and places to stay.'

'And how were they getting there?' I asked.

'The gangs were taking the bus,' Brannock told me. 'The Charleston Police Department in West Virginia had more intel on our Seven Mile Bloods than we did, because they would just wait at the bus stop and look for these guys getting off. It was easy, it's West Virginia; who are all these guys suddenly showing up in their state, right?'

'But then these guys from the gang got smooth,' Robo said. 'After getting picked off the bus, they started to drive down. But then they were getting picked up on the interstate, so they got even smarter and they would get a tow-truck to meet them at the state line and tow their fucking car to the location they were going to.'

'And then they would use the girls to do the selling,' Brannock said.

The gangs' operations were far more sophisticated than I had imagined and a serious step up from car-jackings, robberies and local dope deals.

'So, part of the gang would be the runners, heading south, whilst the rest of them stayed here?' I asked.

'Yeah. The ones left behind would be doing what they call "holding it down",' Brannock told me. 'You know, protecting the neighbourhood, do whatever wild shit that they were doing, whether it was showing up at the school to beat the shit out of some kid, or selling weed, or doing car-jackings or B and Es – breaking and entering in the suburbs or whatever. And that brings us back to this guy who was the ex-DPD officer.' Brannock jerked a thumb at the photo on the wall. 'He was running pills down to Ohio.'

Cops from other cities had told me of problems with gang members or persons affiliated with gangs who had joined their departments for criminal purposes. There were obvious advantages for a gang to have one of their own working in a police department, where they would have open access to reports and records, police radios and other such equipment, as well as knowledge of officers' lives, home addresses and families, not to mention the training and understanding of a department's inner workings. It was a frightening reality.

'Could he have been part of the gang whilst he was a cop?' I asked.

'He could have been,' Robo said. 'If you're dirty, you're dirty, and that cop was dirty.'

I looked up at the boards and walls again, reading the gang names. Six Mile Chedda Grove, Six Mile Chedda Ave, Hustle Boys, Hustle Stack Ball, Hobsquad, Team Eastside – these were just some of the active gangs that Brannock's unit had been dealing with. He and his officers had an impressively intimate knowledge of them. The numerous gangs as well as their many members could have filled an encyclopaedia.

This was a world of cryptic gang names, affiliations, splinter gangs, broken loyalties, violence, murder, revenge killings, drive-by shootings, rivalries, drug dealing and serious criminal enterprises. Trying to get your head around it all was a challenge.

Brannock did what he could to help me understand and later, as I spent more time with him, driving around the neighbourhoods and hearing his stories, a few of the names started to come up again and again, until I too became familiar with some myself. But for every person I managed to get a handle on, there were hundreds of others that I didn't. For every gang that I learnt about – their history, hierarchy, leadership, criminal activities, shootings, murders and deaths – there were dozens more that we never even touched on.

It was a confusing, dangerous otherworld of bullets and blood, far from what would be considered normal decent society – whilst all the time being located right next to it. A person could drive along Woodward Avenue towards downtown to catch a game or have a night out, but they would be passing streets and neighbourhoods that were raging with crime and death.

Brannock dropped a black folder on the desk in front of me. It landed with a heavy thump and contained a huge number of crime reports relating to gang shootings and homicides. He went through some of them, to give me an idea of what he and his unit were dealing with, briefly explaining the case behind each, before turning the page over to the next report.

'This guy's a Seven Mile Blood. A vehicle with out-of-state plates pulled up to his 2007 Mercedes Benz S550 and sprayed it,' Brannock said, pointing to one of the reports. 'He lost control of his car and crashed into a phone store. He lived.'

He turned the page.

'This is a report where two Hustle Boys were shot. One of them was killed and the other lived.'

Next page.

'These are three Hustle Boys that were shot together. Two-two-three rifle ammunition. They were uncooperative and didn't give us a lot of information.'

Next page.

'This was a shooting with our Seven Mile Blood guys, out in the suburbs. This girl was having a baby shower, but her boyfriend – or baby daddy – is a Hustle Boy. These three Seven Mile Blood guys drove into the parking lot of the rental hall, where the baby shower was happening, and opened fire. They shot a fourteen-year-old kid and another man. Then the boyfriend – the Hustle Boy – was shot at again, this time on Mother's Day. There was something like seventy shell casings found at the scene.'

Next page.

'This is the Gratiot car wash shooting. Gutta Hogs against Seven Mile Bloods. Six people were shot here. One of them got his dick shot off.'

Next page.

'These are two Seven Mile Blood guys that shot at each other. One of the guys we arrested beat this case – the jury found him not guilty. They let him out and a couple of fucking weeks later he's dead. They should have kept him in jail.'

'Why are they shooting each other if they're from the same gang?' I asked.

'Because it was believed that one of them was involved in killing the other's uncle. Then, after the guy who beat the case got shot, another member of his gang went looking to take revenge. He gets all pissed and goes looking for some Six Mile guys. Then he sees some poor fucking guy who was just walking his daughter across the street and shoots him. That guy's paralysed now.'

Next page.

'This guy was a Seven Mile Blood. They called him White Boy, because he was a white kid. They killed him; they gunned him down in front of his house.'

49

Next page.

'This is one where some Team Eastside boys were performing – rapping – at the Ace of Spades strip club. When they left the club, the Hustle Boys pulled up alongside them and fired shots into their car and killed two of them. And then the Hustle Boys kid who did this shooting shows up at the hospital the same night. Turns out Team Eastside had managed to fire back and they had shot him.'

Next page.

'This guy was a big-time leader of the Seven Mile Bloods. He was shot and murdered in May.'

Next page.

'This is another leader of the Seven Mile Bloods – he was shot sixteen times and lived.'

The reports went on and on. Brannock kept turning the pages to describe another shooting or another death.

'And these are all gang shootings?' I asked.

'All gang shootings,' he said. 'And all within the past year.'

As we were looking through the binder, two more officers walked into the office. The first, 'Hunter', was black, bald, and looked slightly older than the others. For some reason he looked vaguely familiar to me. The second officer, 'Casper', was Mexican. He was the shortest officer there but he was powerfully built, with dark, shaved hair and a barbed-wire tattoo across his arm.

'Hunter, Casper, this is Mick. He's from Australia,' Brannock said to them.

'England,' I corrected, shaking their outstretched hands.

'Same thing,' Brannock said. 'Kangaroos.'

Hunter looked at me for a moment. 'Mick? Yeah, you've been out with us before, right?'

'I've spent a lot of time in Detroit, mostly with the Narcs,' I said.

'That's right. You came out with our crew a few times.'

That's how I recognised Hunter; he had been a Narc.

'Sergeant Brannock told me that the Narcs had been disbanded,' I said.

'Whoa! Yeah, bad news,' Hunter said, laughing gently.

He and Casper then walked away to a small office behind where AJ had been sitting. Discussion over.

Brannock was getting restless and suggested we headed out. He wanted to show me around the neighbourhoods to give me a sense of the areas we would be working in and to point out some of the gang houses.

'You okay, just the two of you?' Robo asked Brannock as we were leaving the office.

'Yeah. We're gonna take a drive around the Ninth Precinct. If Mick gets shot, I'll take him to the hospital,' Brannock told her.

Robo explained that the 9th Precinct was the most dangerous precinct in the city.

'You taking him to the 4-8-2-0-Die?' Hollywood asked.

'Yeah,' Brannock told him.

'The what?' I asked.

'It's the ZIP code of the area we are going to: 4-8-2-0-5,' Brannock told me, 'except some people in that neighbourhood call it the 4-8-2-0-Die. It's a violent place.'

Brannock was taking me to the deadliest neighbourhood in the deadliest city in America. As we walked out of the office, Hollywood called out to me. In a warning for me not to cross into the afterlife should I get shot, he shouted, 'Stay away from the light!'

4

The 4-8-2-0-Die

'Did you see that gang map on the wall in the office?' Brannock asked as we stepped into his black Jeep. 'The one with all the coloured squares and shit?'

I told him I had.

'Robo did all that,' he said. 'She spent a year going from precinct to precinct, collecting data and putting that map together. I'll make sure you get a copy. As you saw, there are gangs all over this city, but over here in the east is where we have been having the most problems lately.'

'And in this specific ZIP code you work in, the 4-8-2-0-5 ...'

'The 4-8-2-0-Die,' Brannock nodded.

'Yeah, *Die*. Which gangs operate in it?'

'Seven Mile Bloods, Six Mile Chedda, Team Eastside. Then you get down to the Fifth Precinct, which is directly below the Ninth, and that's the East Warren gang, East Warren Kings, Real Warren Kings, Original Warren Kings, Hustle Boys, Gutta Hogs.'

'Are all these gangs black gangs?' I asked.

'Yes. There're no white gangs on the east side. No Latino gangs either. It's all black.'

'And are all the gangs selling drugs?'

'Mostly, although some of the smaller ones, like Everybody Eats, Fast Money Entertainment, they're not so much into the drugs; they're younger kids just doing whatever – robberies, breaking into houses. Everybody Eats is more of a B and E crew.

They go to the suburbs and break into houses; that's their claim to fame. Fast Money Entertainment is just kids from the Parkside Projects that made up a rap group. There's a fucking ATM machine across from the projects and they rob people there all the time. They sell a little bit of dope – dime bags of marijuana up at the party store across from the projects, that kind of stuff – and little street robberies.' ('Party store' is a local name for a small neighbourhood liquor or grocery retailer.)

The GIU's base was located in the 11th Precinct area but the Gang Unit were spending most of their time in the 9th Precinct, just a few blocks to the east. We were deep into the gang areas almost as soon as we set out.

We drove slowly through the streets and Brannock pointed out some graffiti that had been sprayed along the exterior walls of a derelict building. It was bold, colourful, mural-type graffiti.

'See that? That isn't gang shit,' he told me. 'See how they mark their little initials and all that? That's white kids from the suburbs coming down here and spray painting.'

I was surprised; it seemed especially risky to come to these areas of Detroit, just to spray some graffiti.

'That's brave to come here,' I said. Although by 'brave' I meant 'stupid'.

'Yeah,' Brannock agreed. 'But there's a whole culture of tagging in Detroit, and it's more art-based. Their object is to get as many tags up as possible and to get them in the best places. They'll even hook themselves up to apparatus and hang over the expressway.'

Even the famous British graffiti artist, Banksy, had been to Detroit. He had painted a number of murals on abandoned sites around the city. One was of a hooded boy holding a tin of red paint with the words *I remember when all this was trees* written on a crumbling wall. Another was of a little girl, holding a green diamond. It had been sprayed on a wall that was already covered in Latin Kings and Crips gang markings. Banksy was lucky to get away unharmed.

'We had a guy from out of the country that was killed here, tagging,' Brannock said.

He was talking about 23-year-old French graffiti artist Bilal Berreni. A few years before, Berreni had travelled to Detroit to paint murals. Then, in the summer of 2013, he was found by four members of the Young Brewster Niggas gang, near an abandoned tower block in the old Brewster-Douglass Housing Projects – now demolished but once home to Diana Ross and other members of the Supremes. It was later reported that the gang were looking for someone to rob and murder, as they needed to eat.

The gang robbed Berreni and shot him in the face. In addition, it was reported that Berreni's spine, ribs and arms were also broken and his organs had been lacerated. His body lay in the morgue for nearly a year before he was identified. The youngest involved in the crime, a 14-year-old, had been given $50 for his part in the murder – a cut of the money stolen from Berreni, which he then spent on weed and junk food.

'Do many of the kids who come here to spray paint, get attacked or shot?' I asked.

'Yeah, but they don't usually report it,' Brannock said. 'And sometimes we find them in vacos.' A *vaco* is a vacant house.

'You go into these places and find dead bodies?'

'Huh-huh. Yep, sometimes,' he stated unemotionally.

The fact is, it's not unusual to read reports of bodies – adults and children – found in abandoned buildings, with some of the victims set alight in an effort to destroy any evidence.

Brannock stopped the car at the end of a deserted street and stared out. The litter-strewn street had once been lined with family homes but was now, like so many streets in Detroit, overgrown and long-forgotten, a place where abandoned plots had tangled into one another. Brannock pointed at a square of frozen land.

'This was the field where we found these two white kids from Westland,' he said.

'What happened?'

'These kids came over to the east side to buy some pills,' he told me. 'But they were kidnapped and taken to that field.' He fell silent for a moment. Then: 'They were walked out here and executed. Shot in the head with a rifle.'

'Was it a robbery?' I asked.

'Yeah, they were robbing them.'

'And then they just killed them?'

'Yeah.'

The incident was a particularly nasty one. The two boys – white teens from the suburbs – had crossed into Detroit to score some drugs. Two young Detroit men kidnapped them, stripped them down to their underwear and forced them into the trunk of a car. After being driven around for about an hour, the men found 'the perfect spot' to carry out their plan. The half-naked boys were manhandled out of the trunk, walked out to the field here and forced to kneel in the tall grass. The teens made a final, desperate plea for their lives but to no avail. A gun fired and the first boy took a bullet to the head. His lifeless body flopped to the ground. Two more shots rang out. The second boy was shot twice – once in the back and once in the head. He fell next to his dead friend. Their bodies were found by a passer-by, five days after they had been executed.

It was sickening to think what the boys had gone through.

'Could you imagine being the second kid, hearing that first shot?' I said.

Brannock nodded. 'That's what I said when we were standing there at the time, looking at their bodies. You're on your knees, in a field, grass up to your chest and then: BOOM! You see your buddy drop next to you and you know what's coming next.'

We sat in a sad, horrified silence. Eventually I asked: 'When was this?'

'That was in 2012. It was when I was at homicide. Me and my partner Tim responded to the scene.'

'Looks like you dealt with some real nasty shit when you were working homicide,' I commented.

'Oh, it was fucked up!' Brannock said. 'Homicide was *the* worst job. I went down to homicide with fifteen years on the force, so I thought that I had seen everything that I could see. I was like: *I've been out here fifteen years. I've been in fatal shootings. How bad can it be?* And then I went down to homicide and the amount of death that I saw was overwhelming.'

He turned to me. 'That was the worst job that I think I had, being a homicide detective,' he said quietly.

Some officers made a career in homicide but Brannock – and Robo, who had also worked in homicide – had only spent two and a half years there.

'That was enough for you?' I asked. 'Two years?'

'Yeah. Fuck that. Death. Death. Death. That's all. And the amount of baby deaths was just ridiculous. Do you know how many parents roll over onto their kids, while they're sleeping? I even had one where the baby was mauled to death by a pit-bull.'

We pulled slowly – respectfully – away from the execution field and drove towards Gratiot Avenue.

'I call Gratiot "the Heroin Highway",' Brannock told me. 'All the heroin users from the suburbs travel down it, to come here.'

As he talked, he pointed towards two young white guys who were meandering slowly along one of the side streets that cut off Gratiot, kicking at lumps of frozen, dirty snow. The men were dressed in soiled, baggy clothing and looked seriously out of place.

'Those two,' Brannock said. 'They're down here copping heroin.'

If you weren't coming to buy dope, you could avoid ever

turning into the residential areas that branched off from the wide avenues which cut through the city. Other than the occasional glimpse into the devastated streets either side of you, a person could pass them by and never really know what was going on down there, or just how bad it was. Underneath the hazardous freeze, many of the streets had been neglected for so long they looked like the surface of the moon. (A couple of summers previously, some innovative locals who were fed up with the city's lack of action filled a 15-feet-wide crater with water and populated it with goldfish, carp and bill gill, turning the hole in the road into a neighbourhood fishing pond.)

Then Brannock turned off Gratiot and we headed into one of those very streets – Tacoma. The neighbourhood was a total wreck and it's no exaggeration to say that it looked as though a military battle had happened here.

'This block is the result of heroin,' Brannock told me. 'These were all dope houses.'

The narrow street was a horrifying mess of wild plots, derelict, burned-out houses and smashed, ruined sidewalks. It felt like we were there ten years after a great disaster had passed through the area. Being winter, everything was covered in snow and ice, which gave it a peaceful, serene look but I knew that in the summer months the vacant, abandoned houses would be lost in forests of tall grass, weeds and giant bushes.

There were no cars parked on driveways or on the street and there were no people to be seen. However, despite fire damage and plywood boards hammered over missing windowpanes, there were occasional signs of life: a single light-bulb illuminating a bare room, or the shadow of a person – most likely a squatter – lurking around inside.

We drove slowly along the street, dipping and bumping in the deep potholes as hardened snow crunched and sheet-ice crackled under our tyres. Looking at the devastation, I realised that in all the years I had been coming to Detroit, and of all the neighbourhoods I had been to, the area we were now in – the 4-8-2-0-Die – was without doubt the worst. And being Detroit, that was saying something.

Brannock stopped the car and pointed to a ruined house.

'I've been in that building several times,' he told me. 'We would find white kids in there, laying on the floor, sleeping off their heroin high and waiting for their next fix. The life of a heroin addict in the city of Detroit is fucking awful; it's filled with horrible places and dirty needles and sex with strangers. Then you wake up and repeat.'

We drove on, Brannock twisting the steering wheel to avoid fallen branches from dead trees and the large pieces of trash and broken furniture that were scattered along the road and poking out through the snow like half-covered corpses.

I mentioned to Brannock that as bad as Detroit was, I had always thought that it looked like a good place to be a cop.

'True, but it takes its toll,' he replied. 'You gotta fucking see this shit every day. And because of the Ceasefire program, we're getting closer to the kids; we're offering them services, trying to get them out of the gangs. Then you'll be working one night and you see these same kids laying in the fucking street, having been shot fifteen or twenty times.'

It was a good point. Working with the kids was a tactic to try to steer them away from crime and gangs, but it also meant that the officers got to know them on a far more personal level. Brannock told me how he and his officers had grown to like many of the kids, but whether the kids were interested in escaping gang-life or not, they still had to survive these streets and take all the risks that came with living here. Sometimes that meant a bullet.

Brannock turned onto State Fair. Unlike Tacoma, it looked like a reasonably neat street. It had tidy little homes, although many of the roads around it were the usual Detroit misery and horror.

'The gang, Seven Mile Bloods, are all over this neighbourhood,' he told me. 'A bunch of them live up and down on Regent, but this is the main strip. This is the centre of it – the Red Zone.'

The 'Red Zone' was a name that the Seven Mile Bloods had come up with themselves, for the area they controlled (red being the colour of the Blood gangs), and this entire section of the 4-8-2-0-Die had been awarded that title.

'And this is all controlled by just one gang?' I asked.

'Yeah. It's a Seven Mile Bloods area. They control all the dope in the Red Zone.'

'So no one else – no other gang – can sell dope around here?'

'In the summertime, a rival gang *did* come into this neighbourhood and try to set up and sell dope,' Brannock said. 'I'll show you what happened.' He spun the car around and roared off a short distance, just one block north of State Fair, to another narrow, ruined street.

'There was a family and they were claiming "30-Gang" – that's what they were calling themselves,' he told me. 'It's a very large family, with something like twelve brothers and sisters. But they moved onto this block – Rossini and Crusade – and one of the sisters set herself up in a house over here.' Brannock pointed towards a small brick bungalow. 'That house there, with the porch light and the Christmas trees. But then all her brothers started coming over. And then the brothers moved into this vacant house, right here.' He gestured to a burnt-out shell across the street. 'And that's when the shootings started happening.'

The boys from 30-Gang had set up a dope-selling operation in the vacant house on Rossini, well within the Seven Mile Bloods 'Red Zone'. There could only ever be one outcome. One night, a kid from Seven Mile Bloods drove over to Rossini with some of his crew and shot one of the brothers from 30-Gang. Then later that night, Seven Mile Bloods went to Edmore Drive, where there were some kids from another gang – the Hustle Hard Gang –

hanging out. The Seven Mile Bloods aimed their guns and started shooting at them too. This time they shot four kids, killing one girl.

Following on from that, the 30-Gang boys got their people together and on the same night, they went to a Seven Mile Bloods house on State Fair – just around the corner. There they shot a guy who just happened to be standing out in the street, mistaking him for the guy that had shot at them. There had been multiple shootings in a single night, in just a handful of streets, and all the while, with all of that mayhem and death going on around them, regular people and families were trying to live their lives.

'Then the house that 30-Gang had set up their dope operation in, got firebombed,' Brannock said. 'Other houses in the street were also attacked.' He rolled the car slowly along Rossini. 'This house, this house, that house, they all got fucked up.'

'All because of the gangs?'

'Yep.' Then he pointed to another pile of stone and wood that had once been someone's home. 'A white guy was staying here. He was calling the police on them, so they burnt his fucking house down too.'

'But that's right next door to their own house!'

'Yeah, but they don't care.'

'The other gang must have known there would be trouble if they moved in on someone else's area though, right?'

'Right, but they don't give a shit about that either.'

The short but vicious war between Seven Mile Bloods and 30-Gang was a good example of how the gangs operate in these neglected streets, and how their presence destroys these neighbourhoods. Some people move away if they can afford to, like refugees escaping a conflict, whilst others stay and try to survive. And once the gangs have destroyed a street and run out of buildings to use, they simply move on to the next street. For the regular people living in these neighbourhoods, it is like seeing a plague of locusts moving through their area, leaving only desolation behind them.

Although 30-Gang was gone, Seven Mile Bloods were still very active in the neighbourhood.

'What sort of things are the Seven Mile Bloods involved with?' I asked.

'Narcotics, murder, robbery.'

On one of the whiteboards on the wall behind where Whispers sat, I had seen a hand-drawn chart listing the number of shootings that Seven Mile Bloods and another gang – Hustle Boys – had been involved in. The 'scoreboard' listed both fatal and non-fatal shootings. Seven Mile Bloods had four each for fatal and non-fatal shootings, whilst the Hustle Boys had seven non-fatal and four fatal.

'And now Seven Mile Bloods are at war with the Hustle Boys?' I asked.

'Yeah. There've been historic shootings, back and forth, for about ten years,' Brannock told me. 'There're a couple of different stories but to be honest with you, we really don't know what started it. We've been told that it began after two gang members had a fight in prison, but I think it goes back even further. I think it's connected with a homicide, some shooting that happened up at the 007 Club – it's a strip club that has since burnt down. Anyway, that's where they all used to hang out together.'

'So they've been enemies for a long time?'

'Yeah. The Hustle Boys call them the "Seven Mile Slobs". And Seven Mile call them the "Hustle Bums".'

The name-calling was lame, but the consequences could be devastating. When a gang-member gets shot by another gang for calling someone a name, that isn't the end of it – it's just the beginning of something new because now that murder will need to be avenged. And then the second murder will also need to be avenged with a third killing, and then another and another. The cycle of death seems endless. Gangs had even posted 'hit lists' on Instagram, listing rival gang members they wanted to be killed. The hit lists had resulted in a number of murders.

Before I had arrived in Detroit, Brannock and his team had been working with the FBI's Violent Crime Taskforce, targeting some of the most violent gangs in the city, including the Seven Mile Bloods. The operation had come about due to an increase in homicides and shootings in the 4-8-2-0-Die, after a gang war had erupted between the Seven Miles Bloods and an alliance of other east side gangs. Since the war had started, the gangs had been going back and forth at each other, shooting after shooting. But the operation conducted by the FBI and the Detroit police had been a big success, with a number of arrests made and guns seized.

'We targeted all the head guys in the gangs,' Brannock recalled. 'We used a combination of their social media – Facebook, YouTube rap videos – and our police reports to figure out their hierarchy and who their leaders were. They were the most violent people in the Ninth and Fifth Precincts. We'd catch them one at a time with a gun, or this or that. It all came to a head when we did a surveillance operation at a strip club where they were attending a party. As they left the club, we did traffic stops. We had four car chases going on at once. One guy crashed on the expressway. He had an AK-47 assault rifle in the car that came back to several shootings. Each car we stopped had a gun in it.'

'Sounds like a great success,' I said.

'The FBI took the credit for everything,' Brannock grunted. 'They did a press conference the next day saying how they had taken down the Seven Mile Bloods, but it was all off our intelligence. We identified all of the guys. We pulled all the reports. The Feds aren't out there on the street getting these guys with guns and stopping them in their cars, or going inside vacant houses, seeing who is hanging out with who, getting them all together in a gang house. We had to build all that historical shit.'

He drove into Hayes Street. 'Now, this is the Six Mile Chedda Ave area,' he said. 'This is controlled by the Six Mile boys.' He pulled up outside a large square windowless brick building that had half-a-dozen tatty cars parked out front. 'And this is the party store where we just had a thirteen-year-old killed.'

The incident he was referring to had happened just over a month before. A 21-year-old man had been sitting behind the wheel of his Dodge Charger when armed men approached and opened fire on the car. It was done in broad daylight, with witnesses standing all around – some of whom filmed the entire incident on their phones.

As Brannock spoke, I noticed five men outside the party store, watching us. One in particular was paying us close attention. He was a heavy-set black man who stood well over six feet tall. He wore black combat pants, dirty red boots and a big green hooded jacket. The way he stood, the way he stared – he looked dangerous. He walked alongside some of the cars that were parked at the front of the party store, moving towards us menacingly. Then he stopped and returned to the other men, speaking to them but continuing to look back at us.

'We're getting some attention,' I warned.

'Yeah, I know that guy. He's an asshole.' Brannock stopped speaking for a second as the man gave us another close look before entering the party store. 'He knows my car,' Brannock said. 'He's probably got a pistol on him, that's why he's going in the party store. Anyway, back to the story … When the victim pulled up at the party store, he had these two kids – a thirteen-year-old girl and a seven-year-old boy – on the hood of the car. He also had another thirteen-year-old girl, who was a passenger in the car with him. So they go in the store and then they come back out and the seven-year-old and one of the thirteen-year-olds gets back on the hood of the car. At that point in time, two guys come over and they start shooting at the car. The driver got shot in the head and the girl who was sitting on the passenger side is shot and killed also – she was shot multiple times in the body. The driver floors the car and it shoots across and runs into that building opposite and gets lodged in there. Well, the kids that were on the hood fell off and he ran them over but they lived. The girl's leg was completely ripped open. The boy wasn't as bad – he had some bumps and bruises. The driver was k-type (dead) in the car. I've got pictures of it.'

Brannock pulled out his phone and flicked through the screen, searching for the images before passing his phone to me.

'See, there? He's dead inside the car. They shot out the back window, too.' Then he scrolled through to the next image, taken from CCTV cameras that had covered the area. 'This is one of the shooters – we still don't have him identified.'

At that moment, I sensed movement ahead of us and looked up. The man who had previously been watching us had stepped back out of the party store and was now glaring at us.

'There's your friend again,' I said.

'His relatives control all the heroin that comes in here,' Brannock told me. 'That's why he's looking so hard; he's wondering what the fuck we're doing.'

'He looks like a right nasty bastard,' I said, and I meant it.

'Yeah. They're out there selling dope. That's all they're doing, all day long. Heroin, heroin, heroin. And weed. I just confiscated a .45 out of that store. It was supposedly a "community homicide gun".'

The man was still giving us the eye. Brannock, his story finished, drove slowly away from the party store. As we passed close by, the man leant down to get a better look into our car, catching my eye. He looked seriously pissed. I gave him a friendly smile and nodded my head in greeting.

We drove just one block south of the party store and turned into Cedargrove Street.

'The gangs call this Chedda Grove, rather than Cedargrove,' Brannock told me. 'Six Mile Chedda Grove. You'll see that spray-painted around here.'

'Why do they call it Chedda rather than Cedar?' I asked.

'Just something they fucking came up with. Chedda is their word for money.'

'Is there a difference between Six Mile Chedda Grove and Six Mile Chedda Ave?'

'Yes, but not everyone realises that. This is all controlled by the Six Mile Chedda Grove gang, who are a rival of the Seven Mile Bloods. Everything you see around here is all the result of the heroin sales and the gang war.'

I stared at the crumbling streets as we drove through the neighbourhood. 'Can you lead a normal life here if you just work and keep your head down?'

'Yeah, you work for Chrysler or GM and you mind your own business. I mean, shit happens and you're gonna see it,' Brannock said. 'The only problem I see with it is at night, going to the gas station or the places where people gather. You would only go to the grocery store during the day, and only when you need to.'

Going out at night to get food or to fill your car was simply too dangerous, I knew that. Passing by gas stations, fast-food joints and party stores, I would often see shady-looking groups of men hanging around. They were gang members or people working for the gangs, looking to sell drugs, controlling their spots. Or they were 'stick-up kids', who also worked for the gangs, and were looking for someone to rob. Stop at one of these places – even during the day – and not only did you risk losing your car in a car-jacking, you risked losing your life.

A quarter of all violent crime in Detroit happened within 500 feet of gas stations. Recently, in an effort to combat the dangers, Project Green Light had been started. It was an initiative set up by Detroit police in partnership with a number of gas stations around the city. If a gas station had a green light illuminated, it meant that the Detroit police were monitoring it live on CCTV. It was hoped that the initiative would make the gas stations and the surrounding areas safer. Crime would still inevitably be committed at gas stations – including shootings and homicides – but the project had grown in popularity, with restaurants and even cinemas taking part. Even so, I never stopped for gas in Detroit, and apart from downtown and a couple of other areas, I never entered a party store or other business in these neighbourhoods either, unless Brannock or another cop was with me.

There was even a McDonald's restaurant that some cops called 'the Murder-Mac'. When I asked: 'Did you have a shooting there once?' they laughed at my naivety. '*Shootings*,' they said. 'Multiple shootings.'

'Do you have any kind of relationship with the gangs?' I asked Brannock now. 'If you saw them, would you know them by name? Could you just stop and speak to them?'

'Uh-huh. Yep. Plus I have a pretty good memory, so I remember lots of the gang members that we deal with – their faces *and* their real names. And that can be effective, especially out here where it's always "Jig", or "Sonny", or "B-Murder", "Smoke", "Big Smoke", or "Chino". None of the gang members go by their real name and that's one of their things – you're not supposed to be caught with your ID. So when you know their government name and you walk into a party store and they're there selling dime bags of weed, and you're able to walk up and be like, "Hey, John Smith, what's happening, my man," that instantly changes their mind-set of what's going on.'

'They don't like it?'

'Not at all!'

'You know them but they also know who you are. Is there not a fear that they will pull out a gun and kill you?'

'There's always that fear,' Brannock said. 'Who knows what

66

they're fucking high on? Plus, they now drink this shit called "lean". Constantly! It's in every rap video that they shoot.'

'Lean', also known as 'purple drank', was usually a mixture of Promethazine-Codeine (cough syrup), Sprite and Jolly Ranchers candies. Popularised by Texas-based hip-hop stars and DJs, lean had quickly spread around the country. Giving the drinker a sedated and euphoric feeling, it was easy to see why it had become so widely used, when people were surrounded by so much misery. But it could also prove deadly – and some of the very people who had originally popularised lean had since died. The huge amount of codeine that the mixture contained had the same addictive effects as heroin, and lean could also cause the drinker to literally stop breathing. If it didn't kill you or put you in a coma, it could lead to impairment of motor skills and make the drinker feel separated from their own body.

For the cops who police these neighbourhoods, lean is just one more risk factor that may confront them at every stop they make – and every person they encounter.

5

In Memoriam

As we continued with our tour, Brannock pulled the car over by a weather-beaten telegraph pole on a street corner.

'It's not a nice term but I have heard some people around here refer to this as a "ghetto memorial",' he said. 'They put these balloons and shit all over it.'

Taped to the pole were a number of small, weather-faded teddy bears, some with red bandanas tied around their necks. At the base was a huge pile of empty liquor bottles.

The street – Novara – was lined with white-wooden bungalows, many of which were burnt-out wrecks covered in gang graffiti, whilst across the street was a modern-looking building – a middle school.

'This memorial is for a Seven Mile Bloods gang member who was killed,' Brannock informed me.

'What's with all the bottles?' I wanted to know.

'They do that as a tribute or whatever. They'll pour a little sip of their liquor out. Then they'll leave the bottles at the memorial. You'll see it on gang or rap videos, where they will be riding around the neighbourhood on the hood of a car, pouring liquor onto the ground. They're honouring their comrades, they're honouring their dead.'

But there were other kinds of memorials too. As well as the 'ghetto' gang memorials, others had been put up for non-gang members who had also become victims of the violence. We stopped by one. Pinned to another telegraph pole at a crossroad of narrow streets in another depressing neighbourhood was a piece of white paper. It had been stuffed into a plastic envelope that rattled wildly in the freezing winter wind. On the sheet of paper was the fading colour photo of a teenaged white girl, with long blonde hair. Written around the photo were the words: *Blessed beautiful Paige. We love you.* Pink ribbons had been tied around the post, along with a couple of Christmas wreaths.

Paige Stalker was a 16-year-old from an affluent Grosse Pointe neighbourhood, just across the border from Detroit, who had dreamed of becoming a doctor. One year previously, she had been sitting in a parked car with four other teens here at the corner of Philip and Charlevoix. The reason the teens had crossed into Detroit is unknown, although police believed they were smoking pot.

As they sat in their car in the dark secluded street, two gang members, out searching for another gang in order to execute a revenge shooting, mistook Paige's car for the one they were seeking. The men opened fire with an AK-47, shooting over thirty rounds into the car. One girl was hit in the back. One boy was shot twice in the arm and a second boy in the shoulder. They all survived. Paige Stalker wasn't so lucky. One of the bullets had struck her in the head and killed her.

The kids were literally just three blocks west of Grosse Pointe Park. Just three short blocks – but two completely different worlds.

*

There are a number of townships that surround Detroit, and many of them are seriously affluent with multi-million-dollar homes, yacht clubs and a mostly white population. The residents are, in the main, good people; they just live in a totally different world from their neighbours in Detroit, even though that world is sometimes literally across the street.

I had once spent a shift patrolling with one of the Grosse Pointe departments. The Grosse Pointes are five small separate cities, situated south-east of Detroit. The police department I went out with was staffed with friendly, neatly dressed officers. When I had mentioned how different their city was compared to Detroit, the officer I was with told me that in one of the other – 'even more foo-foo' – Grosse Pointes, the cops sometimes had to enforce an ordinance regulating the length of people's lawns. 'Blight ordinances' are common for many towns and cities, Detroit included, but the point the officer was making, was clear – murder and decay on one side of the street, well-trimmed grass on the other.

Whilst on patrol, the Grosse Pointe officer parked his police vehicle along Mack Avenue – a long, wide road that heads east through Detroit towards its more prosperous neighbours, separating one city from another like a tarmac border. North of Mack lies Detroit, south are the Grosse Pointes. The Grosse Pointe side of Mack Avenue was Main Street, USA, with pet boutiques and other such businesses. The Detroit side of Mack Avenue featured boarded-up, graffiti-covered stores. Two worlds separated by four lanes of traffic.

There had also been cases of 'barricades' being placed across roads, stopping Detroit traffic from entering the city of Grosse Pointe Park. One road literally has a brick wall built across it, keeping the residents of one city out of the other.

Another cop I spoke to, from a different department to the north of Detroit, told me that some departments operated a kind of 'border patrol' between their own city and Detroit. But of course this doesn't stop kids from these more prosperous towns from crossing into Detroit, whether to score some drugs, or just for fun and to hang out. And sometimes that has resulted in death.

The reward to find Paige's killers had reached $162,000.

'We had a black girl killed up in the Ninth Precinct, around the same time,' Brannock announced. 'The reward for her is $2,750.'

What made one life more valuable than another, I wondered. Race? Class? Wealth? A ZIP code?

The black girl Brannock had mentioned was 22-year-old Christina Samuel. She had recently graduated from college and was about to begin law school. On Christmas Eve, just two days after Paige Stalker had been killed, as she sat in a car with a friend, two people wearing hoods approached with guns and opened fire, killing Christina.

Brannock was visibly angry at the disparity between the two rewards. 'It just goes to show the value of a black citizen compared to a white citizen,' he told me. 'Both of these girls were innocent victims, so how can they justify the difference in those rewards? They were both gunned down in the same week. How do people sleep at night, putting up a reward like that for just one of the girls?' He shook his head. 'It just doesn't sit well with me at all.'

In both cases, the non-profit charitable organisation, Crime Stoppers, had put up a reward of $2,500, with anything extra being made up by private donation. The donation sizes are another indication of how different people's lives are, on the opposite sides of Mack Avenue.

Both murders are still unsolved, but the father of Christina and the grandfather of Paige have become friends. They meet weekly, and together they attend rallies, and march against violence. Two decent gentlemen from two utterly different – though geographically close – cities, brought together by almost identical tragedies.

We stared at Paige's sad, lonely tribute a while longer.

'Where the hell do the gangs get AK-47s from?' I asked Brannock, breaking the silence.

'Oh, they're a dime-a-dozen,' he told me casually. 'You can buy an AK-47 for two or three hundred bucks at the sporting goods store. I've got two myself.'

*

It wasn't just kids from the suburbs coming *into* Detroit who were putting themselves in danger, Brannock told me: sometimes, Detroit went *out* to them.

A little further on, he pulled in alongside a broken wooden fence on Manning Avenue. Sprayed all across it was gang graffiti. It was completely different from the tagging and suburban kids' graffiti he had shown me earlier. Sprayed in pink was *Mammas baby I love you!*; *RIP Gone but never forgotten!* and *DAT RITE*. At the end of the fence was a brick house. It was still standing, but all of the windows were blown out and black scorch-marks ran up the outside walls, like creeping shadows of invisible ivy. More graffiti was sprayed on the abused body of the house: *U will be missed*; *RIP JAM MONEY*. Stacked on the front steps of the house were teddy bears, deflated balloons, broken candles and dozens of empty liquor bottles. Other wrecked houses nearby had similar markings. Various dead gang members were told to RIP and RIH (*rest in heaven*), along with the gang name HOBSQUAD.

'See where it says Hobsquad?' Brannock pointed. 'They are the younger Seven Mile Bloods gang members. The Seven Mile Bloods juniors were running wild and this one kid – his name was Ihab Maslamani – went off on a spree, and he was robbing banks. He ended up killing this guy from the suburbs called Matthew Landry.'

The Matthew Landry case, like so many others, was horrifying. Landry, a 21-year-old from Chesterfield Township, north-east of Detroit, was abducted at gunpoint in the middle of the afternoon outside of a sandwich shop in Eastpointe – a small city immediately north of 8 Mile, above the 4-8-2-0-Die. His abductors were 17-year-old Ihab Maslamani and 16-year-old Robert Taylor. They bundled Landry into his own car, drove him around for a number of hours and robbed him. Landry's bank card was used to withdraw hundreds of dollars, which Maslamani and Taylor spent on clothes.

Next, they went to a dope house where Maslamani bought crack-cocaine. Landry was made to sit on a couch as Maslamani smoked the drugs.

Finally, Landry was taken to an abandoned house in Detroit, where he was forced onto his knees. Maslamani stood behind him, pointed a gun at the back of his head and pulled the trigger just once. Landry's lifeless body fell to the floor and Maslamani and Taylor simply walked away, leaving the corpse where it lay. At some point the house was set on fire, and after the killing Maslamani took Landry's car to commit further crimes – the 'spree' that Brannock had mentioned.

Maslamani and Taylor had both experienced difficult childhoods. Maslamani had come to Detroit when he was just a child, from Lebanon. Taylor had grown up in a violent, drug-plagued environment. His mother had given birth to him when she was just 13 years old. His father, who had abandoned him, was said to be an alcoholic and crack addict. Despite their ages at the time of Landry's murder, and despite pleas from their defence teams, Maslamani and Taylor were both given life sentences without parole.

'The younger kids worshipped Ibrahim Maslamani,' Brannock told me. 'So they changed the gang name to Hobsquad, because they used to call Maslamani "I-hob". So that's where Hobsquad comes from. In fact, they made a rap video that tells the story about it, and it has news clips in it too. I'll show it to you – it's called *Welcome to Hob City*.'

The rap, *Welkom 2 Hob City* [sic], not only used clips of news report about the Landry case but it also, rather sickeningly, included a recording of Matthew Landry's distressed mother, speaking to reporters after the trial.

As we spoke about the number of homicides that the city saw, Brannock sighed and said, 'Some of the criminals here just don't value life. There was a body found last night in Number Nine (9th Precinct) that was all burnt-up. I mean this poor fucker was burnt-up! I saw the pictures of him.'

'Was it gang-related?' I asked.

Brannock raised his shoulders. 'We'll have to talk to homicide. But the burnt body is a John Doe; we don't even know who it is. There's really nothing to work on. They went to a coroner's office but they couldn't print him. They'll do dental records, I'm assuming, but many people here have never been to a dentist. Usually a family will come forward to claim a body but it can take time. Some guy was involved in robbing people and shit – then he went missing and it wasn't until about three months later when we found his body under a porch. He had been shot in the head.'

We continued on and soon after, Brannock turned into Runyon – a narrow residential street in the 9th Precinct. He wanted to show me another scene of Detroit sorrow.

There wasn't a soul on the street, which consisted of yet another collection of small wooden rundown houses and empty, overgrown plots.

'This used to be a Delta Zone,' Brannock said. 'It meant that police couldn't come here unless there were two or three cars.'

Delta Zones, he explained, were considered to be the most dangerous areas of the city, and police dispatchers had maps, showing them where each of the zones was located. If there was a call for police to one of those zones, the dispatcher would have to send multiple vehicles, for the officers' own safety.

This whole area, Brannock said, was 'narcotic controlled'. Gangs had taken over the neighbourhood, selling drugs and fighting over the territory. As dangerous streets go in Detroit, Runyon was right up there. Even so, and as bad is it looked, Brannock told me that the area had actually cleaned up a little, especially since Mayor Duggan had taken office. Under Duggan's Blight Eradication programme, many of the ruins had been torn down and cleared away.

'The Runyon Boys control this,' Brannock continued, as we cruised along the street. 'There've been multiple homicides here. At one time, this was the most murderous street in the whole of the United States.'

'So, what changed? How come it cleaned up?' I asked.

'The fucking houses being cleared away.'

'You mean everyone just moved out?'

'Yeah. They just left this shit. But there are some people that just can't get out, that are still here.'

I looked out at the few houses that were left and thought about the decent people who were still living here, amongst the wreckage. Once the gangs had taken over, it was tough for neighbourhoods to recover.

'So, for argument's sake, if I was to just drive down here myself, get out of the car and go for a walk, would I be okay?' I asked. It was a genuine question. I knew better than to do it, but there was a part of me that would have liked to just wander along these streets, without an escort.

'During the day … yeah,' Brannock said cautiously. 'But sometimes … Look, if they are out playing basketball and they see your fucking ass coming down here, and they want your car, they'll block the street, come up, pull out a gun and car-jack you.'

'How would they block the road? With other cars?'

'No, with themselves, just standing there.'

'What happens if I just put my foot down and drive at them?'

'Then you run them over.'

6

The House on Runyon Street

Brannock parked up outside a cream-coloured bungalow, and I realised it was the reason we had driven down Runyon Street. The house sat on a small corner plot at the junction of another equally decrepit street, surrounded by a cluster of skinny, snow-covered trees. One of the first things I noticed was a large splash of red across the dented front door and exterior walls. It looked like a splattering of blood, although it was probably just paint.

'This house here, we had a quintuple shooting,' Brannock told me. 'There were five people shot. Four dead.'

The house, he said, had been a 'dope spot' with a marijuana farm in the basement. A rival dealer had paid another man to carry out the hit – but that wasn't the full story.

Michael 'Big Mike' Robinson was growing marijuana and dealing dope from the little bungalow on Runyon Street. The gunman who had been hired to kill him entered the house and opened fire and, as Brannock had told it, five people were shot. A woman who survived had been shot five times, but had managed to crawl away, hiding under the bed of seven-year-old 'Little Mike' – son of the now dead 'Big Mike'.

When the police turned up at the scene, they saw a young man hanging around nearby in the street and assumed he was involved in the shootings.

The young man in question is called Davontae Sanford. Davontae lived in a house a few blocks over from Runyon – and he actually had nothing at all to do with the murders. Seeing and hearing all the commotion, he had simply gone out to investigate. The police, however, picked him up and took him back to the precinct, where homicide detectives, including Homicide Commander James Tolbert, interrogated him. A confession to the killings – containing information only the officers and the killer could know – was typed up by one of the officers and placed before Davontae, who signed it.

It was also claimed that Davontae had drawn a plan of the house, but that is not correct. James Tolbert himself had drawn it – something he later admitted to the Michigan State Police who had been tasked with re-investigating the case in 2015. Then, after being shown photographs of the homicide scene, including the location of each of the bodies, Davontae was told to draw on the plan where each of the bodies was located. The young man then signed the diagram as all his own work. This drawing, along with the confession that had been written for him, was presented as evidence, 'proving' that Davontae must have committed the crime. After all, how else could he have known so much about it?

Homicide Commander Tolbert was later promoted to the rank of Deputy Chief of Police before leaving the DPD to become Chief of Police in Flint, Michigan.

But why would Davontae confess to something so heinous when he had nothing at all to do with it?

At the time of these shootings, Davontae was 14 years old. What's more, he had learning difficulties, and when he was interrogated by the homicide officers and subsequently confessed to the killings, no parent or guardian had been present. True, a 14-year-old with learning difficulties isn't beyond committing murder – even multiple murders – but there is another fact about Davontae that should have caused serious concern around his 'confession'.

Davontae is blind in one eye. So here we have a half-blind 14-

year-old with learning difficulties, who we are supposed to believe carried out the crime of the century – entering a house occupied by a dangerous drug dealer, accurately aiming a gun, opening fire and shooting five people, killing four of them. But this story was believed, and after he took a plea deal, Davontae was convicted. He was sentenced to 37 to 90 years imprisonment.

But things then took an unexpected turn. Whilst Davontae sat in prison, another man, Vincent Smothers, confessed to the Runyon murders. Smothers was a known hit-man, who had carried out numerous contract killings around the city. He didn't know Davontae Sanford and had nothing to gain from confessing to the murders. You could also say that he had nothing to lose. Imprisoned for a minimum of 52 years, for eight killings, Smothers – a former high-school honours student – will not be eligible for parole until he is 81 years old.

Three months after the Runyon shooting, Smothers had carried out his final murder. The hit was against a lady called Rose Cobb, the wife of a Detroit police sergeant, David Cobb. The latter was having an affair, Smothers said, and had allegedly hired him to kill his wife so that he could claim the insurance money.

Outside a CVS Pharmacy on Jefferson, Smothers approached Rose Cobb as she sat in her car, waiting for her husband, who had gone into the store. Smothers raised his gun and shot her in the head, killing her where she sat. Smothers would later state that the gun he used to kill Rose Cobb was one he had stolen from the Runyon house, during the previous killings.

Smothers was arrested for the shooting of Rose Cobb, as was Sergeant David Cobb, after Smothers had put him in the frame. However, with no evidence other than Smothers' claim that Sergeant Cobb had paid him $50 to bump off his wife (having originally agreed to pay him $10,000), Cobb was released from custody. The truth around his alleged involvement may never be known, for five months later, Cobb went to a park in nearby

Stirling Heights, tied a cord around his neck and hanged himself from a tree.

It was whilst he was in prison that Smothers confessed to the Runyon murders. He claimed that he and another man – Ernest 'Nemo' Davis – had carried out the hit. Davis has never been charged with any offences relating to Runyon although he is serving a sentence of up to 15 years in prison for an unrelated shooting of a security guard. Smothers could, of course, have been making the whole thing up for some unknown reason, but there were details that Smothers knew, that were only known to the investigating officers and other persons directly involved in the incident.

As the shooting and murders were occurring inside the Runyon house, another man

came out to investigate the noise from his house across the street. That man was Reverend Jesse King, a Detroit Police Department chaplain. He also happened to be a cousin of 'Big Mike', Michael Robinson.

Reverend King was armed, despite being a man of God. As the gunmen came out of the house, he opened fire on them. The gunmen returned fire, shooting at the chaplain with an AK-47, before making off. King was unharmed and it appeared he had caused no damage of his own on the gunmen.

These details were never revealed to the public, yet Smothers recalled the incident when he confessed to the murders. But none of this mattered. It seemed that no one wanted to give credence to his story; they would rather a half-blind, innocent teenager with learning difficulties sat in prison for 90 years instead.

Many people have campaigned for Davontae's release but the calls were ignored. Brannock, I learned, had worked on the case himself. He had originally been put on it to keep Davontae in prison, and to prove that it was he – and not Smothers – who had committed the murders. But the more Brannock dug, the more he began to believe in the teenager's innocence. Then, quite suddenly, Brannock was asked to return the case file and evidence and instructed not to look into the case any further.

Other detectives had also worked the case, only to find themselves summarily removed from it too. I was told about one officer who, after uncovering a possible connection between Smothers and the then mayor, Kwame Kilpatrick (Detroit's very own criminally convicted civic leader), found himself unexpectedly transferred from a highly respected, specialised unit, to a regular police precinct.

Added to all this is a story that had been given to police by one of their own former bosses, Inspector William Rice, a previous head of the Detroit Police Homicide Unit who had retired a year before the Runyon murders after serving with the department for 35 years.

Rice's involvement in all this is yet another bizarre twist in an already strange and sorry tale. Rice, who was married, was also in a relationship with Davontae's aunt, and had been for about 10 years. His links to the Sanford family resulted in Rice making up an alibi for Davontae, stating that they had been together at the time of the shootings. This lie would end with Rice being imprisoned for perjury – along with unrelated matters of mortgage fraud and drug dealing, together with Davontae's aunt, Cheryl Sanford. And during all this, an innocent boy remained in prison.

Later, when officers in Gang Intel learnt that Brannock had spoken to me about the Runyon case, it was suggested that he had told me the details as an 'insurance policy', in case someone had him killed for knowing too much. The thing is, I wasn't sure if they were joking or not.

As we looked out at the Runyon murder house, Brannock said, 'They've been trying to free Davontae Sanford for years.'

'Do you think he'll ever get out?' I asked.

Brannock raised his shoulders. 'We're working on it.'

It was clear that the case was still eating away at him, and it was important for Brannock that I understood how he had devoted a large part of his career to the Runyon case, as he tried to uncover the truth and expose what really happened – something that he was still trying to do. The Runyon case was full of holes and allegations and untruths. It's a total mess except for two things that seem perfectly clear:

Davontae Sanford is innocent and Vincent Smothers is guilty.

Despite the fact some Detroit police officers had put Davontae in prison and were working to keep him there, his stepfather who, along with many others, has been advocating for Davontae's release, now assists the Detroit Police Department as a mentor on their Ceasefire programme, working closely with Brannock and his team to try and steer kids away from gangs and crime.

As we accelerated away from Runyon, Brannock said, 'You know, there are some detectives who still feel that Davontae Sanford did those homicides.'

'But why would Vincent Smothers admit to it?'

'Exactly.' At that precise moment, Brannock's phone rang. He answered it, then turned to me, saying, 'This is Lance Sullivan. He's a homicide detective working on the murdered firefighter case. Did you hear about that?'

I told him that I had read about the case online before coming out to Detroit, and I had also heard officers talking about it in the office.

Brannock put his phone on speaker. 'What's up, Lance?' he asked.

'You know we talked about you raiding that dope house?'

'Yeah, the guys ran a source through there and we bought some heroin, so we're going to hit it.'

'Perfect.' Detective Sullivan sounded pleased. 'Because this dope house might be coming into that firefighter murder we're investigating.'

Homicide detectives from the Detroit Police Northwest District covered the area where the murder had occurred, but they were already swamped with other cases, including nearly a dozen other murders that they had picked up the week before. Detective Lance Sullivan had stepped in to assist and had ended up taking on firefighter David Madrigal's case himself.

Detective Sullivan had been speaking to people in the neighbourhood who had known the firefighter, and he already had a number of leads. A wallet in a plastic bag, for example, had been flung from Madrigal's stolen SUV. It had been handed to police and found to belong to the firefighter. Detective Sullivan didn't know for sure if the dope house was linked to the firefighter case but it was something that needed to be looked into, all the same.

Brannock's own source, who had bought some heroin there, had described the location as 'banging' – a busy, drug-dealing address. But there was a complication: Detroit homicide didn't want the people inside the house to know that they were being looked at in relation to the firefighter murder, in case it jeopardised their inquiry. That's where Brannock and his team came in. Gang Intel hitting the address wouldn't look so strange whilst at the same time some of Brannock's team – including Brannock himself – had previously worked homicide, which meant they knew what to look out for. Other members of Brannock's team had worked in narcotics, so they too, were obvious assets.

Quickly, I began to see just how specialised, unique and useful the GIU team was. True, they were employed to focus on gangs, but with their combined experience and backgrounds, they could also be used for other criminal inquiries, and as so much of the crime that happened in Detroit – drugs, robberies, homicides – were gang-related anyway, it worked out nicely for all.

'Some kid overdosed right out front of the house, but my own source said that they just kept selling; they don't fucking care,' Detective Sullivan said. 'So it could be a good hit for you.'

'Yeah, no problem, leave it to us,' Brannock said, and he ended the call.

'You're raiding a house tomorrow?' I asked.

'*We. We're* raiding it. You're coming too, Mick.'

7

The Raid

The following day I drove myself to the base. I never use a satnav – not even in Detroit – so I did my best to remember the landmarks from Google Street View images that I had looked at before heading out. At every red traffic-light I came to, I ensured that I didn't stop too close to the cars ahead of me, in case I needed to get away. In addition, I kept my windows up and the doors locked. Car-jackings were epidemic in Detroit. Violence was always a factor and many victims were killed.

Even the police weren't safe. During one of my previous visits to Detroit, an off-duty Detroit police officer, whose second child had just been born the previous day, was dragged from his vehicle and shot multiple times in the head and back by armed men who were described as being on a 'car-jacking spree'. It was the second time that particular officer had been car-jacked, having been shot in the leg during another incident a few years before.

Criminals and gangs need cars, and that often means taking them by force. Even the current Detroit Chief of Police, James Craig, once had to accelerate away from a red traffic-light after he had seen a man racing towards his car – and that car was a police cruiser! Prior to that incident, Chief Craig had wondered why so many Detroit residents were jumping red lights; now he was absolutely clear about the reason. He went on to describe car-jackings as being 'almost like a way of life in Detroit', and warned drivers about the dangers of stopping to fill up at gas stations at night.

As I've said previously, I have never stopped for gas in Detroit – not even during the day. Some may accuse me of being over-cautious, but once you're dead, you're dead, and Detroit had for some years been number one in the USA for car-jackings. In 2008 they peaked at more than three a day. Although numbers are down today, there are still hundreds every year, and it isn't unusual for them to end with the driver being shot dead.

As I drove on towards the base, a thin, scruffy-looking black man in his thirties stepped into the road a few feet ahead of me. He was dragging a huge, rusty chain with enormous fat links behind him, causing me to slow down as I approached. Maybe it was nothing – just some guy taking a chain from somewhere – but the far end of the chain still appeared to be attached to something and I was concerned that he was going to pull it across the road to block my way. Besides, this was Detroit, and I was in one of the most dangerous neighbourhoods in the most dangerous precinct in the city. Hitting the brakes, I spun the car around and drove off in the opposite direction. I'd find another route to get to where I needed to go. 'Better safe than sorry' is good advice in Detroit.

*

Brannock had told me to be in the office for noon and I was bang on time, even after taking a slight detour.

Sitting at one of the empty desks, I looked over at the whiteboard behind where Whispers was sat. A list of officers' roles and positions for the raid had appeared on it. Cooter, Hunter and Casper were all shown 'SH' – Shotgun. Hollywood was shown as being on the 'ram'- the battering ram, to force open any doors. Whispers would be on the Halligan – a firefighter's tool, like a crowbar with a large claw at one end that could be used to force entry into vehicles or buildings. Then, once the door had been breached, AJ and Joe would make the initial entry into the house.

Hunter and Casper both greeted me as they walked into the office together. I followed them into their own room, off the main part of the office, to chat with them as they got kitted-up for the raid. They had both spent years working on narcotics and special operations, and were equipped with black SWAT gear, which included overalls, knee pads, ballistic body-armour, ballistic helmets, face-covering balaclavas, and leg holsters for their back-up handguns, should anything go wrong with the shotguns. Holders for extra magazines of ammunition were strapped around various parts of their body, such as their legs, arms and waist. Hunter and Casper looked like serious shit.

'This is like the old days for you, isn't it? Doing these drug raids?' I said to Hunter.

'True, but with Gang Intel not only do we get the opportunity to do narcotics raids, we also get information for homicides, because there's often a connection. We also get info on gang members and can recover weapons. That's why it's so great working on Gang Intel, because you're not just working solely on one thing.'

'And the gangs are into everything, right?'

'Everything!' he said. 'Obviously, narcotics. And with drugs they generate an income, and when they generate income they need to protect it, so they need firearms. They also need an image, so you'll see them on social media standing around with various guns. And where a gang may begin with just one kid starting out as a rapper, now they're a group doing robberies – stick-ups. Then they start shooting rival gang members and so on and so on. So yeah, everything!'

'This is a fun job but it's also a dangerous job, right? Every house you hit you know that there could be a gun there.'

'Of course! And they could be standing at the door waiting for us.'

'Does it not worry you?'

'It's a mind-set. It's out of my control. When it's my day, it's my day. You just don't know, so you mentally and physically prepare yourself. You train for whatever you need to train for. I've got my helmet, my vest and everything else I need, so the probability of someone killing me, versus me killing him? Well, let's just say, I've got a little more advantage.'

'That Aussie guy here yet?' It was Brannock, walking into the main office.

'I'm here,' I said, stepping out from Hunter and Casper's room. 'You do realise that Australia is nowhere near England, right?'

'It's all the fucking same,' he said. 'You got koala bears in England, don't you?'

'No.'

'Yes, you do. And kangaroos. Isn't that right, Whispers?'

Whispers was sat quietly at his desk. He remained silent and continued to stare at his computer screen but as he took a sip of his coffee, I noticed him smiling at Brannock's foolishness.

I stared at Brannock as he chuckled at his own stupidity. He could be insufferable (in a kind of good way) but he was also extremely funny and I just couldn't help but like him.

'Whispers is a Sheila,' Brannock then said, digging up a piece of Australian slang he must have heard somewhere once; probably in an Outback Steakhouse or in *Crocodile Dundee*, or some shit.

'Sheila is slang for a woman,' I said.

'Right,' Brannock said, agreeing with me. 'Whispers is a Sheila.'

This time Whispers looked up at Brannock, but he still remained silent.

I liked Whispers too. He was calm, softly spoken and unassuming. Whispers was still fairly new and only had a few years on the job, but I suspected that he was one of the smartest cops in the office. When I had asked Brannock about him, and how he had come to be on the unit, Brannock told me how Whispers had been investigating the murder of a guy who was the son of a Detroit police officer's girlfriend. Afterwards, the officer contacted Brannock, telling him that he had a 'super-fucking-smart cop' who needed to learn the streets. As a favour, could Brannock take him under his wing and train him? Brannock agreed and after just two weeks saw the potential in him, noting how 'mature' Whispers was and that he wasn't 'doing stupid shit'. When Brannock was asked to get more people on the Gang Unit, he knew immediately that he wanted Whispers on his team.

After everyone had got kitted up and been briefed about the operation, we headed to the cars. Robo was riding in the front of Brannock's black SUV, so I jumped into the rear with Kap – a keen young white female officer who had been temporarily posted with Gang Intel. Even though Kap didn't have much time in with the department, she was hoping to join Gang Intel full-time. Brannock (not to mention Robo) was eager to have more female officers on the unit, so he was happy to have her.

The house we were going to raid was in a neighbourhood that was besieged by three gangs – Hit Squad, Related Through Money, and Arab Thug Lords. Although they had been told there were no kids or dogs at the house, they had also been told there could be firearms inside, including a shotgun. As with any hit on a house such as this, it would require a fast, hard, aggressive approach. The officers would need to get in and secure the location – and any persons inside – as quickly as possible, to minimise the risk of anyone, suspect or police, getting hurt.

As we headed towards the location, Brannock turned on the car stereo. Violent gangsta rap immediately tore out of the speakers.

'My nigga on the ground, layin' in a puddle of blood ...'

Robo reached over and turned the volume down, so that she could make a phone call.

'This is Gang Intel,' she said down the phone. 'Can we have District Four for a zone clearance? Great, thank you.'

As we reached the street with the target address, Brannock drove along the frozen road, checking it for anything unusual. Outside the house were three vehicles. Brannock picked up his police radio and gave the other units the details of the cars, in case they were linked in any way to the property.

We continued past the address. It was a typical Detroit home, albeit one that seemed well cared for. The small wood-framed building had a fresh coat of white paint on the outside and there were new-looking, double-glazed windows. I noticed that the front door had a metal security gate protecting it. Whispers was going to need his Halligan.

As Brannock reached over to turn the gangsta rap back up, Robo reached over to turn the air con down.

I'm from the streets where young niggas, they'll kill you quick ...'

'You've got the fucking air con on in here!' Robo said to Brannock. 'It's freezing.'

'Relax! Buy some gloves and a fucking hat,' Brannock told her. Then he pointed at Kap. 'You see Kap's prepared. She's got her hat on. The rookie's more prepared than the veteran!'

'I have gloves and a fucking hat,' Robo responded. 'They're in my fucking bag.'

'You're unprepared then,' Brannock told her, before adding, 'I can't believe I have you two in the car with me, fucking up!'

'Only one's fucking up right now,' Kap said.

'Who's fucking up?' Robo asked.

'Last week you lost your prep!' Brannock told her.

'I didn't lose it, I misplaced it. There's a fucking difference!'

Brannock turned and looked at me. 'Mick, can you back me up on this?'

'I'm gonna remain neutral,' I said. 'Besides, I wasn't even here last week.'

'What the fuck? You can get out of this fucking car right now,' Brannock told me. 'Hold on, I'll slow down so you can get out.'

Brannock barely slowed the car down at all. In fact, I think he may have actually sped up a little.

'Okay, go ahead – tuck and roll!' he said, encouraging me to throw myself to my death. Then, changing the subject and becoming serious, he said, 'Listen, when we pull up at the address, we're gonna park right on the fucking grass.'

'You're just going to drive up onto the front lawn?' Robo asked.

'Yes. The neighbour's front lawn. And then we're gonna go back behind the house, whilst Hunter and Casper do their thing at the front.'

'Bang-bang! Motherfucker nigga! Bang-bang!'

Brannock reached the top of the road, spun the car around and came to a stop, facing back down the street. The target house was about halfway down, on the left.

'This is the dope house that everybody comes to in this neighbourhood,' he informed me.

Robo, Brannock and Kap each held their Glock pistol on their lap, checking that they were correctly loaded and making them ready by racking the top metal slide to draw the first round from the magazine into the firing chamber.

A freezing rain began to tumble down from the low, grey sky. As we sat waiting for the other units to reach us, a scruffy-looking white man sauntered past, almost slipping on a patch of slushy ice as he stared hard at us.

'This guy was looking at us when we drove down the first time,' Brannock said. It was a concern. The man had no doubt spotted us as police and if he knew the men in the drug house, there was a chance he could call and warn them of our presence.

Brannock watched the man closely as he passed us by. Then,

picking up the radio, he called to the other units. 'No activity at the house other than those vehicles parked out front.' He turned to me again. 'Mick, if you hear gunfire, get behind this truck. And don't get shot; I still haven't had you fill out your waiver form yet.'

I patted my chest. 'I've got a vest on,' I said.

Hollywood called up over the radio. 'We're at a ruby (*red traffic-light*), then we'll be with you.'

The other units were moments away.

'Know I love that gun sound; Bang-bang-bang-bang …'

Brannock picked up his radio. 'All right, everybody, be safe.'

A split second later, he roared the engine and we charged towards the house. The SUV rocked about as Brannock drove it directly over the kerb and onto the neighbour's frozen lawn. Then all the vehicle doors opened. Brannock, Robo and Kap dived out of the car and rushed the house. I looked ahead and could see three other cars – marked and unmarked – skidding to a halt on the road. Hollywood and Whispers leapt up the front steps of the house. Hunter and Casper, both dressed in their black SWAT gear, followed directly behind them, along with AJ and Joe.

Using the Halligan, Whispers forced open the metal security gate that came before the front door. Then Hollywood moved in with the battering ram. He swung it forward but the door remained shut; it often took two or more strikes to force a door open, especially if they had been reinforced.

Cooter, standing just to the right of Hollywood, realised that the few seconds of delay caused by the metal grill and the door not going in on the first hit, had now put the officers on offer to anyone who was inside. He reached up and used the end of his shotgun to smash in the window at the front of the house. The glass shattered into large shards and Cooter reached through the jagged hole, ripping down the curtains. He lifted his shotgun and peered into the house, covering Whispers and Hollywood, who were still standing at the door.

Hollywood took another swing, and this time the door went in, flying open and crashing against the inside wall. AJ and Joe, closely followed by Hunter, Casper and others, ran into the building. Everyone then began to shout orders.

'POLICE! GET ON THE FLOOR!'

'GET ON THE GROUND!'

'POLICE! DOWN! DOWN!'

'FREEZE! GET ON THE GROUND!'

Silence.

Minutes went by without a word and then I heard, 'ALL CLEAR!'

As I stood by the car, Brannock walked back towards me. 'Nice parking,' I said.

He smiled but didn't reply.

Hollywood was standing at the top of the front steps. 'Mick, are you coming in? It's raining.'

Hollywood was wearing a black woollen beanie, and as I reached him at the top of the stairs, I looked at the words that were embroidered across the front: *Execute cop killers*.

In the house, there was calm and quiet. Standing up, facing a wall in the front living room, like naughty children, were four middle-aged black men. Each had their hands cuffed behind their back.

Some of the officers were sat at a small oval dining table in the centre of the room, filling in paperwork. Robo had opened a laptop computer and was running checks on the people found inside the house. She was asking the men for their names, dates of birth and addresses. Each of the men answered her immediately.

In the corner of the room there was a small, limp Christmas tree. A single, large silver star hung from the top, its weight bending the tree over so severely that the top of the tree was literally pointed at the ground. It looked like the tree from *A Charlie Brown Christmas*.

In the kitchen, three young women, one black and two white, were sat on dining chairs. They were all in their late twenties and they too were facing a wall with their hands cuffed behind their back. Brannock walked in and started talking to one of them.

'Your dad must be proud of you, huh?' he said.

The woman didn't reply. She was slightly built, with pasty-white skin and track-marks across her body that clearly identified her as a heroin addict.

Robo now stepped into the kitchen, holding her laptop, ready to ask the women the same set of questions she had asked the men.

Brannock turned to the black woman. 'Where do you come from?' he asked.

'Flint,' she answered. 'I came here to smoke a joint.'

'You couldn't go to another house to get a joint?' Robo asked.

The woman didn't reply.

'Brannock, you should tell them about the last girl that came here to get fucked up,' Robo said.

'The last fucking girl that came to buy heroin in this city, she met these motherfuckers at a party store and they took her and her boyfriend back to a vacant house. They fucking raped the shit out of her – all three of them. One at a time,' he told the women. 'Then they beat her boyfriend half to death.'

The women all remained silent.

Brannock went to speak to the men facing the wall, leaving Robo to ask her questions.

Moments later, the previously calm living room exploded. One of the handcuffed men had made some sort of threat towards Brannock, who stormed up to him and warned: 'Watch who you're speaking to. You need to keep quiet.'

The man, who stood more than six feet tall and towered over Brannock, said, 'I'm a *man*, with kids – eleven kids!'

'You ain't a man,' Brannock told him. 'You're in a fucking dope house.'

'You take these cuffs off me and we'll see who the man is,' the guy said.

Hunter, always the calm, experienced voice of reason, sidled up to the guy. 'It's all over, man. We're on a whole other page now. Just relax.'

The man grumbled something and Hunter stepped away, joining me by the kitchen door. 'Whoa! That shit was about to go south!' he said.

Robo walked back into the living room. She pointed to the man who had threatened Brannock.

'He's on probation for narcotics,' she said, looking down at her laptop.

'I'm on probation but I ain't on probation for narcotics,' the man said.

'Then what *are* you on probation for?' Robo asked.

'Marijuana.'

'Marijuana? That's narcotics!' Robo said.

'Oh, okay, I didn't know y'all call marijuana narcotics, man.'

'Eleven kids, eh? How much do you pay in child support?' Hunter asked the man, sounding genuinely interested.

'Too damn much,' the man replied.

'Then stop having kids!' Robo said sharply.

But the man wasn't listening. 'They're a real pain,' he complained. 'And the baby mammas are always after a cheque and taking money from my back pocket.'

'You decided to have them!' Robo said. 'They didn't ask to come into this world. Take care of them!'

Brannock walked over to me. 'Have you gone upstairs?' he asked.

I hadn't, so he told me to follow him. We walked up a set of bare wooden stairs to the upper floor.

'It's actually an okay house,' he told me, as we reached the top. 'I haven't seen any roaches yet.'

The room looked like a converted attic, with sloping roofs. Unlike the sparsely furnished downstairs, the upstairs was crammed and cluttered. Piles of clothing lay in crumpled heaps. There were three dirty mattresses on the floor, and litter was scattered around the room along with a number of overflowing ashtrays.

'Those women downstairs, they live here?' I asked.

'Yeah, the two white girls. The black girl is just visiting.'

'So the black guys downstairs, they run the house?'

'Yeah. They're the sellers. See all the fucking needles and heroin wraps?' Brannock asked, pointing to the side of one of the mattresses. I looked down. On the floor were half a dozen used needles and screwed-up needle wrappers. Small pieces of pink paper lay nearby.

'They're lotto ticket forms. They get those at the party store for free,' Brannock told me. 'The dope boys grab them by the stack-full and use them to wrap their heroin.'

'And that's how the dealers sell them?' I asked.

'Uh-huh. Ten bucks apiece.'

Ten bucks for a wrap of heroin didn't sound like much, but when you had no income and needed multiple hits a day, you either stole or you used what you had – for the women, that meant their bodies.

'But why are the women here? Is it just to get free drugs?' I asked.

'Yeah, they fuck the dealers and they get free drugs.'

Brannock reached down and picked up a huge, plug-in dildo.

'Let's go see the guys down at homicide,' he said, waving the dildo around like a Light Sabre. 'We can tell them we found the murder weapon.'

Hollywood walked into the room. 'Are they going to go through this room some more?' he asked.

'No, they're done. Homicide won't search this shit, that's why they brought us,' Brannock told him. Then he picked up a white fur sleeveless jacket. 'Hollywood, put this on.'

'God damn it!' Hollywood said, smiling but stepping back, away from it.

'I'm gonna give it to Robo,' Brannock said, smirking. 'Remember she said she wanted something like this?'

'She did say that she wanted a fur jacket,' Hollywood said. 'But I don't think she meant cat!'

'This isn't cat. This is some kind of rat,' Brannock replied.

Back downstairs and Robo was in the kitchen, tapping at the laptop.

Brannock walked over to her, holding up the jacket. 'Hey, Robo …'

Robo looked over. 'Ah Jesus! I knew it was gonna be a dildo or some shit.' Even so, she took the jacket from Brannock.

'I got it for you for Christmas,' Brannock told her.

'Oh, you're so sweet,' she said.

'It's cat. But it's clean cat.'

Robo pulled the jacket over her arms and twisted her body to take a better look at it.

'I think there're bugs in it,' Brannock warned her.

Robo made a face, quickly pulling the jacket off and leaving it on a chair.

Brannock laughed and walked into the living room to speak to the handcuffed men. 'There's heroin shit all upstairs so this is a …'

'I don't know anything about that,' one of the men said, cutting Brannock off.

'There's cocaine and heroin stuff in the house and this girl right here is a fucking heroin addict,' Brannock said, pointing to one of the white women.

'Okay, but that doesn't mean I know anything about it,' the guy said.

The man who had previously threatened Brannock shuffled restlessly in his handcuffs. 'Man, I've got places to be, dawg,' he said.

'It's 2.33 in the afternoon, it's not like you're at fucking work,' Brannock said, before adding, 'Well, you kinda are at work, when you're selling dope, I understand that. But you should be at Ford, Chrysler, Dunkin' Donuts, something, anything! Well, I'm going to give you a place to go – jail.'

'I do have a job, *sir*,' the man hissed, annoyed.

'Why ain't you at it then?' Brannock asked.

'I gotta be there at four o'clock.'

'Not today, you won't be.'

'That's messed up,' the man replied.

'You chose to hang out at a dope house, so it is what it is,' Brannock told him.

'You're taking food out of my kids' mouths.'

'Taking food out of your kids' mouths! Why ain't you at home with your kids then, instead of a dope house?'

The man didn't answer.

'All of you have a bunch of excuses for your fucked-up behaviour,' Brannock scolded them.

We walked back into the kitchen, where Robo was checking each of the women's criminal history on the laptop. They had all been arrested multiple times for crimes including retail fraud, burglary and drunk driving.

'I'm not proud of what I've done. I got caught stealing, you know?' one of the white women said. She had a long ponytail, a pockmarked face and was dressed in a baggy black T-shirt and a tight pair of green shorts.

'And now you got caught in a dope house,' Brannock said.

'What is worth stealing that is worth your freedom?' Robo asked.

'Nothing!' the woman answered immediately. 'There's nothing that's worth my freedom. I know that now.'

'You've learnt a lesson?' Hollywood asked.

'I'm not saying that I'm completely reformed yet, no. I have a lengthy [criminal] history.'

'But why?' Brannock asked. 'You're a decent-looking girl.'

'Hanging out with the wrong people,' she said sadly.

'Do you bring your mom over here?' Brannock asked the woman. 'Your mom come visit you here?'

'Yeah.'

'Yeah? Your mom comes here and plays NBA2K with your fucking boyfriends and shit?' (NBA2K is a basketball video game.)

'No,' the woman told him. She sounded sad, defensive and weak. 'She comes over here just to see me.'

'She comes over here to play dice and shit?' Brannock asked, pushing her emotionally.

'No, she comes here and brings me food.'

'Does she shoot you up between the toes and all that shit?'

'No, she does not.'

'No?'

The woman lowered her head, staring down at her lap. 'I just want to be with my parents down at the beach.'

'No, this is better for you; just keep slamming that shit into your veins,' Brannock told her.

'You've got $13,000 worth of warrants,' Robo told the woman, reading from the laptop screen.

The woman didn't reply.

'Too bad your mom wasn't visiting when the police came in here and raided your fucking house,' Brannock said to her. 'At one time, when you were a child, this neighbourhood was beautiful. Now look what you brought to this motherfucker.'

'Any of you got kids?' Robo asked the women.

The women with the ponytail didn't but the other two did.

'I have one,' the second white woman said. 'She's at an aunt's house.'

'How old is she?' Robo asked.

'Six.'

'She's not at school today?'

'Today is a day off.'

'So why aren't you spending the day with her?'

'I had stuff to do this morning.'

'Like come to Detroit and smoke a fucking joint?' Brannock asked.

The woman didn't reply, because it was true.

'And you got kids too, ma'am?' Robo asked the black woman.

'I've got two. They're at school,' she said.

'Who do they live with?' Robo asked.

'Their grandma.'

Robo turned to the woman with the ponytail, who didn't have any children. 'You're not planning to have any, right?'

'Not right now,' she answered, sounding offended.

'I would hope that you wouldn't have any at all!' Robo said to her.

'Oh, thank you,' she replied, annoyed.

'I'm just saying, you can't even look after yourself so why would you bring a child into the world? I see way too many kids coming into the system because of this shit. They didn't ask for it. Then they're thrown away like fucking trash.'

'And if they grow up then they're going to end up like me, right?' the woman said, challenging Robo.

'If that's what you do, what do you think your kids are going to do? Do you think they have any chance?' Robo had raised her voice, trying to get her point across to the woman, who seemed to believe that being a heroin addict, living in a dope house and having a child was a reasonable option.

The woman was now in tears. 'I don't want to be like this,' she said, sobbing. 'I never wanted to be like this.'

'But you choose to be, right?' Robo asked.

'No.'

'No?' Robo's voice was now softer, more sympathetic. 'Well, there're a lot of places that can help you.'

'But I've got nowhere else to go,' the woman said.

'What about your mom's house?' Robo asked.

'I only go there to visit.'

'She won't let you stay there?' Brannock asked.

The woman didn't reply.

'Probably because you stole from her,' he said accusingly.

'If you told your mom you were trying to get clean and … 'Robo started to say but was cut off by the woman.

'Her husband's a fucking asshole,' she said. 'He's fucking violent and I won't put up with that.'

'You saying that you couldn't go into any church and ask for help?' Robo asked.

The woman cried some more.

'These are the things you need to do; you need to get into rehab,' Robo told her, now sounding like a caring, older sister. 'And something else you need to do is not to come back here.'

'All my things are here,' the woman said, sounding as though she was searching for an excuse not to leave.

'I don't give a shit! What is here? You have to change your whole, entire life!'

'I know but I need my clothes. I mean … I need my clothes.'

'You don't need shit,' Robo told her. 'I'm telling you, when you go to rehab, you don't need shit other than yourself.'

'You can't take none of that shit into rehab,' Brannock told the woman. 'Everything from your past, you have to leave behind. You take your body and the clothes on your back, that's it.'

Brannock walked away. Robo remained in the kitchen, trying to convince the woman to leave the house and seek help, but the woman seemed seriously conflicted. She clearly wanted to break away from the life she had found herself in, but at the same time she was tightly in the grip of heroin. It could have all been an act to garner sympathy but there was no need for her to play any of us – she wasn't under arrest, she wasn't going to jail. She could simply wait it all out and then, once we left, continue exactly from where she had left off – up those stairs, fucking drug dealers, injecting herself, and slowly dying.

But somehow, Brannock and Robo had managed to break through and the woman was trying to reach out and take hold of the lifeline that they were throwing her. It was like watching a hospital patient, who could hear everything that was being said around them whilst being unable to communicate back; struggling to lift a finger to show they were still alive, still worth fighting for, still worth saving. Behind the dirty, tatty clothes, the track-marked flesh and the wasted eyes, there was a smart and pretty woman.

'I want to stop doing this shit,' she said, sobbing.

'If you don't want to be doing this shit, why are you?' I asked.

She looked up at me. 'Because it's a physical thing,' she said. 'When I withdraw I get deadly sick.'

'But how did you get into it to start with?' I asked.

She looked down at the ground. 'Somebody else made me do it.'

'Made you take drugs? Made you inject yourself?'

'No, he ...' The woman started to sniff back tears. Then her face changed, she became angry and started to cry again. 'A man made me do it, yes! A man made me do it, and he shot it into my arm. He had a gun at my head and he made me do it.' She sniffed loudly. 'Like I said, I didn't choose to do it the first time. But I'm not going to talk if I'm going to be laughed at.'

'Who's laughing?' Hollywood asked her.

'It was a genuine question,' I told her. 'I wasn't laughing at you.' Nobody was.

Tears glided down the woman's nose and dripped onto her bare, bony knees.

Robo stepped forward, holding a business card for a rehab centre – a house that was run by nuns. 'I want you to take this, okay?' She put the card in the woman's pocket. 'I'm telling you, call this number.'

'If you want to get clean, you have to stop seeing everyone you know who does drugs,' Hollywood told her gently.

'I know that. I know that. It just hurts …'

'Of course.'

'I didn't make these choices,' she told him and began to cry again. 'I've been through too much.'

Hollywood stepped closer towards the woman. 'He wants you to get clean,' he told her, pointing a finger upwards.

I looked up. Did he mean *God*?

'I know,' she told him sadly.

'Listen to me, He still loves you. Do you understand that?'

'I'm trying. I want to be better than this.'

'He just wants you to get better. He always loves you. All you have to do is ask Him for help, I honestly believe that. I'm a big believer in God. Now go back over there, think, and get your shit straight. My partner just gave you a card; the next step is on you.'

'I know. Can I wipe my face on something?' the woman asked.

Robo tore off some sheets of kitchen roll and used them to wipe away the sticky tears and globs of snot from the woman's face.

'Thank you,' she said.

'Listen to me, He didn't give up on you,' Hollywood told the woman, pointing to the heavens again. 'He didn't give up on you. Do you know who I'm talking about?'

'My dad. I know that,' the woman replied.

'No,' Hollywood said. 'God.'

'Call that number on the card I gave you,' Robo told the woman. 'The place is very close. My sister went there.'

'I will.'

I looked over at Robo. *Her sister?*

'It's a church, right?' the woman asked.

'Yes, but listen, it's not going to be easy. My sister's already gone through it a second time.'

'I want to get myself out of this house but I need someone to come and get all my stuff before I go anywhere,' the woman said.

'Will someone come here and get it?' Robo asked.

'Yeah.'

'What's your mom's number?' Robo asked, holding her phone in her hand, ready to dial.

'My mom just changed her number,' the woman said, sounding as if she were making excuses again, but then she offered her dad's number instead.

The woman's dad answered when Robo rang him, and Robo began to speak to him, explaining who she was and the reason she was calling.

As Robo spoke to the father, I asked the woman if she had been serious when she told us that a man had injected her by force. Hollywood, equally interested in what the woman had to say, leant forward to listen.

'Yes,' she told us. 'I was on pills. I was on oxys and the guy who gave them to me, he did it – he injected me. My ex-boyfriend, he was addicted to them and then I started doing it with him. I thought that if I was spending all my money on him, I might as well get high too.'

'That was the dumbest ...' Hollywood started to say.

'It was the dumbest thing I have ever done. I know,' the woman said, starting to cry again. 'Seriously, it's the biggest regret I have. If I had never have done that, I would have been fine.'

'Okay, listen, she's going to help you out,' Hollywood said, pointing towards Robo, who was still talking on the phone. 'Don't fuck it up!'

'I won't. Trust me, I won't.'

'The hand is here,' Hollywood continued. 'All you have to do is reach.'

'Thank you for giving me that chance.'

'And don't forget what I told you – He always loves you. You just gotta ask Him for help.'

'I know. And if you look around a little bit you can see that I try and make the place look nice. I even put the pictures up,' the girl said, laughing gently at herself. 'And these guys here, they look after me. They make sure I eat every day.'

'Who? Those men out there?' I asked.

'Yeah.'

'They're looking after you? Really? You really believe that?'

'Yes. One of them was my friend. And this is his family. I had nowhere to go and he said that he had a room upstairs I could rent.'

I thought about the dirty needles I had seen upstairs. I thought about the stained mattresses on the floor, the used wraps of dope, the sex toys. These men weren't her friends. They weren't helping her. They were using her. In her desperate state and crushing need for heroin, she either didn't see it or chose to ignore it.

As the woman was still handcuffed, Robo stepped forward and held the phone to the woman's ear, so she could speak to her father.

'Hello? Oh, hello, Dad.'

Brannock, who had been outside searching one of the cars, walked back into the kitchen at that point. He asked how things were going with the woman. I told him that Robo was trying to get her father to pick her up and take her to the rehab centre.

'She thinks these men are her friends,' I told him.

'No, they are not!' Brannock said firmly.

'She says they look after her.'

'Yeah, because they're all fucking her, that's why. She's got a heroin habit. She don't have no job. She's got to be slamming that shit into herself at least five or six times a day.'

Then Brannock stepped up to the black woman, who was still

handcuffed and seated; she was the owner of the car that he had been searching.

'You've got a half-eaten donut in that motherfucking car,' Brannock said to her.

'I was going to eat that!' she said.

'That's disgusting. Plus you got all that leopard print on your car seats and shit in there!'

'You don't like the leopard print?' the woman asked Brannock, smiling.

'No! It looks like a bad porno happened in there,' he said teasingly.

The woman laughed out loud.

Hollywood interjected with, 'There's no such thing as a bad porno!'

This caused more laughter.

It was a different situation in the living room, however, where the handcuffed men were getting restless. The man who had threatened Brannock was making noises about 'getting the show on the road'.

'Okay, man, you're going to jail, just relax,' Hunter told him.

A mobile phone on the dining table had been ringing and buzzing the entire time we had been in the house. Everyone had ignored it but finally Hunter bent down to read a text message on the screen.

'I've got five. Would you do a girl?' Hunter read out to me.

'What does that mean?' I asked.

'Girl is slang for coke or crack,' he said. 'Someone's looking to buy. Girl is cocaine and Boy is heroin.'

A uniform cop, who had taken part in the raid, walked over to where I was standing with Hunter. 'There're probably three to four hundred rounds of ammunition back there,' he told us. 'So, if nothing else, we got that. There's probably a 9mm [gun] too, we just haven't found it yet.'

'We've found some cocaine, as well,' Hunter told him. 'And we've got a bunch of Ziploc bags, so we know they're selling.'

One of the men who had been arrested was concerned that his car, which was parked outside the house, would be stolen after he had been taken to jail. An officer had called the man's wife on his cell phone, which he then left on the dining table, on speaker-mode. The handcuffed man stood above it, leaning forward. He wanted his wife, who was nine months' pregnant, to come and collect his car, but by the sound of things she didn't seem too keen.

'I'm about to go to jail, damn it!' the man shouted down the phone at her. 'It's not like I wanted to go to jail! Come and get the car, man. The keys are here, at the house. I'll leave them in the mailbox. There are some diapers in the car too. You hear me?'

As we were leaving, Robo spoke again to the woman she had given the rehab card to. 'When was the last time you used?' Robo asked her.

'Yesterday,' the woman replied.

'Yesterday? So you're looking for a fix up at this point?'

'Not necessarily.'

Robo stared at her for a moment before saying, 'Make sure your dad gets that card.'

'Do you think that girl will actually follow through with it all?' I asked Robo later as we returned to the car.

'Yeah, I do,' she said.

Brannock shook his head. He was a little more sceptical. 'She's putting heroin into herself right now,' he said.

'Her dad told me that they had been talking about rehab just last week,' Robo said. 'But you can only hope and pray at this point. My sister went there. She was addicted to prescription drugs. It's a good place.'

Brannock started the car and drove away from the house.

'Oh, I forgot my clipboard on the fucking table!' Robo said, as we left the neighbourhood.

'You lost your fucking clipboard now?' Brannock huffed.

'I didn't fucking have it in my possession last,' she said defensively.

Brannock caught my eye in the rear-view mirror and picked up his radio. 'Hunter, Brannock. Did someone grab Robo's clipboard with all the names on it and everything?'

'Yeah, confirm, we've got it,' Hunter called back.

Satisfied, Brannock put down his radio.

'Did you see how in the beginning they came up with every excuse as to why they were in that house?' he asked me.

'The women, do you mean?'

'Yeah. And then by the end they were crying and shit? You've got to make it the worst fucking experience of their life, so the next time they think about doing that shit, they're going to be like, "Fuck that. I'm not going in that house".'

'Did they find anything yet from the firefighter case?' Robo asked.

'No. Absolutely nothing,' Brannock told her.

'How did that girl say she got hooked on heroin?' Robo asked.

'Guy put a gun to her head and injected her,' Brannock told her.

'She said she started on oxys,' I said.

'OxyContin? That's how my sister started,' Robo told me.

'They're done beyond saving,' Brannock grunted.

Robo looked over at me. 'We have a difference of opinion on that.'

'Do you have sympathy for them?' I asked Brannock.

'Fuck that. They're nasty fucking heroin addicts,' he said.

But I didn't believe him. Spending time with Brannock, out on the streets, listening to him tell me stories of killings and murder, hearing him speak about the people and the city, I always detected a tone of compassion and empathy. Brannock *did* care, but I suspected his contrary attitude was put on to try and wind up Robo. He was just being obnoxious for the fun of it.

107

'I, on the other hand, do have sympathy for them,' Robo said. 'But I will say this, my sister did relapse – just on alcohol though – and had to go back to rehab. She did a year and a half there altogether, and her daughter could stay with her on weekends. She says she's clean now, but you never know until the bottom falls out, sometimes.'

'A heroin addict is always a heroin addict,' Brannock told her.

'That's not true,' Robo said.

'But it's always there.'

'I'm sure it is,' Robo agreed, but sounding pissed off. 'They're an addict for a reason.'

Brannock's phone rang and that was the end of the conversation. Robo turned her head and stared out of the window in silence.

Brannock had gone in hard on the woman in the house, but he had done it to try and encourage her to leave and seek help. Between him, Robo and Hollywood, the approach seemed to have worked. Brannock did care and he was well aware of the situation these people – and especially the women – found themselves in. Brannock had a teenage stepdaughter and he told me that he would sometimes bring her to certain areas of Detroit to show her what could happen to her and where she could end up if she dropped out of school. He didn't want her, or anyone else, to end up in the same situation that he often found these women in – addicted, selling their body, living in filth, abused and sometimes dead.

His dislike for the dealers and pimps was something I could relate to. I had spent a number of years working in a high-vice area of London, and whereas I could empathise with the prostitutes, who worked long hours doing a dangerous, dirty job, I considered the pimps to be nothing but repulsive parasites.

*

108

By the following day, everybody who had previously been staying at the house had left. The raid had resulted in the arrest of the four men, who each had warrants for various matters ranging from misdemeanours to felony crimes. There was also the seizure of a small amount of drugs and a quantity of ammunition. The raid had also led to a drug house being closed down – a blessing for the neighbourhood, at least until the next one opened up. I hoped the raid had also resulted in at least one woman turning her life around.

I pestered Robo for days afterwards, trying to find out if the woman had gone to the rehab centre. Robo told me that the centre never gave information about who was or wasn't there. Instead she tried to call the woman's father, but he never answered or returned the calls. We all hoped that she had entered the programme but I suspected, sadly, that she was back on the streets.

8

Jerry Bell

Sunday, 10 January 2016

It was the weekend and the Gang Unit had no commitments. They had originally been warned to come in to assist the FBI on some gang surveillance but the job had been called off due to the dangerous winter weather. Everyone was now getting a couple of days at home, and Brannock had called to tell me not to bother coming in.

On the Sunday night, I arranged to meet up with an old acquaintance called Jerry Bell – a former gangbanger turned good. I had first met Jerry more than ten years before and had kept in touch with him; we had managed to see each other on and off, over the years.

Before I came back to Detroit for this visit, I had seen in the press that Jerry's cousin had recently been shot dead by a federal agent. I had also heard that, in an unrelated incident, Jerry too, had been shot – or rather, shot again; he already had a number of bullet-holes in him from his gangbanging days.

As a kid, Jerry had grown up in south-east Detroit and had run with a local gang but being a gangbanger hadn't defined who he would become in later life. When I first met him, it was through his then wife who was a sergeant with the Detroit Police Department. I was staying at their house for a week or so on one of my regular visits to the city. At that time, they lived in a beautiful, large home in the city, but being Detroit, across the street from them was a huge pile of blackened wood and stone that had once also been a house.

I liked Jerry from the first time I met him. He was a black Detroiter and he was friendly, open-minded, inquisitive, keen to smile and quick to laugh. Despite the two very different worlds that we came from – or perhaps because of it – we hit it off straight away. One evening, his three young sons from a previous relationship were staying over. They enjoyed listening to the English guy's accent and we had lots of fun impersonating each other. Jerry was happy that his sons were learning about another country and another culture.

One morning I was greeted by his boys with the words, 'Yo, yo. What's up, dawg?' Jerry was keen for me to reply to his children with, 'Yo, yo. What's up, my niggas?'

Jerry's wife wasn't at all impressed. Neither was I.

'Jerry, I'm not calling your kids "niggas",' I told him.

'Why not?' Jerry seemed slightly puzzled and a little hurt.

'For a start, they're kids. And secondly, I'm just not comfortable with it.'

'Mick, Mick, Mick!' Jerry said, trying to reassure me. 'It's okay; you're white on the outside but you're black on the inside!'

Based on this logic, we agreed to a different approach and each morning his boys would greet *me* with, 'Yo, yo. What's up, my nigga?'

When I first met Jerry, he was in the process of buying his own hydroplane – basically, a fast motorboat. Hydroplane racing, like Formula 1 on water, is a sporting event that is held yearly on the Detroit River. These boats can travel at up to 200 mph. They can flip in the water and accidents are not unheard of. In fact, a number of racers have died in what was once called 'the world's most dangerous sport'. In recent years, I'm glad to say there have been many safety improvements.

As a child, Jerry had become fixated with the boats. He was just a poor black kid and hydroplaning was a white man's sport – usually a rich white man's sport at that. But Jerry would hang around the waterfront, watching, learning and trying to get to know people. His dream was to one day own his own boat and compete. It was a dream that he would realise, although it wouldn't be easy. There were plenty of people looking to obstruct him – and Jerry believed it was because he was black. The arguments reached city council and made the press, and Jerry's tenacity eventually won him the right to compete in the races, where he finally got his own boat and team. A black Detroiter fighting against racism to realise a childhood dream and compete in powerboat races … that was a long way from his previous life as a gangbanger on the dangerous streets south of 8 Mile.

Although I was aware that Jerry had once run with gangs, I had never really spoken to him about his past. I was keen to hear about his younger years, and to understand what it was like for him, growing up on these streets. This free Sunday seemed like the ideal opportunity to start the conversation, and Jerry, being Jerry, was only too happy to tell me.

Jerry now worked long hours as a cab driver, with few days off. He was working tonight and he told me to meet him at a small hotel, just east of downtown. I checked Robo's gang map. The hotel was in the King Homes gang area – the only gang shown in that part of the city and one that Brannock had already warned me about. The King Homes was another name for the Martin Luther King Apartments – a low-income housing project made up of low-rise apartments and row houses. Over the years, drugs, violence and gangs had infested what would otherwise appear to be a pretty little housing complex.

I wasn't happy. It was late and dark, and with the atrocious weather the roads had become deadly ice traps. From above, the city must have looked like a huge frozen cobweb, made up of wintry side streets and arctic thoroughfares. It was also an area that I didn't know. Getting lost on those streets, at night and in this weather, would be unthinkable.

A fresh dumping of snow concealed the sheet ice that already covered the surface of the tarmac. The wheels of my car spun wildly if I tried to move too quickly, and the vehicle travelled diagonally if I hit the brakes too hard. I had no choice but to drop the speed down to a slow crawl.

The hotel was in an area that was completely new to me but being on a main road – East Jefferson – I found it fairly easily; too easily. I was early and Jerry was late. I parked out front and left the engine running, firstly to keep warm but secondly so that I could drive away quickly if anyone approached the car. I watched my mirrors closely.

Few cars were travelling along East Jefferson. Snow was falling again and the temperature had dropped further as a furious wind carried the cold through the streets like a weapon.

After about twenty minutes, Jerry pulled into the parking lot in his yellow cab. I stepped out from my toasty car and into the deep freeze. We greeted each other quickly, with the usual, complex handshake – up, down, grip, bump – and stepped into a tiny lobby area of the hotel. The Middle Eastern guy behind the counter knew Jerry and they exchanged their own verbal greeting. Jerry explained to the guy that I was a friend and we took a seat by the large, ice-coated windows as a blizzard raged outside.

In the light of the hotel lobby, I noticed a 1-inch scar on Jerry's left cheek, and I guessed it had something to do with his recent shooting.

Jerry yawned. He looked utterly exhausted. 'I'm sorry,' he said. 'I've been up a day and a half, working.'

'Looks like you need some time off,' I said.

'I work seven days a week, but man, this body gotta rest at some point.' He yawned again and squinted his red eyes. 'So, what brings you back to Detroit?'

Although I was unsure about how he might react, I told Jerry about the book I was writing and about the Gang Intel Unit that I had been embedded with. Despite being previously married to a Detroit cop and already knowing about my own past as a police officer in the UK, I was afraid that Jerry's opinion of the police might have hit the gutter after learning of the death of his cousin. It turned out I needn't have worried.

Jerry's 20-year-old cousin, Terrence Kellom – a father of one, with a second child on the way – had been shot dead just a few months previously by an Immigration and Customs Enforcement (ICE) agent who was part of a multi-agency unit which had attended Kellom's home in Detroit to arrest him for an alleged armed robbery of a pizza deliveryman. When the officers knocked, Kellom's father told them that Terrence wasn't in, but the officers entered the house and found him hiding in the attic. It was claimed that Kellom had dropped down through a hole in the attic floor and had threatened officers with a hammer. As Kellom lunged at them, the federal agent in question opened fire. Terrence was shot four times and killed.

The young man's family disputed the officers' account of what had happened, claiming that the police were not looking for Terrence over an armed robbery of a pizza guy, but because of a violation of probation over a weapon. The family believed that the federal agent had executed Kellom; they argued that Terrence had never dropped down through a hole in the attic, as had been claimed. As they told local reporter Charlie LeDuff, it was impossible for a person to do so. Even the family's lawyer said that 'a small baby couldn't have fit through that hole'. However, LeDuff, who at 170 pounds weighed 60 pounds more than Kellom, tried it and managed to drop through with relative ease.

Evidence also showed that the dead man's clothing had visible traces of drywall, wood chip and insulation fibres.

The family also maintained that Kellom had never been armed with a hammer, even though a hammer containing traces of Kellom's blood was recovered from the scene.

The Wayne County prosecutor, Kym Worthy – the first African American and the first woman to hold the position – decided that the federal agent who had killed Kellom shouldn't face charges over the shooting. At a press conference she said these words: 'Yes, black lives matter – of course they matter – but you know what else matters? Credible facts matter. Supportable evidence matters. Provable evidence matters. Doing justice matters. And the truth matters.'

Like the county prosecutor, the federal agent who had shot Kellom was also black and Kellom's father believed that had the agent been white, the killing of his son would have received wider coverage.

All in all, it was a sad tale and I felt terrible for Jerry. I brought the subject up as delicately as I could.

'This is a difficult thing to talk about and ask you, Jerry,' I said quietly. 'Before I came out here to Detroit, I read online that your cousin had been shot.'

Jerry looked up, staring me in the eyes. 'When? Which one? Which time?'

It wasn't the response I had expected – after all, how many of his cousins had been shot? But I put his reaction down to exhaustion.

'Terrence Kellom,' I said.

'Yeah. Terrence got shot, yeah,' Jerry said calmly, nodding his head. 'He got shot by a federal agent. They're saying that he had a weapon and we're saying that he didn't. So, it's a mystery, right there.'

'Has it caused big problems with your family?'

'Well, no. If anything, it's caused problems for the federal agent. This guy is not going to have a normal life,' Jerry said. 'He's probably going to be looking over his shoulder.'

'People are after him?' I asked.

'I can't say that they are after him but they won't let him go that easy. So that's why I keep my nose clean, away from the situation as it stands right now.' Then he leaned forward, lowered his voice and said, 'Because I know what's all involved.'

The term 'all involved' was one that was often used by gangs. It basically meant anyone who was totally immersed in gang life and everything that was associated with it – shootings, murder, etc.

It's no secret that, over the past few years especially, race relations and policing in America have been having a tough time of it. People with anti-police prejudices, people with genuine concerns and argument, and others who feel marginalised, have once again been finding a voice. If the Civil Rights Movement of the 1950s and 1960s was Act One, then what is happening now feels like Act Two, albeit without a clear leader or spokesperson such as Martin Luther King or Malcolm X.

I spoke to Jerry about the trouble that had erupted in places such as Ferguson and Baltimore, and elsewhere, following police shootings of black men. There had been accusations of police wrongdoing, followed by protests, demonstrations and riots. The Black Lives Matter movement had become increasingly vocal and prominent. None of that had happened after Kellom's death, however. There had been a small demonstration with banners that read *Liberate the Hood*, but there had been no violence, no rioting and no solid Black Lives Matter involvement.

I wondered why. Had Kellom's father been right about the federal agent being black, leading to less interest in the case? Or, I wondered, was it the fact that Detroit's Police Department being majority black, had helped to calm the anger? The city is over 80% black, whilst the Police Department is almost 70% black –

so although it isn't entirely representative, it's not far off. This is in contrast to other cities, such as Ferguson, Missouri, for example, where at around the time of the rioting which followed the fatal shooting of Michael Brown by a white cop in 2014, the city, which is two-thirds black, had just four black police officers out of a total of 54.

Jerry believed that the absence of violence and trouble following Kellom's death was due to the prosecutor ruling in favour of the officer rather than in favour of the family, and because people respected the investigation process.

Jerry didn't agree with the prosecutor's decision, however. 'She's full of crap,' he told me. 'I don't think she did that investigation well. I think she knew that if she ruled in favour of Terrence, then it would have started a big ordeal.'

'So why haven't there been any problems with rioting?'

'Because people respect our city and we don't want to tear it up. We've got to live here. What we gonna tear it up for? So I don't think people would even give them that kind of pleasure, of rioting and looting and all that other stuff. We don't really want that here.' Then Jerry fell silent for a moment, looking at the ground and nodding his head. 'Yeah, Terrence,' he said sadly.

*

Jerry could easily have been another shooting-death statistic himself. His upbringing mirrored that of many Detroit kids. After his parents had separated when he was a child, his mother had moved him and his two older sisters around the city, before they finally settled on Ashland Street in Precinct 5's area. By the time he was 16 years old, he was running with a gang called Mack Town, named after nearby Mack Avenue, and Jerry was given the gang name 'Chico', which was something his mother had called him, after one of her boyfriends.

'You know, you go to school and you get beat up a lot, so you try to get protection,' he told me. 'That was the way you got it – you joined a gang.'

Jerry's 'initiation' into the gang had been a violent one. Locked in a closet with another boy, they were made to fight.

'If we didn't fight, then our Older Gs, which is what we called the older guys in the gang – they would do things to us,' Jerry told me. 'They would throw buckets of hot or cold water into the closet. I remember this one gang member called Darren; he never really wanted to fight. We were in the closet and he said, "Man, I don't want to do this no more." And then they threw a bucket of ice water on him. But he still didn't want to fight, so they pulled me out of the closet and two guys went in there and beat him up pretty good.'

After the fighting, Jerry and other potential gang members were made to do other 'gang stuff', such as running through graveyards at night and going to schools to confront anyone who was giving their own gang members hassle. The Older Gs handled any real violence though, and Jerry soon found himself being used to work on the drug-dealing side of gang business.

'We were using weed to get high but we were selling crack cocaine to make money,' he told me.

Jerry had been in the gang for almost two years when he got shot. He had been at a party that his cousin had been giving, just a couple of blocks away from his own house. At the time, the thing to wear was a big, thick coat by a manufacturer called Triple F.A.T. Goose. These were essential for the deep freeze of Michigan winters but also essential for anyone wanting to have 'the look'.

Some other gang members, from Cleveland, Ohio, were also at the party and there was some envy over the coats. As Jerry and a group of his friends left the party, the Cleveland gang approached them. One of the gang took a swing at Jerry, but Jerry ducked. As he dodged the punch, one of Jerry's friends swung back at the other guy, knocking him down.

'And that's when the gunfire erupted,' Jerry told me. 'And that's how I got shot. I always had a fear of being shot, and I had been told that it would burn – and that it did! It was almost like someone took a hammer and hit you in that spot.'

One of the Cleveland gang opened fire with a .25 Auto; Jerry knew what gun it was because someone had picked up some of the spent shell casings. It was a defensive, compact gun that fired relatively small rounds, and it was one of these bullets that had entered Jerry's right side. Then, as he dropped down, a second round struck him in the head.

'That second one grazed me,' he said. 'If I had never ducked … Well, you can see right there where it took my hairline away. It goes up and around a little bit. Yeah, this guy damn near took me out, man. Big time.'

Another bullet struck Jerry's friend in the neck, with a second hitting him in the shoulder. Like Jerry, his friend survived the attack. Jerry spent two days in hospital.

That was the breaking point for Jerry and he knew he had to leave the gang. Other gang members were being shot and some were being killed, and Jerry's mother was begging him to leave before he too ended up in the morgue. Then a gang member who Jerry's sister was dating, was shot and killed. Jerry's sister had been present at the shooting, and that was enough for Jerry's mother; they moved house, away from the block, and out of the area.

The hotel manager walked over to where we were sitting. 'Hey, Jerry, wanna go to the gas station and get me some cigarettes?' he asked.

'No!' Jerry said, laughing.

'Why not?'

'Because I'll get robbed!' Jerry turned to me. 'Never go to a gas station in Detroit at night!'

'I don't even go during the day,' I said. 'I get my gas outside the city.'

Jerry nodded his head in approval.

'How about the shot under your armpit?' I asked, turning the conversation back to his gunshot wounds. It was one of his older injuries that I had been aware of, although I had never been told how it had happened.

Jerry laughed again, but this time he looked embarrassed. 'I was so stupid, man. Damn! We used to walk around with our guns hidden under our arms. The gun was a .25 Auto. It was so small you could just hide it. Then one day it went off and shot me in the side. It was a through and through – went in one side and came out the other.'

'Was this when you were with that gang?'

'Yeah, I was doing stupid stuff. I'm so mad about that, man. I'd have nightmares, thinking about what could have happened. I went to the hospital and they took out some bullet fragments and stitched me back up. I got my butt whupped too. My mom stomped me, man. She beat me bad!'

'Where were you getting all these guns from?' I asked.

'You can buy 'em off the street, or a crack-head may come up to you and say, "Hey, I stole this gun. Give me twenty dollars for it, and you can sell it and you'll probably get fifty dollars for it." But nine times out of ten, we'd keep the gun rather than sell it on. We're gonna take it and do something with it.'

All of this talk was leading to one thing – Jerry's latest shooting. The scarring on his face was clear to see and knowing Jerry as I did, I knew that he would want to tell me all about it. It's not that he was proud of being shot, just that this was his life – this was Detroit – and he knew that I was interested. When I had called him to arrange meeting up, it was one of the first things he had said he wanted to talk to me about.

'I was inside the cab,' he said. 'I was working for Checker Cabs and I got shot. Almost killed me, man.'

On that day, Jerry had gone to pick up a fare, just a few blocks from the hotel where we were now sitting. The man – a big, middle-aged black guy, who stood over 6 feet tall – said that he wanted to be taken to Mack and I-75. When they reached the destination, the guy wouldn't pay for the ride and instead tried to rob Jerry.

Jerry started to drive to the nearest police precinct, as per company policy. The guy then pulled a gun – a .357 Magnum – and opened fire. The protective screen between the driver's seat in the front and the passengers' seat in the back was bullet-resistant – but only to a degree. Bullets from the Magnum tore through the screen and one of them hit Jerry in the leg. Then the man leaned his arm out of the passenger window and shot through Jerry's open window. The bullet ripped through Jerry's cheek, hitting his teeth and breaking his jawbone before coming out the other side of his face.

'After he shot me in the face, I started driving like this,' Jerry said, leaning over an imaginary steering wheel. 'I was acting like I was dead. Just playing dead!'

With the taxi still moving, and believing that Jerry was dead, the man began to climb out of the side window to escape. Jerry watched the mirror, with a half-opened eye, as the man managed to get his body onto the open windowsill.

'And as he started climbing out the back, I just thought, *I got him!* I was looking in the mirror and I was like, *Oh, I got him!*'

Jerry rammed his foot on the accelerator and aimed his taxi at a tree.

'BOOM!' Jerry said, with a broad smile. 'He tried to climb out the back window – his butt was actually sitting on the window – and I took the side of the car up against the tree and it hit him! Here, let me show you.' Jerry laughed at the memory of that moment. He picked up his smartphone and began to flick his finger across the screen, looking for pictures.

'Here,' he said, turning the screen for me to see. 'That's the side of the car. The guy's blood is right here.'

The photo he showed me was of his yellow Checker Cabs taxi. There were five bullet-holes in the front windscreen, where rounds had gone through as the man had been shooting at Jerry. The front of the taxi had completely wrapped itself around a thick tree trunk. The side of the taxi was scraped, dented and smashed and there were long streaks of blood running down the bodywork of the vehicle.

'Did you kill him?' I asked.

'No. But he was messed up. Oh, he was messed up! He was in court. He had stitches. The guy was pretty messed up, man.'

Jerry stood up and lifted the leg of his pants, to show me where one of the bullets had gashed him. It had struck him above the right knee but hadn't gone in. 'It wasn't a bad one,' he said. Then he lifted his shirt. Running down his chest was a large scar, with another scar running across his belly.

'You get shot there too?' I asked.

'No. When I crashed the car into the tree, the seatbelt I was wearing caused the laceration in my stomach. That's how hard I hit the tree.'

'What about the scar down your chest?' I asked.

'That's when they opened me up.'

'For what?'

'To fix it. They had to remove four inches of my intestines.'

After the shooting and crash, Jerry spent eight hours in surgery and six days in the hospital. He had to wear a K-wire for eight weeks to hold his jawbone together. In all, it took him two years to recover from the incident.

The man who shot him got 50 years imprisonment.

'It was terrible, man. It was terrible. But God is good. I'm here.'

'So, you've been shot five times in total?'

'Yep,' he said, suddenly sounding weary.

'Do you think that's normal for Detroit?'

I knew it was a stupid question as soon as I asked it, and judging by the look on Jerry's face, so did he.

'Nothing's normal when you get shot,' he said. 'But it happens. Some people make it, some people don't. I'm just one of the fortunate ones that made it.'

Surviving shootings such as these wasn't actually that unusual. Spending time in gang areas of various American cities, I had come to realise that more often than not, people did survive being shot. I have spoken to a number of officers who have told me how the hospitals 'save everybody'. One cop told me that if the shot person still had a heartbeat when they reached the Emergency Room, nine times out of ten they could be saved, with charitable foundations and the taxpayer often covering the medical bills and other such costs.

Gang members too, are well aware of the success rate of hospitals in keeping their members alive and, when faced with possible closure, some gangs have even campaigned to keep their local hospital open. But gangs shoot to kill, not to maim, so hospitals will sometimes change patients' names or make other clandestine moves to protect the identity of the wounded in their care.

'I've had some close encounters, man,' Jerry continued. 'Some very close encounters. I'm still doing it though, I'm still a cab driver. I'm not scared.'

'You're not?'

'Nope.'

Jerry believed his lack of fear came from the time he had spent with his gang.

'I guess it's because I was taught so much in the gang life that nothing really scares me. It was an experience and it helped me get street smart. I'm very street smart. If it was two people – me, and a person from a different country – and they move us into one of these neighbourhoods, I'll make it out of there alive; probably that other person wouldn't. So everything you learn comes from time and experiences. It helps you to become brave, it helps you, you know, to make right decisions, and that's how it was with me. But I left the gang eventually, yeah, I got out of there.' Jerry gave another little laugh.

It was late and Jerry was exhausted. The roads were a deadly nightmare of solid ice and I was keen to head back to where I was staying. Before I left, Jerry wanted to know what I thought about the changes in the city.

'Downtown has changed so much,' I said. 'But the outside areas, the neighbourhoods, like where you grew up, they're still bad.'

Jerry nodded his head in agreement. 'I think what they're gonna do is rebuild downtown first and then it's gonna spread out.'

'You got high hopes for Detroit?' I asked.

'Oh, yeah! High hopes? I've got super-high hopes for Detroit! Because Detroit, oh man, it's been so good to me. It's been so good to me!'

I looked at Jerry in disbelief. '*Good* to you? But you've been shot five times!'

'I'm still here though, ain't I? I'm still here to talk to you.'

And that was how Jerry judged the place as having been good to him: he was still alive. Living in Detroit hadn't been easy; he hadn't had a privileged upbringing or a decent education but he still believed that Detroit had been good to him, simply because he wasn't dead. That was all it took. That was the difference between good and bad – being alive rather than being in the ground.

Being alive has allowed him to achieve things for himself. He had children, he had been married to a cop despite his gang past, and he had realised his own childhood dream to become a hydroplane racer – against all the odds. By not being *dead*, Jerry had managed to find himself a life outside of Detroit and its gangs. He didn't hold any bitterness towards the city, only thanks and appreciation.

'Even with all the changes and investment, the gangs will never leave though, right?' I asked.

'No, they ain't going nowhere,' he said. 'If anything, they'll go underground. You wouldn't see 'em. You don't see 'em now. And if you did, you wouldn't know who they are. It's hard to recognise a gang member. They fly under the radar, man. And believe me, these ones here in Detroit are organised.'

'Are the gangs different now, to how they were in your day?'

'I no longer affiliate myself with gangs or want to be around them, but just that one area that you have been spending time in, in the north-east, that area is gang-infested, man! The gangs pretty much tore down or burnt down every house there already. Why? Because they don't have nothing else to do.' Jerry stood up, getting ready to leave. 'That's a bad area, man,' he told me. 'You wanna be careful or it'll be you getting shot next.'

9

God, Guns, Family

The officers of Gang Intel often finished work late, usually well after midnight. At the end of each shift I always asked Brannock what time I should come in the following day, and he always gave me the same answer: noon. So that's when I would turn up.

Sometimes I would be the first one in. I would then sit around, catching up on my notes, chatting a little with the officers as they began to filter in, all the while wondering where Brannock was. Usually he would roll in sometime after 1 p.m. Occasionally he wouldn't turn up for many hours, as he would be at headquarters for a meeting or some other place. I had learnt not to be concerned; he would show up eventually.

Brannock, along with the rest of his unit, put in a huge number of hours. I just never understood why he always told me to be there at noon each day. By the time I got back to where I was staying in the basement of a cop friend's house, in a town north of Detroit, had written up that day's notes, checked and replied to emails and seen to other general admin, it would be deep into the early hours. I would have liked a longer lie-in but I was always afraid that something would happen and I wouldn't be there. In the end though, I suspected that Brannock was just screwing with me.

*

As I walked into the office on that Monday morning, the only other person there was Hollywood. He was standing by Brannock's office, heating up some food in the microwave.

'How's it going, Mick?' he asked.

'Good, thanks. No Brannock?'

Hollywood looked at his watch, more for effect than anything else, and shook his head.

'Did you get your tickets yet?' he enquired.

'Tickets for what?'

Hollywood flexed his muscles, showing off his large biceps. 'For the gun show, baby!' he said.

We both laughed. Hollywood's image was important to him. He was solidly built, with muscles that had been worked on for many years. He was also a thoughtful, sensitive soul who could sometimes seem intense and serious. Even so, he was always friendly and easy to be around. He was one of the first in the office to really make me feel welcome, and he had even laundered one of his own Gang Unit T-shirts so that he could give it to me as a gift.

However, I had also noticed that Hollywood was often singled out for gentle, and sometimes not so gentle, teasing from some of the others. And although everyone found themselves on the receiving end of ribbing from time to time, such is the high-spirited nature of professions like the police, Hollywood just seemed to get a little bit more. 'Gun show' comments didn't help his case, I guess.

The microwave pinged and he walked into his office, spooning some steaming food into his mouth. I followed him in.

As it was just the two of us, I took the opportunity to find out more about him. The first thing I wanted to know was why he was called 'Hollywood'.

'I did a TV commercial for the Super Bowl a few years ago,' he told me. 'I've also been in a tattoo magazine.' True enough, Hollywood's arms were covered in colourful ink.

He started looking through the papers on his desk, searching for the magazine to show me the spread – an article about cops and their tattoos.

'A tattoo will tell you what a person is all about,' Hollywood said. 'That's Saint Michael,' he told me, pointing to the large archangel, who is the patron saint of police officers, on his forearm. Saint Michael was standing in front of an American flag and was using a spear to kill a demon. On his other arm, Hollywood had numerous tattoos of faces. 'This one is Alexander the Great of Macedonia,' he said.

'You're Macedonian?' I asked.

'Yeah. My father was Macedonian. He was born there. All these people you see on my arm are Macedonian freedom-fighters.'

As I had witnessed at the house raid, Hollywood was also a religious man – a devoted Christian. 'A hundred per cent,' he told me, when I asked him about his faith.

'Do you carry your religion with you in your work?' I asked.

'Absolutely.'

'But at the same time, you carry a gun, ready to kill.'

'Absolutely.'

I mentioned how in America, for some people, guns and God often seemed to go together.

'Oh yeah!' Hollywood said, agreeing with me. 'It usually goes: God, guns, family.'

'But some would question, if you are a religious person, and you have a gun …'

'That what?' Hollywood asked. 'That I should stand by and watch people butcher my family? No. Absolutely not. Do I believe in God? Absolutely. Do I believe in Jesus Christ, my Lord and Saviour? A hundred per cent. But I'm not a fool. I'm not going to let someone come into my house and rape my wife or shoot my kid.'

'Have you ever shot anyone?' I asked.

'I've been in a shoot-out but I don't know if the person I was shooting at was shot or not. I was off duty, on my way to work and I stopped to get gas. There was a car in front of me being driven by a small Hispanic man. He had got out and was pumping gas. Then another car pulls up and two guys get out with handkerchiefs over their faces and they point a gun at the Hispanic guy's head. Then one of the guys takes his gun and hits the dude in the head with it. Blood pours out and they're beating him with the gun. Then the storeowner comes out and takes a shot at the guys. They duck down and then I open my car door and I start shooting – POW, POW, POW, POW. They start shooting back and – BING! They hit the fucking mirror on my car. FLOOM! It goes flying. And this is my personal car!

'I crawled around to the passenger side and then I started unloading again. They shot again and hit my door. I shot back and blew out their back window. I aimed my last shot and I thought I hit the motherfucker in the head. I was praying to God that I fucking hit him. But then they drove off and we don't know if the guy was shot or not because no one went to the hospital. But who knows? Then Internal Affairs came out and asked all kinds of questions. "How many rounds did you fire?" I go, "I think three or four." They said, "You fired fourteen." I didn't even know! The whole time I was just thinking, "Man, I hope I don't get into trouble!" You know? It's weird – I know that I have the right to shoot but I am still worrying about getting into trouble!'

His end comment did not surprise me. I have known officers who have killed people. After a shooting they are put on administrative leave. They sit at home watching the news and listening to criticism from the anti-police brigade, the armchair critics, hindsight experts, and family members of the deceased.

They rightly face an investigation into their actions but they also hear calls for them to be imprisoned for murder, before any findings have been released. Whether a shooting is 'justified' or not, it is obviously an awful thing for the family of the deceased to go through, but it is also something that takes a terrible toll on the officers and their families. Despite what some want to believe, no cop actually *wants* to shoot someone. Why on earth would you?

In 2016, police in America shot around 2,000 people. Of those, just under 1,000 were killed – almost all men, although 40 were women. Over half of the people killed were armed with a gun at the time of their death, while 48 were listed as being unarmed. Almost half of those killed were white, and a quarter black. But there is disproportionality in that figure as blacks make up only around 13% of the US population. There must be reasons why the numbers are unbalanced but I believe those reasons are more socio-economic and due to the failure of government – federal and local – rather than any kind of racism or prejudice on the part of the police.

Although police officers must take responsibility for their actions, they – along with the citizens they police, who are mostly just trying to get by in life – are the ones who have to live in, deal with, and take the blame for the societal mess created by others.

Hollywood went back to searching for the tattoo magazine, whilst continuing to talk to me. 'Listen,' he said. 'If I can retire from this job, not killing anyone, that's great – that's a good career. But if I have to, I will.'

'Do you think you would feel remorse, if you did? Especially as a religious man.'

'Depends on the situation. If there was a guy on top of a little girl, trying to kill her, then no, I don't think I'd feel remorse. Did he shoot at me and maybe this was his first time, and I killed him? Then I'd probably feel a little remorse. But who knows?'

'Do you believe that God would punish you?'

'Absolutely not, I don't believe so. Didn't He have angels that fought? Saint Michael fought demons – he *killed* demons. What's the difference? That's how I look at it. I could be completely wrong and be going to Hell, though! We'll see. I just try and do good.'

As we had been talking, other officers had started to filter into the office. Brannock, who had been at a meeting downtown, arrived about an hour later.

'Has Hollywood been behaving himself?' Brannock asked Cooter.

Cooter swivelled around in his chair to face Brannock. 'What are you asking me for?' he asked.

'Because you're his babysitter.'

'I've been busy working. I don't know what anybody else is doing.'

Hollywood stepped out of his office. 'Why are you trying to start shit with me?' he asked Brannock.

Brannock ignored him and turned to me. 'Has he been behaving himself, Mick?'

'He's been telling me about his Macedonian heritage,' I said.

'Macedonia is a shithole,' Brannock said.

'You've never even been there,' Hollywood said.

'Yes, I have,' Brannock said. (*No, he hadn't.*)

'It's the jewel of the Mediterranean,' Hollywood told him.

'It's not even a country any more.'

'Yes, it is! You don't even know where it is, do you?'

'Yes, I do,' Brannock told him. 'It's in England, which is in the middle of Australia.'

'I used to be a happy person before I joined this unit,' Hollywood told me.

'You were a piece of shit,' Brannock said. 'Your career was in the toilet.'

'And you saved me!' Hollywood said sarcastically.

'And I resurrected your life!' Brannock told him.

'I'll be out of here this time next year anyway, once everything comes through,' Hollywood said.

'What's coming through?' Brannock asked, suddenly sounding concerned that he might actually lose Hollywood.

'My modelling career.'

'You're full of shit!' Brannock snorted. 'They don't need a double for "drunk Robert De Nero"!'

'By the way,' Hollywood said, cutting over him, 'Mick bought some tickets today.'

'He's not going to the fucking gun show,' Brannock told him, knowing exactly where Hollywood was heading with his 'tickets' comment.

'You're very protective of him,' Hollywood said.

'That's because he's writing a book about me.'

Hollywood waved a dismissive hand at Brannock. 'Why am I even talking to this guy? Now I'm just getting angry,' he said, and walked away back to his office. His sanctuary.

Then Brannock turned his attention to AJ, who was quietly typing at his computer, minding his own business.

'AJ's doing something with his keyboard,' Brannock said. 'It doesn't have shit to do with police work, but he's doing something.'

'It does have something to do with police work,' AJ said defensively.

'Don't lie to me!'

'It is, man. It's union-related.'

'Oh Jesus Christ!' Brannock said, shaking his head.

Brannock went into his office and called me in. He sat in his large leather seat and leant over his computer, tapping at the keyboard, searching for videos on YouTube. During our tour around the 4-8-2-0-Die, he had mentioned a couple of times about how the gangs were all making rap videos. Gangsta rap could be big business. Get noticed, get signed by a label, and not only could you make a load of money, you could get out of Detroit. The chances were slim though, and some would never leave The D. Even when they were signed, some would still affiliate with their old gang, committing crimes, getting shot, getting killed. And although most would never get signed, it didn't stop them churning out the professional-looking videos. These rap videos were an established part of the gang culture. Yes, they hoped it would bring fame and riches, but it was also a way to promote the gang, show off and intimidate rivals.

The first video Brannock wanted to show me was one that had been filmed on Runyon Street.

'I want you to see this video,' he said. 'You'll see how different it looks on the video compared to what we saw the other day.'

'When was this filmed?' I asked.

'The year 2009 – right before their collapse,' Brannock said.

'Whose collapse?'

'This gang. Everyone you see in this video is either dead or in prison, all except one of them, and he was the youngest Runyon boy out there. Some of them killed each other.'

The video had been filmed in the street and showed a large group of black men, walking along, talking directly to the video camera. Many of the men were wearing black T-shirts with *Runyon Ave* printed across the front in large white letters. Even though it was officially Runyon Street, many people referred to it as Runyon Ave.

'*Show y'all how we do it on a daily basis, y'all hear? That's the crew back there – Seven Mile Niggas, where it's at,*' a man on the video said to the camera.

'See, they're coming south, down Runyon,' Brannock said. 'Look at all the houses.'

As with now, it was winter and there was some snow on the ground. The difference was that the short street was lined with houses, and cars were parked along the kerbs or on private driveways.

The men walk down to a small party store at the corner of Runyon. Inside, a couple – the owners – are standing behind a security screen, along with their young son. They laugh along with the men, who joke around as they are buying some small items of junk food. I couldn't imagine what life must be like for this family, hiding behind a screen, selling beer and Twinkie bars to armed gangbangers all day long.

As the men on the video leave the party store and walk back up Runyon, some of the older members reminisce about how the area used to be. Although it didn't look as bad as now, there were already a few vacant lots on the street.

'*I can remember when this bitch* (Runyon Street) *had a house on every motherfucking lot,*' one man says. '*But once '85 got here, and that crack shit came, it was over. It started making its name around '85. Crack fucked everything up. It made the smart motherfuckers* [rich], *but it deuced the dumb motherfuckers.*'

It was interesting to hear the man talk like this, remembering how crack cocaine had come into his neighbourhood and changed everything for the worse. For cities like Detroit, crack was the narcotic equivalent of the atomic bomb. Easy and cheap to produce and sold for $5 or less a 'rock', crack quickly become the drug of choice for many. With huge profits to be made, it wasn't long until firearms became a must-have accessory. Corners and territories were protected and fought over by dealers and gangs, and bodies soon started to fill the morgues.

A gang known as the Chambers Brothers had controlled much of the crack-cocaine trade in Detroit in the 1980s and were possibly the first gang to introduce the drug to the city. The Chambers had left absolute poverty in the Deep South and came to Detroit hoping to better their lives. Getting involved in the crack trade, and running their operation like a business, made them multi-millionaires. At the time, the Chambers were regarded as one of the most successful drug-dealing organisations in the entire country. It also made them a public enemy, and eventually the Chambers Brothers would end up behind bars. The early 1990s movie, *New Jack City*, was based on a story about the Chambers, though the setting was moved from Detroit to New York.

There had been numerous allegations in the 1980s and 1990s that crack cocaine had first entered the US after the CIA had allowed the Nicaraguan Contras to ship in the drug as a way to fund their Reagan-supported war against the country's leftist government. Although there were clear links between the CIA, the Reagan Administration and Contra rebels (some of whom *were* involved in cocaine trafficking), the allegations against the CIA – that they had conspired with the Contra rebels to bring crack cocaine to America – were never proven. Investigative reporter Gary Webb, who wrote about these allegations in his 'Dark Alliance' series in the 1990s, was later found dead, with two bullet-holes in his head. It was believed – genuinely – that he had committed suicide.

Brannock brought up an online rap video filmed in Detroit by one of the gangs. Shot in a residential street, it featured around 20 young black men and one black woman, who had long, bleached-blonde hair.

'What gang is this?' I asked.

'This is P-Rock – Plymouth Rock. They're a west side gang. Plymouth and Sussex area.'

'P-Rock, nigga!' an armed man says angrily at the start of the video.

Brannock stopped the video almost as soon as it had begun and pointed to one of the men on screen, who was holding a gun.

'That's a 50-calibre Desert Eagle handgun,' he told me.

'Is that a serious gun?'

'Yeah! It's 50-cal! You use it to shoot elephants and shit,' he said.

Brannock pressed play, but almost immediately paused the video again.

'An AR-15 with a 100-round drum,' he said, pointing out another man, who was holding an assault rifle.

Play.

'Bitch.' 'Nigga.'

Pause.

'AR-15 pistol, with a 30-round magazine and Magpul sights.'

Play.

'I can't wait to finger-fuck you. Before you get to me, someone on my team will slug you ...'

Pause.

Brannock pointed out another man holding a gun. 'Green laser and a 100-round drum on that AR,' he said, before gesturing to another man. 'AK-47 pistol.' Then another. 'AR-15 pistol.'

Play.

'Hunting guns, hunting clips, lock and load. Getting shot, dirty bitches, all code. P-rock! P-Rock! I'm from P-Rock!'

Most of the men in the video were holding some sort of firearm. Many were brandishing high-powered assault rifles – the sort of weaponry you would expect to see Special Forces fighting with in a war zone.

Brannock shook his head as we watched the video. 'I mean, how are they even filming that?' he asked. 'This is obviously filmed right on the street corner of Plymouth and Sussex. There are at least six or seven assault rifles in that video.'

'And no one is calling the police?'

'No. Each one of those guys is holding an assault rifle, whilst standing in front of a brand-new Corvette. And it's in broad daylight!'

Even if the police were called, I wondered what they could do against such firepower. Cops carry a handgun on their hip, and in their patrol car they may have a shotgun, AR-15 or other such rifle, but when faced with a large group of men armed with AK-47s and other military grade weaponry, in reality, what could they do? It certainly isn't unusual for cops to find themselves outgunned. If you were hiding behind the flimsy door of your police car, armed with just a handgun, and these guys were coming at you, you were as good as dead.

There has been much talk about the 'militarisation of police' in America but as the saying goes: you don't take a knife to a gunfight. Is it any wonder that officers want access to better firepower and armoured vehicles when they know what they may have to face? After the much-criticised police response to rioting in Ferguson, in 2014, President Obama prohibited the sale of certain types of military equipment to police. Two years later President Trump lifted the ban.

I personally don't like the military fatigues and look that some police employ – it is everything that police were *not* supposed to be – but the issue isn't that police are being equipped with military vehicles and weaponry; the issue is that they need to have them to begin with. If you want to de-militarise the police, then first you must de-militarise the general population and criminals. Until then, I would rather the police outgunned the criminals than the other way around.

Brannock pointed to one of the men on the P-Rock video. 'This is Drew the Boss,' he told me. 'He's the manager of the Déjà Vu strip club in Highland Park. It's right there at Six and Woodward. From what I heard, he played in the NFL but got hurt.'

Drew the Boss, whose real name was Andrew Davison, had indeed played professional football for both the Dallas Cowboys and the New York Jets, despite having a bullet lodged in his arm after being shot in Detroit. He died in 2017 at the age of 37, from a heart condition.

Play.

'I'm strapped up for real, bitch, and I got the 100 round clips for real, while y'all niggas just talking, bitch ...'

'All they talk about is killing, shooting, doing drugs,' Brannock commented.

'Would you go and investigate that?' I asked.

'For specific ones we do but there are thousands and thousands of these videos. It's hard. Plus they are always moving the guns around. And they can always say it was just a prop.'

'It's frightening,' I said. 'Those guys are out there with these guns and the cops are out there armed with just a Glock.'

Brannock nodded his head and pulled up some images on his phone.

'Look at this gun we got out of a house recently,' he said, handing me the phone. The picture was of an AR-15 assault rifle, with a large, 50-round magazine.

'It was in the house with two flak jackets,' he told me. 'Along with a Tec-9 – a semi-automatic pistol that looks a bit like an Uzi – and some old, bullshit rifle.'

He pulled up another photo.

'That's an AR-15 assault rifle with a laser scope, collapsible stock and a 100-round drum. And two pistols – a Glock and a Smith & Wesson – with 30-round magazines. This was all in the trunk of a car.'

'A gang car?'

'Yeah. P.D.Q. – Puttem Down Quick.'

'They're better armed than you are.' I said. I wasn't joking.

'These are the mags that they stick in their guns, and this is our shit.' Brannock showed me an extended magazine that held 33 rounds, used by the gangs. Then he showed me a standard police-issued magazine that held 15.

'Where do they get these weapons?'

'At a Gun and Knife Show; some girl will buy it.'

'So, do you think there should be better gun controls?' I asked.

'That won't stop the criminals from getting the guns,' he said. 'They're still going to get them, whether it's breaking into houses or whatever. You're only hurting the people that are legally wanting to get guns.'

In all the years I have been visiting police departments in America, only one police officer has ever expressed any strong interest in gun control. That officer was from a tiny Delta community in Mississippi, where a man had recently shot five officers, including the Chief of Police who took a bullet through the neck. The officer said that she wanted 'all guns to be outlawed', telling me that it would make her job 'so much safer'.

But despite what she – and I – saw as a clear advantage for police officers, many I have spoken to in America are against gun control. For obvious reasons the cops wanted to be armed but they were also happy for citizens – the decent, honest ones, at least – to be armed too. There are cultural, legal and historical aspects to this, of course, but even so, I always found it strange that police officers, especially in a country where they face so much personal risk from guns, would be in favour of civilians being armed and having access to so much serious firepower.

People often say, 'Guns don't kill people; people kill people'. Another way of looking at it could be: 'People *with* guns kill people.' But this is an argument that has been raging in America for decades and one that may never be resolved.

The video ended and Brannock immediately searched for another.

'You'll like this one,' he said. 'Listen to this voice at the beginning.' He brought up a rap video from 50 Band Gang, titled 'Me and My Burner' (gun).

On screen, a pair of black women dressed in skimpy, torn underwear walk around a dark house, carrying guns. A man starts to speak as music plays in the background. The man says: 'You know, if you are confronted with an immediate threat to your safety, you're not going to have time to dial 911, so it becomes an issue of: the threat's here, I have to respond to the threat.'

The rap then starts. *'KILL, KILL, KILL! MURDER, MURDER, MURDER!'*

Brannock paused it.

'Recognise the voice at the start?' he asked.

The words sounded familiar but I couldn't place the voice.

'Chief James Craig,' he said.

That was it. That was why I recognised the words. The gang had rather audaciously inserted a recording of the Detroit Chief of Police at the start of their video. The words were from an interview Chief Craig had given to a television news station, in which he had expressed his support for the residents of Detroit to arm themselves and fight back against criminals if they had to. At the time his comments had caused quite a stir. But he was simply being realistic. This was Detroit, not Nantucket.

Towards the end of the rap video, as a large black man smokes and more women in torn underwear point guns at the camera, the music is overlaid with the sounds of screeching car tyres and heavy gunfire. A man continually makes threats and 'nigga' is angrily spat out every three or four words.

Many gangs made these types of videos and they were usually in the same style, with groups of men and a few barely dressed women, hanging around a street corner, staring into the camera and waving around the biggest, baddest guns they could get their hands on, whilst one or more of their number rapped. The videos were raw, fierce and extreme. These were real gang members, filmed in their own territory, possibly showing off real guns.

*

The rap videos were also used as a show of force: to intimidate or insult another gang. In response, that gang might leave its own messages online, mocking the videos and the gang members who had appeared in them. In turn, these messages of disrespect could be answered with the very weapons that the gangs had been showcasing in the videos. If you wanted to start some trouble, all you needed to do was leave an insulting message on someone's YouTube channel or Facebook page. It was that simple and that petty. People were being killed because somebody called someone else a name.

More shootings; more killings.

However, the record labels did notice some gang rappers and some even got signed. But they were still from Detroit and they still ran with their crew. Even when a gang rapper was close to making it, a bit of 'beef' (trouble, feud or grudge) with another gang could end it all.

Dex Osama (real name, Byron Cox) was a perfect example of this. Dex was a 26-year-old Detroiter who had grown up fascinated by guns. Some of his family members had the same dangerous interest, and in Dex's teen years, two of his uncles were shot dead. Dex was part of the Choppa Boyz – a west side gang. The word 'choppa' is street slang for an assault rifle, such as an AK-47. Dex was a big guy ('greedy', his mom called him). He liked to have things and he could be seen flashing around piles of cash in videos.

Dex first came to notice after he released a rap song titled 'Death On Me'. The song had a rather ominous history. Dex claimed that he had once seen a 'dark shadow' hovering over him. His mom told him that the shadow was Death. It was a warning, she said, that he 'had death on him'. Inspired by that incident and his mother's words, he wrote the song. Sadly, the warning proved to be true.

After releasing the song, he was spotted by hip-hop star Meek

Mill and signed to his record label. Things were seriously looking up for Dex Osama and he was starting to experience a life that so many kids in Detroit could only dream about.

At the time, Osama was dating a girl who danced at the Crazy Horse strip club. One September night in 2015, Osama attended the club and saw another man requesting his girlfriend to dance for him. Knowing that Osama was watching, his girlfriend looked over for approval, but he told her 'no' – he didn't want her dancing for the man. There was an argument, and in his anger, Osama opened fire in the club, shooting in the air. Another man, who had just been released from prison after serving over 20 years for second-degree murder, complained to Osama that he was ruining his good time. They began to argue and the argument spilled outside. Osama was armed, but so was the other man, who pulled out his gun, pointed it at Osama and shot him in the chest. More rounds were fired (25 in all) and Osama – still alive at that point – ran off, collapsing at a nearby gas station. It was there, on the gasoline-stained concrete forecourt, that he died.

At the time, there had apparently been beef between Osama's gang – Choppa Boyz – and another gang called Bandgang, with claims that there had been insults traded over social media. In addition, Osama had allegedly been rapping about robbing the other crew and had mocked Bandgang over the death of one of their members – 'Dotts'. There were further claims that in one of his rap videos, titled *Clean Up Man*, Osama had admitted to killing Dotts. In retaliation, Bandgang then released a couple of rap videos of their own, that were part titled: *Dex Osama Diss* and *Choppa Boyz Diss* (Diss meaning disrespect). The titles were a straight-up insult. Despite all that, the man who had shot Osama apparently had no connections to either of the gangs; he was simply a newly freed man, looking to have some fun.

Whatever the reasons for his death, Dex Osama was a young man, from one of the most deprived cities in America, who had possessed some talent, been noticed, and placed on a path that could change his life forever. Yet Detroit would never let him go, because he could never let go of Detroit. As one online commentator had put it, Osama wanted to 'keep kickin' it in da 'hood'.

In April 2017, a year and a half after Dex Osama had been killed, his little brother, 'Big Ducie', was found dead in Detroit. He had been shot in the head.

*

There has been much criticism of the gangsta rap genre, with many claiming that it glorifies and glamorises violence, crime and guns, that it represents women as nothing more than sexual objects – 'bitches' and 'hoes' – and that it reinforces the stereotype image of poor blacks. Rappers counter these claims, stating that the music and the lyrics simply reflect their reality. This is their truth. The violence in the songs matches the violence that they witness daily on their streets and in their neighbourhoods. The songs aren't a cry for help so much as a way of telling the story of their lives.

And are these songs really all that different to the commentary and anger expressed by Billie Holiday when she sang 'Strange Fruit', with its brutal and powerful lyrics, or Nina Simone singing 'Mississippi Goddamn', which was banned in a number of states, and saw records broken in half and returned to the record company by radio stations across the nation? There are plenty of examples of supposedly safe pop music containing violent and misogynistic lyrics, despite not having the background – the reasoning and truth – rap has.

Wherever you stand on the debate, one thing is for sure: the music has made some people a ton of money, whilst many of those who were creating it to begin with, have been left behind … and continue to die.

In one gang's rap video that Brannock showed me, there were three young teenage boys standing behind an adult male rapper.

'So, this is how they get you, when you're a kid,' Brannock told me. 'The older guy in the video, who is fucked up and has done homicides, and beat homicide cases; he's doing his whatever – his hustle, robbing motherfuckers, selling dope. These three kids you see in the background, they're all still in school – they're the little guys. So, what would you rather do? Would you rather go sit in a classroom or would you rather be on YouTube, standing behind Cocaine Sonny (a Seven Mile Bloods gang leader), shooting a rap video, getting chedda and smoking weed and hanging out? And you know, you don't have a dad, so hey, *"come with us; now you're part of something"*. Plus you're protected at school – you're wearing red and you're a Blood, so nobody's going to fuck with you.

'So what else is there for these kids? When they wake up every day and look out of their window and they see the challenges and struggles in front of them, what else is there? They borrow each other's clothes because they only have a couple of outfits. They don't have shit! All they have is each other. That's why the "no snitching" thing in Detroit is so strong.'

'So you sympathise with them, with their situation?' I asked.

'When you ain't got shit, what else is there? Maybe if I could play sports and maybe get a scholarship, or whatever, but if you can't do that and you can't rap, what do you do? Do you sell dope? Do you bother going to school? Why go to school? Every day you come home you see your mom struggling. The kids are hungry; your brothers and sisters aren't eating. Mom has to take the Gratiot bus to fucking K-Mart for nine dollars an hour, or whatever. And you're sitting in class, hungry. Fuck that! So that's why they do what they do; the pull is strong. And then you see the dope boys in the neighbourhood, drinking lean, driving around in a Mercedes Benz S550, money, Gucci belts, fresh clothes. I mean, what would *you* do?'

I knew that Brannock was right. The draw for these kids, to the gangs, was understandable. To eat, many of the kids living in the neighbourhoods survived by using Government Assistance cards, such as the 'Bridge Card', which they spent at party stores, to buy junk food. Other kids resorted to crime – robbing, stealing, selling drugs. There were free lunches at the schools, but many of the kids refused to eat it. There was a stigma attached to it and many felt embarrassed to be seen eating the free school food.

As Brannock had said, there were similar problems with clothing. Pride prevented many kids from resorting to charity, and instead they traded or shared clothes with their friends and family members, using belts or string to make larger items look as though they fitted.

When you have nothing and are surviving day-by-day, the life of a local gangbanger or dope dealer must be enticing.

Brannock shut down the computer. He didn't have any paperwork to do and he wanted to take me out to show me more of the 4-8-2-0-Die. Robo said that she would come with us, but we needed to head downtown first, for a Ceasefire meeting at headquarters.

We left the base, and moments later on a nearby street, rail-crossing barriers dropped down and red warning lights began to flash.

'These fucking trains!' Brannock said. 'Every time I need to get anywhere, these fucking trains come!'

I couldn't see the problem. It was only a train, after all, and it shouldn't take long, but as minute after minute dragged by, I started to see his point. The train was a freight train, and it was literally miles long. Coming through the centre of the city and residential neighbourhoods, also meant that it had to drop its speed down to a crawl. Brannock was seething.

'Can't you find another route?' I asked.

'These tracks are all over this neighbourhood, so no matter

where I turn, this train will still be there, blocking our way,' Brannock said. 'I hate these fucking trains!'

As we waited for the train to pass, I looked over at a nearby party store, on an otherwise derelict street.

'Why are these corner stores called party stores, in Detroit?' I asked.

'That's just what they call them around here,' Brannock said. 'That's just how they're known. They sell lotto, groceries, cigarettes and liquor, and they accept the Bridge Cards, WIC cards – all the benefit assistance cards. And those guys you saw on the videos will walk to these stores twenty times a day. That's also where you get your weed and everything, although not from the guys in the store. Well, sometimes, but not always. Everything in the neighbourhood, in Detroit, is centred around the party store. So for example, there's one at Eight Mile and Cherrylawn, and fucking everybody, from Roselawn, Kentucky, all these streets, they all walk to that party store. That's where they socialise, that's where they get their beer, their cigarettes, their lottery – and you're playing lottery every day.'

'Why on earth would you open a store in these neighbourhoods?' I asked.

'The owners don't usually work in them,' Brannock told me. 'They get immigrants and students to work in these places. Same with the gas stations.'

'I take it certain gangs will stay away from certain party stores? They won't mix together?'

'Yeah, the gang runs the party store. Like, Runyon Boys control their party store, so another gang isn't going to go up there to sell dope. They will gun you down. Did you hear them say on the video, "If you're not from over here, you ain't gonna be over here"? That's how it is. They control the party store, or the gas station, and that's their corner.'

'That party store on the Runyon video, I take it that I couldn't

just pull up there and walk into that store and buy a can of Coke?'
I asked.

'Yeah, you could,' Brannock said, although it was in a tone that
suggested I shouldn't. 'But you might get fucked with. They'd
want to know what your ass was doing there. They'd ask if you
was the *po*-lice. Then they'd probably take all of your shit.'

'So you wouldn't just go in there and buy ...'

'I go wherever the fuck I want to go,' Brannock said, cutting
me off.

Finally, the end of the train passed by. The warning lights at
the rail crossing stopped flashing and the barriers lifted. Brannock
put his foot down.

*

The Ceasefire meeting was being held in a large room, with a glass
wall and a huge meeting table. It was due to start at 1 p.m. and
we were a few minutes early, despite the train. Sat around the table
were the various agencies with a stake in Ceasefire: DPD,
Michigan State Police, FBI, senior officers from the 9th and 5th
Precincts, the Prosecutors Office, and Wayne State University. It
was getting close to standing room only but I found a chair at the
back of the room, positioning myself away from the main table.

Brannock knew most of the people in the room and he
introduced me to them. After each introduction, he told the
person, 'Mick's writing a book about me.' This statement was met
with various responses, including: 'It's gonna be a short book.' 'Is
it a children's book?' And my personal favourite, 'Is it a re-write
of *The Thing*?'

Assistant Chief Dolunt charged into the room. He always
seemed to be rushing around from one location to another, as
though he were doing the job of five people all at the same time
which, knowing Dolunt, he possibly was.

After a few more introductions and some basic admin, we settled in for the start of the meeting. As we did so, a couple of officers walked in late.

'Oh, apparently the meeting starts at 1.15 and not 1 p.m. So you're right on time!' Dolunt said, making a joke but getting his point across at the same time.

The meeting got underway and a list of the previous week's Ceasefire-related crimes and shootings were projected on the wall. A lieutenant from one of the precincts shuffled some papers and then began to go through the list.

'There was a shooting at the Eastland Mall,' the lieutenant said. 'Three in custody, with confessions.'

Dolunt scribbled some notes and said, 'Great job by Gang Intel.'

'A gang shooting where one suspect shot through the victim's windscreen,' the lieutenant continued. 'Second suspect pulled the victim from the car. The vehicle was found burnt out.'

Everyone had their head down, making notes as he continued through the list.

'NBA, drive-by shooting …'

'NBA?' someone asked.

'Niggas 'Bout Action. Guy was shot in his car after a fight at a barbershop. Looks like a retaliation shooting. Lots of shootings on Nottingham – the disruption team are looking into it. A victim was being robbed and she drew her gun but shot herself in the hand during the struggle. Six Mile Chedda gang – two brothers were fighting and one of them pulled a gun and shot the other one. Someone was shot after someone fired their gun into the air and the bullet came back down and hit them in the head. A victim was found in a car with two gunshot wounds to the head – it's believed that the victim was moved there from the actual scene of the shooting.'

The list went on for some time.

Towards the end of the meeting, Dolunt turned to the lieutenant from the 9th Precinct. 'Final shooting numbers for your precinct, for the year?' he asked.

The lieutenant looked down at a piece of paper, reading the figures. 'Two hundred and one non-fatal shootings and forty-six fatal,' he said.

The 9th was just one of twelve precincts across the city. By anyone's standard, it was a huge number of shootings and killings for just one area: the 9th Precinct is less than twelve square miles with a population of around 70,000. It was now even clearer to me why Brannock's team had been told to concentrate their efforts on that area.

*

'Shit,' Robo said as we stepped back into Brannock's car. 'I left my radio at the meeting.'

Brannock huffed theatrically. 'Mick, are all your officers in England as incompetent as ours?'

Before I had a chance to reply, Robo turned to Brannock and said, 'Because you've never left anything anywhere, right?'

'Ever!' Brannock said, smirking.

'I'm sure you haven't,' she said. 'Because you're the fucking man!'

'I know. That's why Mick's writing a book about me. When you have something that has this much perfection, like me, you write a book about it. They put Jesus in the Bible, didn't they?'

'Fuck!' Robo said. 'I just remembered where I left it. It's in the conference room.'

'Great. The Chief is about to give a press briefing in there. Right, so now you had better fucking go in there and tell the Chief of Police that you lost your five-thousand-dollar radio,' Brannock told her. 'And I'm not going in there with you.'

'Okay, don't! I'm a big fucking girl!' Then Robo turned around to look at me. 'So, the cops in England are assholes too?' she asked.

'You're cutting into my lunch period with your fucking bullshit,' Brannock told her.

As angry as he pretended to be, I knew Brannock loved that Robo had given him a reason to pick on her. Any excuse to turn on the mock anger was welcomed in Brannock's mind.

Robo hopped out of the car and ran into the building.

'She loses stuff all the time,' Brannock told me. 'Just watch, I gave her my badge to get in there and I bet she loses that too.'

Ten minutes later Robo stepped back into the car holding her radio. She handed Brannock his badge and pass.

As we drove through downtown, Robo pointed down one of the streets. 'A few years ago, I went ice skating and I parked my car down there,' she said. 'When I came back out, my car was gone. Stolen. I had my gun on me but everything else, including my badge, was in the car.'

'See?' Brannock said. 'If you didn't have your legs attached, you'd lose them too.'

'Shut up,' Robo said.

'Probably leave them in some fucking hotel room.'

'Would you stop already?'

Brannock smirked and headed back towards the 9th.

'I was showing Mick some of those gang videos online,' he told Robo.

'Did you see all the weapons they were carrying?' she asked me.

I told her I had, and wanted to know how common it was really, to see assault rifles and AK-47s on these streets.

'Are you kidding me?' she asked. 'They have them and they use them. I'll show you.' She handed me her phone. 'Press play, on the screen,' she told me. 'It's an actual dispatch recording of an incident here in Detroit. DPD were following a van that was involved in a kidnapping. You want to know if these motherfuckers have AK-47s? Listen to this ...'

I pressed play and listened.

The incident had happened in 1998. Officers were following a van that was believed to have been involved in an abduction. The commentary between the officers and the dispatcher starts off calmly enough, falsely giving the impression that nothing much is going to happen. As officers give out their location so that others can back them up, pieces of information start to trickle through, including that the occupants of the van are possibly armed with 'a lot of weapons'.

Without warning, one of the officers following the van yells over the radio: 'WE'VE GOT SHOTS FIRED! WE'VE GOT SHOTS ...' Next, an officer transmits that his 'PARTNER IS DOWN!' and that both he and his partner have been shot. He says that his partner is 'HIT BAD!' and he himself has been shot in the neck and shoulder. As the officer gives out their location, desperately crying out for a medic and EMS (Emergency Medical Services), he states that his partner has been shot in the head.

The audibly distressed dispatcher does all she can to get units to them, trying to reassure the shot officers that help is on the way.

The transmissions are gut-wrenching. This was a piece of horrifying history, recorded forever, of the final moments of a police officer's life.

'So the guy in the van basically just stuck the weapon out of the window,' Robo told me, as I handed back her phone. 'The officers never saw the weapon – just the muzzle that came out the back window. And then they just lit them up as they were chasing them.'

'What were they firing?' I asked.

'An AK-47,' Brannock said. 'One officer was killed – Shawn Bandy.'

'Of the other two officers, one had his eye shot out,' Robo told me.

'Lloyd Todd – his eye was shot out,' Brannock said. 'Ramon Childs was all right though.'

Robo showed me a photo of Todd. 'That's him, right here. He's blind in one eye. He can never work again. A bunch of officers from the Number Nine went over to his house this summer,' she told me. 'They helped to mow his lawn and fixed his roof and stuff like that.'

'Did he get out with a pension?' I asked.

'Duty disability, but after the city bankruptcy thing, we got screwed,' Robo said.

The City of Detroit declaring itself bankrupt in 2013 had a direct effect on employees' pensions and benefits, including the police. The city took away employee medical coverage and handed disability claims by Detroit police officers and firefighters to a private company.

'Originally, they were saying that if we were shot on duty, we wouldn't be covered,' Robo continued.

'But surely that's when you *should* be covered?'

'Right,' Brannock agreed. 'They overturned that but they still messed with their medical and with their disability.'

'I was working the night of that shooting. We ended up going over there,' Robo said. 'I started the academy in '96, graduated in '97. This happened in '98. It was a horrible night. Horrible. Horrible.'

'For me and Robo, that was our first police funeral,' Brannock told me.

The occupants of the van had kidnapped a woman and her 12-year-old son in relation to a drug dispute and had held them for ransom. After they were spotted and followed by the police, the men had opened fire with an assault rifle. Although it was often reported as being an AK-47, court documents state it was a 'dawoo rifle' – possibly meaning Daewoo. Three of the chasing officers were hit.

Officer Shawn Bandy was the passenger of the first, marked police unit. He was shot in the face, twice. He was a 23-year-old, 4-year veteran of the Detroit Police Department. The driver of the second police unit, 34-year-old Michael Lloyd Todd, was shot in the right eye and now has a prosthetic replacement. The right side of his brain was also damaged, resulting in limited mobility to the left side of his body. He now uses a scooter to get around and has suffered unimaginably ever since. Flying glass wounded the third officer.

One day after the shooting, Shawn Bandy's family, including his father, Max, who was also a Detroit police officer, had to make the decision to turn off Shawn's life-support machine. Shawn Bandy was engaged. On the night that his life support was turned off, Shawn's family found out that he was to be a father.

I had originally planned to transcribe the entire dispatch recording here, in this book. It made for extremely distressing reading but was a perfect example of how an incident can escalate so rapidly from calm to chaotic, and how deadly the job can be. I spoke to a number of DPD officers about whether I should or shouldn't document the recording. My concern was for Shawn Bandy's family. This was, after all, the final moments of his life, and a recording of his murder. Attempts to contact his family on my behalf were made but with no luck. Sadly his father Max had died just three months before, and Shawn's mother had already endured the hell of listening to her son's final moments three times in court, and so I felt it was right not to include the transcript in this book.

Four men were convicted of first-degree murder for the killing of officer Shawn Bandy. They each received a life sentence. One of those men is the son of a retired Detroit police officer.

Even though the incident had happened nearly 20 years ago, Robo still held onto that recording and carried it with her. The event had clearly had a huge impact on her and Brannock, as well as many others. And since it occurred – and at the time of writing

– twenty more Detroit police officers have lost their life in the city, most of them violently and most of them by gunfire.

Robo and Brannock never wanted to forget what had happened that night, and after listening to this recording, I felt the same.

I was well aware of the dangers faced by officers on these streets, but the recording was a shocking reminder of how quickly a routine incident can escalate and how deadly the city could be. And then, moments later, I was reminded again.

10

The Gun Show

As soon as we reached the 9th Precinct, a call came out over the police radio that spiked Brannock's interest – a report of a shooting, in a nearby street. Uniformed 'District' units were already making their way there. Brannock and Robo decided to head towards the area and hang around, just in case it turned out to be anything gang-related.

As we drove closer to the location, Brannock pulled up to a kerb and stopped the car. We were on Mack Ave, the major thoroughfare that runs between Detroit and the more affluent townships to the south and east.

'Recognise the cow?' he asked me.

Robo turned to look at me, a broad grin across her face.

I looked out of the window. In front of us was a small cream-coloured building that looked as though it had once been a kiosk of some sort. On the roof of the building was an enormous white bull's head. And yes, I did recognise it. I had seen it a number of times before, on previous visits to Detroit. The bull's head had become an unofficial tourist site and had attained a curious amount of pride amongst Detroiters. The reason? The building had featured in the Eminem movie, *8 Mile*. In one particular scene, characters from the movie drive by the head and open fire on it with a paintball gun.

'Yep,' I said. 'I recognise it. *Eight Mile*, right?'

Robo nodded her head, still smiling.

'That's the one,' Brannock said. 'Now, let me show you something else. I want to show you the house where I dealt with a double homicide on Mother's Day.'

We turned immediately to our left, directly opposite the bull's head kiosk, and crossed into Lenox – a narrow, scruffy-looking residential street. As we drove slowly along, I could hear the sound of ice crunching under the tyres of Brannock's car. Main avenues such as Mack weren't so bad but everywhere else was a dangerous warren of frozen roads.

The house Brannock wanted to show me was on the left side of the street. Most of the lots on that side of Lenox had had their ruined buildings cleared away and were now just empty snow-covered plots, whereas the right side of the street was, for the most part, still lined with houses, albeit mostly rundown ones.

Brannock gestured to one of the buildings on the right side of the street. It had nothing to do with his double homicide, but he wanted me to see it all the same.

'That's the Hustle Boys' home base, right there,' he said, pointing to a dilapidated and grimy wooden house.

I looked over at it, and as I did so, a man walked down the front steps and across a small front yard, heading towards the road.

'There's someone coming out of it,' I said. The man had now stopped on the sidewalk and was staring towards our car.

Robo peeked out of the rear windscreen. 'Oh, he's just a young kid,' she said, sounding unconcerned.

'This is the house, right here,' Brannock said, pointing to one of the few houses that occupied the opposite side of the road.

As he spoke, I noticed him simultaneously using his rear-view mirror to peer at the kid, who was still standing in the street behind us. He soon lost his train of thought.

'No, it wasn't that house – it was this one…' Then Brannock stopped speaking and concentrated on his mirror. 'What's he got in his hand?' he asked, sounding uneasy.

'I can't see,' Robo said.

'The kid?' I asked. I looked around and saw that he was now standing by a van, at the side of the road. He was staring directly at us, occasionally turning to look back towards Mack, as if he were checking to see if anyone or anything else was coming into the street.

'What the fuck is he doing?' Robo asked.

'I don't know,' Brannock replied slowly, still watching.

The kid was gripping something with his right fist. The object was small and black but bigger than a phone.

'He's got a gun,' I said.

'Shut the fuck up!' Robo said.

I looked again but now I was in no doubt. 'He's got a handgun. It's in his right hand.'

Brannock got straight onto his handheld radio. 'Hey, anybody close on Lenox?' he asked.

I continued to stare at the kid, now unable to take my eyes off him or the gun. 'He's definitely got a black handgun,' I said.

'Yeah,' Brannock said in agreement. 'Yeah, he has.'

'Fuck, yeah!' Robo said, now seeing it too.

Brannock got back on the radio. 'Hey, anybody close on Lenox?' he repeated.

Then the kid moved; he returned to the house and went inside. As he did so, Hunter came on the radio. 'Hey, Brannock, do you want me to head towards Lenox?'

'Fuck, yeah!' Robo said, looking at Brannock.

'Yeah, I've got a guy with a semi-automatic handgun, standing out on the street.' Then turning to me and Robo, Brannock told us, 'I'm gonna flip back around and see if I can pick him up again.'

Brannock sped away from Lenox, the wheels skidding on the thick ice. He took a turn to the right, followed by another and then a third. We were back on Mack. The bull's head was just in

157

front of us. Then Brannock turned right a fourth time and we were back on Lenox. This time, he stopped a couple of houses down from the Hustle Boys house.

'That motherfucker was just standing there, by the side of that fucking van,' Robo said, shocked at the brazenness of it.

'I knew he had a gun,' Brannock said. 'I could see it right in my fucking rear-view mirror.' He picked up his radio. 'Hunter, how far out are you?'

'I'm just leaving the base now.'

There was a collective 'fuck' from Brannock and Robo.

'Had to grab my vest,' Hunter explained over the radio.

Vest. I looked down at the seat next to me. My personal set of ballistic body-armour was somewhere under our collection of winter jackets and bags. As I scrabbled around, digging through the clothing and equipment, I found it and quickly yanked it out. I also found Robo's set.

'You want your vest, Robo?' I asked.

'No.'

It wasn't the answer I was expecting but I had noticed that Brannock wasn't wearing a vest either. Regardless, I quickly pulled mine over my head.

Brannock got back on the radio. 'He came out as we were slow-rolling by the house. He had the gun in his hand. I want to try it again and see if he comes back out. If he does, I'll have you guys snatch him up.'

Brannock and Robo had their own guns drawn and were holding them on their laps. Robo was racking hers, making sure it was loaded and ready to fire. I looked at her hands and noticed that she was gripping her Glock pistol with newly French-manicured nails. It was quite the contrast.

Brannock lowered his radio and we sat in silence, staring towards the house, waiting for our back-up to arrive. Our car began to rock as a fierce wind blew along the street, forcing up small, ghostly puffs of snow from the ground. Other than us, the street was empty.

As I fiddled with the Velcro straps on my body-armour, the door to the house opened. It was the kid. This time, I was able to get a better look at him. He was young but he was no child. He was slightly stocky and looked to be in his twenties.

'Heads up!' Robo said, also seeing him. 'He's got his fucking hand down his pants.'

I looked. The guy had one of his hands stuffed down the front of his baggy jeans, as though he were holding something. This wasn't good and we all knew that there was a real chance that he had hold of the gun.

Brannock picked up his radio. 'I've got him walking northbound. Got him walking northbound, coming right towards us.'

'This motherfucker is gonna pull his fucking gun out!' Robo said.

Brannock continued to talk on the radio, sounding more urgent. 'He's heading northbound, straight towards us. We're gonna have to take him down. Stand by.'

Robo reached for the door handle.

'Hold on, hold on,' Brannock said. 'Wait till he gets closer.'

'I'm telling you, he's gonna light us up!' Robo said, sounding increasingly anxious.

'No, he ain't.'

'Bullshit!' Robo sounded convinced that rounds were about to come flying through the windscreen.

By now, I too was seriously concerned. The guy was walking directly towards us, as though he were on a mission and we were the target. He was looking at our car, staring into it – staring at us. His hand was still pushed down the front of his baggy jeans. At that moment I wanted a gun of my own. Robo's words – 'he's gonna light us up' – were bouncing around in my head. Being in a gang area, alone, back-up still some distance away, watching the guy striding purposefully towards us, almost certainly with a gun, my own mortality had begun to scream at me. I wanted to be armed. I wanted a gun. I wanted to have a chance to fight back if I had to. But I didn't have a gun; all I had was a pen, a notepad and a camera. I started taking pictures.

Brannock slowly reached for his door handle. 'Okay,' he said. '*Go!*'

Brannock and Robo simultaneously opened their doors and I did the same. The guy continued towards us, undeterred. Brannock and Robo immediately raised their handguns and pointed them directly at the man.

'POLICE!' Robo shouted. 'PUT YOUR HANDS UP, MOTHERFUCKER, OR I WILL FUCKING SHOOT YOU!'

The guy immediately pulled his hand from his jeans – it was empty – and he threw both arms in the air.

'GET THE FUCK DOWN! GET THE FUCK DOWN!' Brannock ordered, marching forward, one hand outstretched, pointing his gun directly at the guy.

'GET THE FUCK ON THE GROUND!' Robo shouted. 'DON'T MOVE YOUR FUCKING HAND!'

The guy kept his hands in the air and fell to the ground, lying face down in the snow-covered front yard of another house.

We moved in closer, Brannock and Robo still with their guns pointed at the man, who was now completely prone on the icy ground. There was no gunfire. The only sound I could hear was the crunching of our feet on the snow and ice, and the sound of my camera clicking rapidly.

'Mick, watch the house,' Brannock ordered. 'If anyone comes out, shout.'

I looked towards the gang house, wondering what I would do if others did come out. There were just the three of us – and only two were armed. For the second time in less than a minute, I thought: I need a gun.

Brannock and Robo holstered their weapons and sat the guy up. They asked him his name but he refused to answer. Robo then stuffed her hand into his jeans, hunting for the gun. As she did so, a car pulled into Lenox from Mack Avenue. It rolled slowly towards us.

'Heads up, we've got someone right there,' Robo warned, looking towards the car as it inched closer.

Brannock took hold of the guy on the ground, grabbing his jacket around the shoulders. Robo stood back up, pulling her gun and watching the car. Two young black men sat inside, looking at us with fixed stares as they passed slowly by.

'We need the others to get their asses down here, quick,' Brannock said.

Then there was another car. It seemed that word was out about us being on Lenox. This time it was Brannock who pulled his Glock. He held it by his side, following the car with his eyes as it drove by, just as slowly as the previous car had. The car came to a stop a couple of houses up from the gang house. Brannock kept his gun down by his side, as he faced the car, sideways on, ready to raise it; ready to open fire. Then the car quickly pulled away and drove off.

We were seriously exposed, standing out on the street, with no one else around. Anyone looking would guess that we were police but that didn't necessarily make us any safer. We had a gang member cuffed in the snow, we were in their area and there were only three of us. It was starting to feel increasingly hairy.

After the second car had taken off, Robo returned to searching the guy's pants.

'Got it!' she said. She pulled her hand out. In it she was holding a large handgun. It was a SIG Sauer .45 calibre pistol.

'I come down here and you try and light me up?' Brannock said to the guy, accusingly.

'Y'all stop outside of my house like y'all gonna do something,' the guy replied glumly. 'What else was I meant to do?'

'I don't know? Call 911?' Brannock suggested.

'What's the 911 do for us? You know our house just got shot up. What did 911 do? Nothing!'

A few weeks before, there had been a shooting in the street and the house had been the target. It was the reason the guy claimed he had come outside to challenge us. He thought his house was going to get shot up again.

'Got anything else on you?' Robo asked, sitting the guy up.

'Come on, man, y'all just searched me, what else can I have on me?' He spoke softly, in a defeated tone.

As we stood on the snow-covered street, I could hear the sound of police sirens getting closer.

Over the radio, dispatch was giving other units an update on our situation. 'Units to respond; officers holding one on a CCW.' (Carry Concealed Weapon.)

'On scene,' I heard an officer say over the radio. It was Hollywood. He arrived in an unmarked, black Crown Vic, with police lights flashing from within the front grills. The car slid a few extra feet across the ice as he brought it to a stop. He got out, wearing a heavy black down jacket.

'We've got the gun off of him,' Brannock told Hollywood as he stepped delicately over the ice towards us.

'Stand up,' Hollywood ordered the guy. As he got to his feet, Hollywood began to search his pockets. The guy immediately began to protest.

'They've already checked these pockets. Why do you have to do it too?'

'Because you had a gun on you,' Hollywood said.

Cooter arrived in a 4x4 and walked equally cautiously across the ice. Brannock then told Hollywood and Cooter the full story.

Other gang officers began to arrive and for the first time I noticed that many of them wore olive-green cargo pants and black jackets. Despite being a plain-clothed unit, this green and black ensemble appeared to be an unofficial uniform. Then I looked down at myself. The entire time that I had been with Gang Intel, I had coincidentally been wearing exactly the same outfit. For someone on the streets – someone armed with a gun – I would have been indistinguishable from a cop. (The following day, I would go in wearing jeans. Naturally, the others then also started wearing jeans.)

As we stood there, the adrenalin started to wear off and I began to feel the weather again. It was freezing. The wind was now blowing gently but the temperature had dropped so low that it felt as though razor blades were being dragged across my skin. I walked around in a small circle, clapping my hands together, trying to warm up but the forced movement only resulted in me slipping multiple times on the ice. As I rubbed and blew on my fingers, Cooter went up to Brannock and said something quietly in his ear. Brannock stepped away.

'He walked up on us!' Brannock said to him, sounding defensive. I guessed that Cooter had questioned why we were there and why Brannock and Robo hadn't waited for back-up before taking the guy down.

'He was walking away,' Cooter said.

'*No!*' Brannock replied. 'He came out of the house and walked up on us.'

I was surprised to hear Cooter challenging Brannock in this way; after all, Brannock was the unit sergeant. But Brannock didn't get angry; he simply explained the situation. There was genuine concern from Cooter about the danger we had been in, and Brannock had accepted those concerns, without pulling rank. I realised then that Brannock respected his officers' opinions and experiences, and that they respected – and cared – about him.

A marked police unit turned into Lenox from Mack. The guy was handed over to a pair of uniform officers, who then placed him in the rear of their car, to take him to jail.

Finally, we stepped back into our own vehicle. My fingers were frozen to numbness.

From the front passenger seat, Robo turned to face me. 'Hey, you like that?' she asked, smiling broadly. 'That'll be great for your book!'

'I thought that guy was gonna pull that gun and start shooting,' I said.

'Oh my God, I'm telling you right now, it was close,' Robo said. 'Fucker! He didn't even run!'

'He couldn't run with that gun,' Brannock said, as he started the car. 'It would have dropped down his leg.'

Robo had the guy's gun on her lap and was checking it. 'Fucking loaded with one in the chamber,' she said. 'Fucking A! It's a forty-five, too. That would have fucking hurt bad,' she said. Then she handed me the gun and one of the rounds.

I looked closely at the gun. It was large, heavy and solid. It was also scruffy, with a build-up of grime and dust in the corners. Then I looked at the bullet that Robo had handed me. It was short and fat – a 'stopping round' – with enough power to immediately incapacitate its target. If it hit you, you wouldn't be getting up again.

'You see how big the fucking rounds are?' Brannock asked. 'Look at that!'

'You could kill an elephant with these bullets,' I said, not even joking.

'Yeah. We would be dead,' Robo said.

'Did he have a whole magazine of these?' I asked.

'Five rounds,' Robo confirmed.

Brannock and Robo were still on an adrenalin rush from the incident. It had been a fast-moving, highly dangerous situation. The way that Brannock and Robo had spoken to the guy – loud, aggressive, swearing – had been utterly necessary. It was important that the man immediately knew who they were, who was in charge and what the consequences would be if he didn't comply or if he was crazy enough to draw his weapon. No one wanted to get shot and Brannock and Robo didn't want to have to shoot. The aggression was all part of taking control of the situation and ensuring that everyone lived. Go in soft, appear weak, lose control … and there was every chance that the fresh white snow would have been soaked red with someone's blood.

'That's how fucking quickly that shit can change,' Robo said.

Brannock nodded in agreement. 'There was a second there where he wasn't going to drop that gun. He bladed his body.'

I too had noticed the gunman's positioning. As he had approached us, he had turned his body side-on (blading), presenting less of a target. It was a standard defensive – and offensive – technique, should rounds start to go off.

'We were awfully close though – we would have lit up his ass!' Robo said.

'Oh, I would have shot that guy,' Brannock added.

'There was nothing in our backdrop,' Robo said. 'We weren't in each other's way. I was over here, you were over there.'

'And I was stood behind the engine block,' Brannock added.

'I had no cover,' Robo said. 'I was exposed.' She went quiet, reflecting on how dangerous the situation had been and how vulnerable she had left herself.

'He wouldn't have had a chance,' Brannock said, reassuring her.

We drove through other gang streets, all just as depressing and dangerous as Lenox had been. The chatter in the car dropped off and I started thinking about the incident and how it could have gone differently. What if the guy *had* drawn his gun? What if he *had* started shooting? And what if Brannock or Robo had killed him – or if Brannock and Robo had been killed? What would I have done? What if others had come out of the house or one of the cars had opened up on us? I didn't believe for a second that my regular travel insurance would cover me.

'Surely he would realise you were cops though, right?' I asked aloud.

'That's why I made sure he saw my badge, right the fuck away!' Robo said, holding up her metal Detroit detective badge.

'It was brave of him to come out and face us on his own,' I said, rashly.

Neither of them replied.

*

Brannock found a parking space as close to the doors of the base as possible. As we entered the building and walked along the chilly corridors, he reached up with one of his arms, rubbing and twisting his shoulder.

'You okay?' I asked.

'Yeah. I'm on restricted duties,' he replied.

I thought I had misheard him. 'Who's on restricted duties?' I asked.

'Me!' He said, laughing. 'I fell over on vacation in Mexico and broke my collarbone; shattered it.'

I stopped walking and stared at him. 'But you just arrested some guy with a gun.'

'Yeah,' he said, still amused but wincing in pain as he continued to manipulate his shoulder and arm.

Robo gave me a 'that's Brannock' look.

As we were about to pass by an open door, leading to another office where a female officer was sat at a desk, typing, Robo poked her head in, showing the officer the .45. 'See?' she said. 'We go out and this is what we get!'

Now Brannock looked into the office. 'Mick, tell her I'm a hero.'

'He's a hero,' I said, with as little enthusiasm and emotion as I could muster.

'Right!' Brannock said. 'And he's writing a book about me!'

'Is it called *The Blob*?' the officer asked.

'Don't give him all that praise, Mick,' Robo said, cutting in. 'I think I did my job too.'

'I was the one that fucking saw it!' Brannock said. 'I was looking in the mirror and saw the goddamn fucking gun!'

Robo ignored him and walked off towards the Gang Unit office.

After that incident, everything changed. It was as if a level of trust had suddenly developed between Brannock and myself. The incident was enough to bring me into the fold, and I immediately felt more accepted.

As Robo and Brannock walked into their respective rooms to de-kit and write up their report and statements, I took a seat at the large meeting table, making notes of my own.

'Robo, what time did we make that arrest?' Brannock called out from his office.

Not hearing Brannock fully, she called back, 'The time for what?'

'The arrest!' he shouted.

'Two-fifteen.'

'The time for what?' Brannock mimicked, mocking Robo's words but speaking loud enough for us all to hear. 'THE TIME THAT OPRAH COMES ON TV!' he called out sarcastically.

This annoyed the hell out of Robo. 'I DIDN'T HEAR YOU, YOU FUCKING DICK!' she screamed at him. 'FUCKING GO AND MAKE YOURSELF BUSY!'

From his office, I could hear Brannock chuckling to himself.

It was clear that Brannock and Robo had an 'old married couple' type relationship, but despite their bickering, they were good friends. They were also old friends, having grown up in the suburbs and gone to school together, long before either had considered joining the police.

167

At school, Robo had hated Brannock. 'He was an asshole,' she told me. 'If you think he's bad now, imagine him at puberty!'

They had both joined the DPD within months of each other, without realising that the other had also joined. At a time when the city still had residency for its workers, they had ended up living in the same apartment block, literally across the hall from one another. And although they had both worked in homicide, it wasn't until they came to Gang Intel that they finally started to work together. And now here they were, shouting obscenities at one another all day long.

Despite the language and insults, Robo was kind and thoughtful. She was also tough. A survivor. She had known from a young age that she wanted to be a cop and described herself as 'a thrill-seeker'. She loved city life and had never wanted to do a regular job. Robo hated going to college and sitting in class, so as the Detroit police didn't require a degree or college education, she dropped out of school and joined up. Financially, it wasn't easy. When she first joined the force, she was only making $25,000 a year: the wage was so low that she actually qualified for food stamps. She never took any government assistance, however, stating that she would rather work two or three jobs than accept hand-outs. Robo could have joined a suburban force and earned better money, but she enjoyed working in the more challenging environment of Detroit.

Robo had been married to a cop who worked in one of those better-paid, suburban forces. They had a daughter together. Working with DPD provided her with health insurance and a pension that she could claim after 25 years, when she would be just 46 years old. All in all, things were looking pretty good. But then it all fell apart. First, her marriage broke down and she got divorced. Next, the city went bankrupt. Now when she leaves the force, her health insurance will be taken away. Her previous police pension was also stopped, meaning she will no longer receive the income she had been expecting. Instead she is enrolled in a new scheme, but with so few years left to work, she is unsure how much she will actually get back from it. And with no college education or degree, Robo believes her prospects of getting a well-paid job outside of the DPD are tough.

'What do I do?' she had told me, with a shrug. She seemed resigned to her situation.

*

By midnight most of the officers had headed off home to get some rest before doing it all again in the morning. Brannock was in his office typing up a report, so I wished him goodnight. He raised a friendly hand without taking his eyes away from the screen.

As I went to step out of his office, I stopped and turned back. 'You have an interesting bunch of officers working for you,' I said.

Brannock stopped typing and looked up at me. 'I hand-picked them,' he said. 'When I was asked to start this unit, I told them I wanted to pick my own guys – people that had been tried, tested and proven. I wanted guys that had been involved in shootings.'

'Why was that important?' I asked.

'Because we are dealing with gangs. You've seen it for yourself. This is dangerous work and I need to know that my guys have what it takes to pull the trigger if they have to. I don't want to get into a gunfight and find the guy next to me is having a panic attack. A lot of guys aren't putting in to do this job. This is a lot of work and a lot of hours. You have to sacrifice your family life and then you're in the shit for thirteen hours a day. You live this. This becomes your norm.'

'But it's also real cop-work,' I said.

'Yeah, but with real cop-work comes real fucking problems, like drinking and post-traumatic stress disorder, and getting in trouble, and getting indicted. You become your environment; a lot of officers do. Listen, I have the best police job in America. I'm in charge of the Gang Unit in the most dangerous city in the country, but we're not playing out here – this is serious shit.'

*

In the yard, my car was buried beneath a thick layer of fresh snow, as deep as a couple of house bricks. Solid lumps of dirty ice had congealed around the wheel arches. I had to knock them off with repeated, forceful kicks. A solid film of ice coated the windscreen. I scraped off as much as I could before getting into the car and switching on the heater and blowers as high as I could get them. The display on the car's dashboard showed that the temperature had dropped to 14 degrees Fahrenheit (minus 10 degrees Celsius). I pulled up the zip on my heavy winter jacket and wrapped my arms around my body as I waited for the glass to clear enough for me to be able to drive.

As I waited, I thought about the people who lived in the ruined houses in the gang neighbourhoods. Many were without electricity, heating or running water. Drug users, dealers and prostitutes were crashed on the hard floors or on soiled mattresses in vacos, where all utilities had long ago been turned off.

Desperate people had already ransacked most vacos. Pipes, wires, and anything with any kind of scrap value had been ripped out and sold, leaving just a wooden shack with boarded-up, missing or smashed windows. Even the houses that were legally occupied were often without power. Families lived in darkness, although some stole power from their neighbours, or directly from the power companies, by literally climbing up electricity poles and hooking up wires.

I had been talking to Robo about it earlier in the day, when I asked her how people survived the winters.

'These people have nothing,' she had said, shaking her head at the sadness of it all. 'They just hope and pray that they make it through the winter. You and I have Christmas; these people don't have Christmas. Christmas is whatever they can take. Look how cold it is; if you don't have a coat and you don't have the money to buy a coat and you're freezing, what do you do? You steal, you rob, because you're cold and you want a coat. I remember I went into one house and everyone was fully dressed. They had their coats on the entire time. The people that don't have electricity are usually all curled up together on the couch, using each other's body heat.'

One of the consequences of the cold weather was that the attendance rates at the schools go up a little.

'The kids know that they are going to be warm there,' Robo told me. 'Although a lot of problems at the schools blow up because of that.'

So many of these homes in Detroit were filled with hungry, cold children. Around them, older kids were killing each other. The winter weather only added to the misery. It was truly pathetic.

Over forty million Americans live in poverty. Whether it's in the dangerous, forgotten corners of Detroit, an Indian reservation in the Midwest, or tiny Delta communities in the Deep South, the poverty, hunger and hardships I have witnessed in America are amongst the worst that I have seen anywhere.

For instance, soon after my visit to Detroit, officers raided an apparently abandoned house that was believed to be used for drug-taking. The house had no beds, no windows, no heating and no toilet, yet inside, officers found a man and a woman living there, along with their seven children aged between 9 months and 9 years. Also in the house were two guns and a dead dog.

*

As I drove home through the dark warren of streets, my wipers were struggling against the onslaught of the blizzard. I pushed on, leaning closer to the windscreen, trying to get a better look at the road ahead. Snow and ice were building up dangerously on my headlights, as their glow was rapidly becoming weaker. I wanted to leave the area as quickly as I could, but going too fast, I risked losing control of the car. Crashing or getting stuck in these neighbourhoods didn't bear thinking about. Driving slowly, however, felt nearly as risky.

A light ahead of me changed to red. *Damn.* I feathered the brake, cautious not to force it. Even so, the back end of the car twisted left and right, before the vehicle eventually skidded to a halt, at an angle, halfway across the stop line. I was stopped at a crossroad that contained a gas station, a prison, and a graveyard. I noted how the graveyard was better kept than most of the streets around it.

A narrow street to my right was severely overgrown, almost lost in a tangle of tall weeds, spiny bushes and dark, skeletal trees. There were perhaps four houses – all burnt-out shells – concealed in the undergrowth. A pair of twisted street signs warned, *Do Not Enter.* Why would you? I wondered. It was like something from a terrifying fairy-tale. And yet a few days later I watched as two young boys strolled in carefree fashion along the centre of the street, returning from school, swinging their bags casually in the frigid air.

I shivered violently. The car heater was already cranked up as far as it could go, but I checked it again, trying pointlessly to turn it higher. I twisted the blowers in my direction, aiming a couple at my frozen fingers.

I glanced back at the gas station. Despite the weather, a couple of shady-looking men shuffled on the forecourt under a faint light. No cars pulled in to fill up. In fact, there were no other cars at all, so I took my foot off the brake and continued through the red light and deeper into the blizzard.

But despite it all, I felt happy. I felt happy to be back in Detroit. Even with its many imperfections and some deeply troubling issues, I loved this place because, as one local business put it: 'Detroit Hustles Harder'.

11

Hell Zone

Tuesday, 12 January 2016

A city newspaper, the *Detroit News*, was running a story about my visit to Detroit. I had met the reporter, George Hunter, a few days before, over breakfast at a local diner. He was a crime correspondent, and after the interview we had got talking about the high murder-rate in Detroit. I asked how he managed to report them all but he surprised me by saying that he didn't. It was only the more interesting or unusual cases that got column inches in the paper. Each case and each death mattered, he told me, but there just wasn't enough room for them all.

Then he surprised me a second time. When we talked about how dangerous some streets and neighbourhoods were, he revealed to me that he had seriously considered arming himself with a gun. Most reporters wouldn't dream of such a thing and many would feel that it would go against everything their occupation represents. But George explained that he often had to go into dangerous neighbourhoods, knocking on doors to get a story or to interview people. Most of the time the locals wouldn't have a clue who he was – just some stranger on their street – and he was out there alone and on offer for anyone looking for a victim.

Being a reporter doesn't guarantee protection anywhere, but especially so in Detroit. In the 1970s, for example, the then editor of the *Detroit News*, Martin Hayden, had a box delivered to his office. The box – possibly sent by the mafia – contained a human head, its eyes propped open with toothpicks. More recently, in January 2017, a retired TV news anchor had Molotov cocktails thrown at her house, after a Detroit resident blamed her for the rising crime-rate. And then in March 2017, two Detroit journalists were shot at in the street whilst covering a story about the shooting of two Detroit cops the day before.

George ended by telling me that when he checked with his editor to see if he would be allowed to carry a firearm, he was informed that it was against company policy. So that was that.

Today, the newspaper was sending a photographer to the base to get a picture of me, to run with the article. The rest of the Gang Unit wanted to be left out of the image, but Brannock agreed to be in it with me.

Everyone was sat in the office, drinking coffee, as Brannock and I waited for the photographer to arrive. I was parked at one of the empty desks, catching up on some notes. Whispers was sat at his desk, searching through gang videos on YouTube. Brannock was in his office, speaking to the homicide detective about the firefighter case. Hollywood and Scrappy were each slouched in one of the leather armchairs, chatting about religion.

'Our priest was speaking the other day, and he says, "When you're giving to the homeless, you're not just giving to the homeless, you're giving to me. Are you going to refuse me?"' Hollywood said.

'Your soul will deviate,' Scrappy said.

'There are still good people who are atheist or agnostic,' Whispers said, looking up from his screen.

'A hundred per cent,' Hollywood agreed. 'But I believe that with religion, you lead a better life. For me, anyway.'

'You can be atheist or agnostic and still be a good person but I believe you are being a good person towards everybody else; I don't think you are being a good person towards yourself,' Scrappy said. 'If you talk to an atheist, man, he's got a lot of anger issues.'

'You atheist, Whispers?' Hollywood asked.

'No, I'm Christian,' he replied.

'Brannock's an atheist,' Hollywood said.

'Brannock's the devil,' Scrappy snorted.

Whispers stopped tapping at his keyboard and sat back in his chair, thinking for a moment before saying, 'One day he's going to be talking and he's just going to explode. I truly believe it.'

'He's gonna grow fucking horns!' Scrappy said.

We giggled like school kids making fun of their teacher.

'You know what's crazy?' Scrappy continued. 'We're sitting here and we have all these different faiths in this room, yet we get along, we go about our day, we have each other's back. We've got Christians, atheists – and Reef's a Muslim. There're a lot of people outside the US who would just have a hard time grasping that idea.'

'Not just *outside* the US,' I said.

'I think, at least for us, we just want a normal life,' Hollywood said. 'I go to work, I have my friends, I have my neighbours and that's it.'

Robo was busying herself, ordering some stationery for the office. She walked around the room with a clipboard, asking people what they needed. Whispers, who until now had been one of the quietest and most mild-mannered of the GIU officers, seemed to have become affected from being in Brannock's company for so long and was a little feistier than usual.

When Robo asked Whispers if he had any stationery requests before she submitted the order, he said, 'Some of those knobbly wands we saw at the house we raided.'

'Knobbly wands?' Robo asked. 'You mean the dildos? We can't order dildos; I only have seventy-two bucks to spend.' Then she pointed at Brannock, who had now joined us all in the main office, warning Whispers, 'And don't you start copying him.'

Turning to glare at Brannock, she said, 'And don't you encourage him.'

'I'm infectious,' Brannock told her.

'You're an infection, more like,' she said.

'Your voice is like nails on a chalkboard,' he responded.

Whispers held up a metal clip, asking Robo to order some of those.

'Do you know what they're called?' Robo asked.

Brannock jerked a thumb at me. 'Ask English,' he said. 'They have them over there. They're called koala bears.'

'The clips?' I asked.

'Yeah.'

'They're called bulldog clips.'

'Bulldog? Like a bull with horns, and a dog?'

'Yeah. Like a bulldog. And a clip. A bulldog clip.'

Robo looked down her list. 'They're called "binder clips",' she said.

'At least you're now calling me English, rather than Australian. That's progress, I guess,' I said to Brannock.

'They're still the same thing,' he shrugged.

'And what's your heritage?' I asked.

'Irish and German.'

'Well, that explains everything. It's no wonder you hate me.'

From the first moment we met, Brannock had been full of wisecracks, teasing abuse and ridiculous amounts of attitude. I noticed that when he had brought his wife and stepdaughter into the office on one of the days I was there, he spoke to them in exactly the same way he spoke to his officers. I wondered if he had always been this way, or if the job had made him what he now was. The answer, probably, was a bit of both.

Over the time that I spent with Gang Intel, I had gained their trust, and my relationship with Brannock had developed into one where we were able to speak frankly. There was a friendship developing between us; we amused each other and had grown to like one another, also. One of the consequences of that, however, was that the level of insults and abuse intensified. But I had spent long enough as a police officer myself to understand that teasing, as vicious as it sometimes seemed to outsiders, was all part of being a cop, and helped get you through the day. Besides, I mostly enjoyed it and liked to give back as good as I got. Brannock could be extreme with his abuse, but that was fine with me.

The saying about a person's bark being worse than their bite fits Brannock perfectly. He reminded me of the last sergeant I had worked under in the Metropolitan Police in London; they were both equally but comically obnoxious – and the worse Brannock got, the funnier he became. He was still a bit of an enigma though, and I wondered what his own history had been. What had turned Brannock into Brannock?

When he returned to his office, I followed him in and asked if he would tell me about how he became a police officer in Detroit.

'We could be waiting a while for the photographer,' I said. 'He keeps calling to ask for directions to the base.'

'Well, if you're going to write a book about me, I guess you need to know a few things,' Brannock conceded.

He told me to sit down, and then he began to speak.

'I'm an only child and I was always a spoiled prick,' he started. 'My family came to Detroit when I was ten, so Detroit was a huge shock to me. But I knew I wanted to become a police officer, as my dad was a police officer in Baltimore. I was always fascinated with that shit. I was going to college but I was fucking up. When I finally got my shit together, I was doing loss prevention, in stores. It was a good job and I really enjoyed it – it's a lot like law enforcement. I was in the city of Inkster and they had an auxiliary police department, which I joined. You could be an auxiliary officer and you got to carry a gun and everything, so that was my first real policing experience and I fucking loved it.

'A couple of guys that were doing the auxiliary shit there, said that they wanted to apply for Detroit. "Oh, Detroit's doing a mass hiring! You gotta go!" they said. I was like, "I really don't want to work in Detroit." They said, "All you gotta do is go and fill in a postcard." I was like, "Okay, I'll go down." It was at Cobo Hall or Joe Louis Arena – rows of people. So I went down, filled out the form and I got hired. The two guys that dragged me down there, they *didn't* get hired. They didn't pass the background checks.

'I did the whole academy thing, but when I came out I was still a typical suburban asshole. I didn't know the culture and I was an arrogant prick. I basically started my police career just doing stupid shit. I was injuring prisoners, getting into fights that I didn't need to be getting into, driving like a fucking maniac, doing all the wrong things – all the rookie mistakes that police officers make when they first get that badge and come on the job. I was arrogant, I thought I knew everything.'

Brannock's wild behaviour quickly got him noticed by the senior leadership at his precinct – for all the wrong reasons. After a couple of incidents ('injured prisoners', 'dumb car chases') things came to a head and one of his bosses warned him that should one more prisoner get injured or should he get into any more trouble, they would be looking to kick him off the force. But with his arrogance, Brannock couldn't see what he was doing wrong.

'I wasn't admitting that it was me that was the problem,' he told me. 'I'm thinking, "It's this city!" you know? But it wasn't the city, it was me that was fucked up. It was my attitude that was the problem.'

After a female prisoner began to injure herself in the back of his police car, by repeatedly banging her face against the cage, Brannock was convinced his time with DPD was up, but it wasn't. Despite feeling that he 'just couldn't win' and that he was 'a shit-magnet', he managed to hang onto his job.

'Shortly after that happened with the prisoner, we had a big storm. It was Fourth of July 1998 and all the power was out through the city. Me and my partner, who had about two months less than me on the job, were at a restaurant and a police run was given to us, to a man on a porch firing a shotgun. So, wanting to look cool, I pulled out of the restaurant, you know, lights and sirens, squealing tyres, all that dumb rookie shit.'

Brannock left the restaurant and headed towards the shooting. With the power cut due to the storm, all of the traffic-lights were out. Brannock headed towards an intersection. As he did so, a lady who should have stopped at the junction instead continued into it.

'I T-boned her,' Brannock said. 'I shouldn't have been going lights and sirens. Sure, some guy was reportedly shooting his gun but it's Fourth of July in the city of Detroit, so everybody is out shooting off guns and shit. So I T-boned her car and her car rolled on its side. The lady's twelve-year-old daughter was on the back seat of the car. She was ejected out of the vehicle. She was okay though. She had some bumps and bruises and she had to go to the hospital but she was all right.'

'What about you and your partner?' I asked.

'Our car – a brand new scout car – was totalled. Me and my partner? We weren't hurt at all. Of course! You know? The two jackasses that caused the whole thing are unhurt!

'That was it for my commander at the time – she was like, "Fuck this guy". She took my department driver's licence away and I had to walk a beat for about three months, all by myself, up and down Plymouth Road. Other officers at the precinct were told not to pick me up. I wasn't allowed in any scout car at all. Don't get me wrong – I fucking deserved it! So, I really had to adjust everything – my attitude, my perception of the city. I had to grow the fuck up. I was nineteen, twenty years old, I was still a fucking high-school kid doing stupid shit that affected other people's lives. I'm a cop, I'm supposed to be trusted out there.'

That incident – and somehow not being fired – did change Brannock, but the car crash was just the beginning of his transformation: there was more he wanted to tell me. The second part of the story caused him to lower his voice, sounding more reflective, even humble.

'I'm not a religious person but I do believe that everything happens for a reason,' he told me. 'I had to go through these experiences as a rookie to make me the officer I am today. I had to fuck up. I had to learn the hard way. And throughout my career, I've felt that someone has been watching over me and guiding me in the right direction.

'So, after my car accident, I'm walking a beat. My lieutenant at the time was basically done with me but he tells me that they were giving me one more chance. He said, "I know you're a smart kid, you've just got to grow up. This is real-life shit, this isn't that shit that you were doing in high school."

'So they gave me another chance. Then he calls me one night at home, and he says, "Well, Brannock, you fucking blew it." He goes, "Where's your badge at?"

'And I said, "Lieutenant, it's in my wallet. I have my badge!"

'He goes, "Did you have another badge made, and lose it?"

'I was like, "No! I have my badge!" I'm panicking, so I run in the bedroom to check, and thank God, my badge is in my wallet."

'So, he says, "Well, Internal Affairs wants to talk to you. They found your badge on the People Mover (an automated transit system), downtown."

'And I'm like, "I've never even been on the People Mover. I don't know what you're talking about."

'So he was like, "Well, you're going to have to go down there and explain that – but don't you lie! If you lost your badge, then you tell them that you lost your badge and that you didn't make a police report on it."

'I said, "Okay, but I didn't lose my badge."

'So the next morning he calls me and says, "Hey, everything's been resolved. We figured it out, it's not your fault."

'Well, turns out that back in 1995, there was a horrible car accident involving two Detroit police patrol cars. In one of the patrol cars were Officer Lindora Smith and Sergeant Earl White, and they had a ride-along in the car with them – a police cadet named Aaron Phillips. They were in a car chase and they were T-boned by another scout car. All three of them died in the car.

'Officer Lindora Smith had the badge number 2283. It's the same badge number that I had. When an officer is killed in the line of duty, they retire the badge, but somehow, in the shuffle, it got mixed up and I ended up with her badge.'

'How did her badge get on the People Mover?' I asked.

'I don't know for sure but I was told that they had made some other badges and presented them to the family at the funeral. So, the department assumed that one of the family had it and was carrying it around and lost it.

'So, they send me down to the basement at headquarters and some old, crusty white guy is down there and I tell him the story and he's like, "Oh, that's interesting. Well, we'll fix that." He then takes a soldering iron thing and flips the "3" off of my badge and solders a "4" on the end. So, my badge number changed to 2284. That's all they did. Here I am thinking that I'm gonna get a whole new badge and everything, and that's all they did.

'As soon as that badge number changed, I got back to the precinct and I was put into Special Ops. I started working with these two cops. One had twenty-eight years on the job, and the other had thirty-five years. So I got these two badass cops to learn from and shape me and take care of me and look after me. And ever since then my career has been nothing but good things. Nothing but good things!

'I truly believe that Lindora Smith and Sergeant White were

looking over me, and I was going through all that because I had her badge number.

'I know that sounds fucking crazy but then some other things in my career happened later down the road and it just felt like they were looking over me.'

After Special Ops, Brannock moved onto homicide, and it was whilst he was there that he was promoted to sergeant. With the promotion came a move within the department.

'I had all these open cases and all this stuff going on at homicide and then I get promoted and I'm told that I am getting transferred to the Ninth Precinct – which had the reputation of being the shithole of the world! And I had never worked on the east side really, except when doing the homicide and narcotics stuff.

'As a supervisor I was terrified to go over to Number Nine. You know, here I am, a new boss, and I'm going to the worst precinct in the city. The very first day at the Ninth Precinct, there was an influx of new supervisors. Eric Jones, my new inspector, has us all meet up and he starts telling a story about a sergeant that moulded him and how when he first got on the job he was injuring prisoners, not doing things the right way. He told us that this sergeant took him under his wing and kinda brought him up and showed him how to be the real police. That sergeant was Earl White!

'I never met Lindora Smith or Earl White – they were killed before I got on the job – but I just always felt that connection. So, I went to DC for Police Week and I went to The Wall and I thanked them, and I ... you know, do that little ...'

Brannock made a hand gesture, as if he was making a pencil rubbing. 'The Wall' he was speaking of is the National Law Enforcement Officers Memorial in Washington DC. Included on that wall are the names Lindora Smith and Earl White. Brannock had made a pencil rubbing of their names, onto a piece of paper.

That rubbing was pinned to a board, in his office. He told me that he kept it as a reminder to always do the right thing.

Brannock believed that Lindora Smith and Earl White were the reason his career had been as positive as it had been. Maybe he was right but he also needs to give himself due credit. Brannock is a great cop, a hugely experienced officer – hardworking, tenacious, sarcastic but funny, street-smart. If you met him once you would think that he was hard – hard on crooks, hard on his officers, hard on you, hard on himself even. But get to know him, spend time in his company and you will see a man who cares deeply for his officers, for the job, for the department, for the city and for the people.

Taking yourself too seriously in a job such as policing, as many officers do, can be damaging to your health. It can also be damaging to the people around you, to colleagues and the public. Not every situation requires a zero-tolerance 'Robocop'. Brannock understood the absurdities of the job and the absurdities of life. He, and everyone else around him, was all the better for it. And then there was this – his belief in his own guardian angels.

'Lindora Smith and Earl White will be with me my whole career,' he told me. 'I believe that a hundred per cent. And I'm not a superstitious guy or believe in fucking ghosts and all that other bullshit. It's just a gut feeling. I always felt they were there. I was lost and I was doing dumb shit. I'm lucky to be alive, with the shit that I was doing.'

*

The newspaper's photographer finally found the base and arrived. He was a slim, middle-aged black man who looked tired but he was keen and friendly and ready to go, with his large digital SLR camera slung over his shoulder.

Brannock thought the office, with its walls plastered with gang intelligence, was probably not the best place to grab a snap. As we had been planning to go out and look at some gang areas, I suggested bringing the photographer with us. Brannock agreed and we all jumped into his 4x4.

Brannock drove us just a few blocks east of the base, to show me some of the Hell Zone gang houses. On one street, I noticed a two-storey house that had been gutted by fire. The door was missing and the windows were just blackened holes. Burnt timbers hung from walls and ceilings, and half the roof had collapsed into the building itself. It was basically a typical abandoned house in Detroit. It would be ideal for the photo.

'How about this one?' I asked.

Brannock peered at the house and slowed the car down to a crawl before coming to a stop outside.

'That'll work fine,' the photographer said.

We could be accused of feeding a cliché, the usual negative narrative, but then again, having me stand in front of a beautiful mansion on a leafy street in the Sherwood Forest or Palmer Woods neighbourhoods would be odd. Although Detroit did have a handful of these affluent areas, they weren't the places where I was spending my time or the places I was writing about. I was here to record the work the Detroit police were doing in the gang neighbourhoods, and about the people who lived in those areas. A burnt-out, graffiti-covered house represented just that.

I gathered my camera and notebook, ready to step out of the car, but then Brannock reached over with his hand, indicating for me to stay where I was.

'Are they doing what I think they're doing?' he asked.

I looked up. Ahead of us, just a couple of doors along from the burnt-out house, two young black men were fiddling with the front door to another abandoned, but mostly intact house.

'Let me tell you what's going on here,' Brannock said. 'They're gang members looking for an abandoned house to sell their drugs from.'

'They're breaking into that place?' I asked.

The photographer peered forward, between the two front seats, where Brannock and I were sat.

'Yep, looks like it,' Brannock said.

The two men noticed us watching. They stopped pulling at the door and stared back at us. Then, from between a couple of other houses on our right, another young black man started to walk towards us. Just in front of us was an old sports car, stopped in the street, with its engine running. The two men at the house looked as though they were talking to the driver, though we couldn't hear what they were saying. There was no one else on the street. Then the men stepped away from the building and started to walk towards us, one of them with his hand stuffed in the waistband of his jeans. The man on our right was also stepping closer.

I heard the clicking sound of metal – Brannock had drawn his gun and he held it on his lap. 'I think we may need to find another house,' he said.

'That's a good idea,' the photographer agreed.

Roaring away at speed could have spooked the men and invited all sorts of trouble. Instead, Brannock brought down his window and began to cautiously creep along the road. The men continued to step forward, slowly surrounding us. Brannock raised his gun and rested it on the open window, so that the men could see it, as he continued to roll along the road. The men stopped walking and stood in the street staring at us with deadpan expressions. No one spoke. Brannock kept his gun in view until we had passed them by. Then he picked up the speed and we drove away. None of us said anything more about it, simply accepting it as a normal hazard in these neighbourhoods.

Just two blocks away, we found another house to use for the

photo. It was a small, single-storey brick building – not as dramatic as the other place, but it was still a house used by the Hell Zone gang, with the outside walls covered in their graffiti. As with the other house, the door and windows were gone. Inside, the exposed floorboards were rotting away and covered in trash – bottles, food wrappers, old flyers and other general litter. Across the interior walls was more Hell Zone gang graffiti: HELL ZONE #49 FREE MY BRO'SZ!!!

'Forty-Nine?' I asked Brannock.

'Telephone keypad,' he said. 'Four for H, nine for Z. HZ – Hell Zone.'

'Free my Bro'sz?'

'Someone got locked up.'

As the photographer took his pictures, I walked around the house with Brannock. The other rooms were empty, each a smaller version of the main room – bare wooden floors, trash, graffiti.

The photographer asked me to stand by one of the graffiti-covered walls so that he could take some snaps, and I did my best to look sombre and journalistic.

After the photographer had taken his pictures, we dropped him back at the base before Brannock and I headed into the streets once more.

As we hammered along the frozen, slushy road, away from the base, Brannock took a call on his phone. It was Reef, one of his officers, who was currently off work.

Brannock's tone was uncharacteristically upbeat when he spoke. 'Hey, Reef! How's it going down in Texas, my man?'

'Yeah, it's going good,' Reef said. But he sounded tired and sick.

'Those nurses treating you well?' Brannock asked.

As they spoke, I heard Brannock using words such as 'treatment' and 'hospital'. Occasionally, he would make some wisecrack that got Reef laughing a little bit.

'Did the guys tell you about Reef?' Brannock asked me, after the call.

'I've heard people mention his name, but that's all,' I said. 'Seems like a popular guy but other than that I don't know anything else about him.'

Brannock nodded then explained what was going on. Reef had recently been diagnosed with leukaemia. His diagnosis had come out of nowhere and it had been a shock for everyone who worked with him. He was married and had kids, but the department only paid for so many days sick, before they stopped paying altogether. With Reef's regular household bills still to meet, together with the extra medical costs, officers from the department had come together to help him out. Brannock told me that Detroit police officers had given up their own paid leave days and donated them to Reef, so that he could continue to earn a wage whilst getting treatment for his illness. Fundraisers had also been arranged, and money had been collected to help send Reef to Texas, where he could get the best treatment available.

The police often come in for criticism and sometimes that criticism is justified, but this here was the police that I had always known; officers banding together to help a sick colleague. Everyone hoped that Reef would respond to the treatment and everyone hoped that he would be able to return to work, but no one knew for sure. They had already given their money and their time; hopes and prayers – and sometimes wisecracks to make him laugh – were all they had left.

*

Brannock had mentioned to me a number of times that he was going to tell me about 'the worst homicide I ever dealt with', but he never seemed ready to reveal the details of it to me. The more that time went on, the more certain I became that it was simply because he wanted to get to know me better first. I figured that the story was very personal to him, so I hadn't pushed him into telling me about it. But things now felt different between us, so I went ahead and asked.

'You keep threatening to tell me that homicide story,' I said. 'The worst homicide you ever dealt with.'

Brannock nodded. He thought for a moment, driving in silence, but then began to speak.

'This guy was dating a girl but the girl had a case against him after he shot a gun at her. Then one day she was with her friend and this guy kidnapped them. He put these two girls in the trunk of his car and disappeared. He then walked them out to a hole that he had fucking dug and laid them in it. Then he fucking executed them.

'But there was another guy that had brought the perpetrator the shovel to use to bury the girls, and he flips and gives information to homicide. I was in homicide at the time, and the state police came out with dogs and everything and they covered the field where he had buried these two girls. It was the most horrific fucking thing I had ever seen. Just to be there in the woods and know what these girls went through. Knowing that they were going to die, walking them into the woods.'

Brannock had images of the homicide scene on his phone. He had originally taken them for evidential reasons when he had been investigating the case, and had kept them in case anything came up in future. But he also kept them as a reminder to himself of what he had had to deal with – not as some kind of macabre trophy, but because it was now a part of his own history.

He brought the pictures up on the screen and passed me the phone.

'This is where we started – this is the woods. You had to walk along this path to an old baseball field that's been covered over. These big tree stumps were on top of the hole. So we had to roll them off and then dig the girls out. They were huddled together – see how he had duct-taped their shoes and their hands?'

'How old were these girls?' I asked.

'I think, eighteen.'

'He duct-taped their ankles and wrists?'

'And their faces, yeah. Dumped them in the hole and then fucking shot them. So we had to dig this mud and we had to do it in sections because we needed to find the bullets and shell-casings and fragments … and you can imagine the smell! But to see two clothed bodies like that …'

'How long were they in there for?'

'I don't know, maybe three weeks to a month, or something.'

Brannock had told me homicide stories before – it was one of his things. Every time we went out of the base we usually ended up in some neighbourhood or other where he had dealt with a murder or murders. Perhaps he really did consider me to be his personal biographer and was using me to record his policing history. But I always suspected something else.

Policing can take a serious toll on a person – especially when you work somewhere as busy, desperate and violent as Detroit. With Brannock, I always felt that he was telling me about these murders as a way of preventing the victims from being forgotten, and to release some of his own burden. It was important that others knew what had happened in *this* street, or in *that* house. Being the only person holding on to that knowledge and those terrible memories, can be a depressing weight. From my own experiences, I understood Brannock's need to talk. Every bloodied body, every half-decomposed corpse, every dead kid, had become part of who he was.

Those two girls, executed in that pit, never knew Brannock and he had never known them, yet destiny had brought them together in the most awful of circumstances. Brannock couldn't just walk away from those memories, or from that case. Of all the homicides he had investigated, those two girls had hit him the hardest. Under that gruff armour there was a huge heart, but there were also years and years of sorrow. With Brannock, it would be easy to believe that what you saw was what you got, but if you cared to look deeper, you would see that there was actually much, much more.

*

We had been driving out to the 10th Precinct, just to the northwest of downtown. The precinct hosted a number of gangs – Dexter Boys, Niggas from Linwood, Total Take Over, Trust No One, and Niggas Bring Crack, to name just a few. I had wanted to see where the 1967 riots had started and Brannock had agreed to show me.

He pulled the car over at the corner of Rosa Parks Boulevard – which was called 12th Street at the time of the riots – and Clairmount, next to a small park.

'This is Gordon Park,' Brannock said. 'This is where the '67 riots started.'

There was a freezing wind raging outside, so I remained in the car and stared at the park through my window.

'It doesn't say anything about it,' he said, correctly guessing that I was looking for a plaque or some other monument. At that moment, there was nothing. In July 2017, however, fifty years after the events, an historic marker was finally erected in the park.

'So, as you can see, the riot spread north and south from here,' he continued, pointing up and down the road. 'Look at how many houses are still burnt-up over there.'

I gazed at rows of large ruined houses and destroyed businesses. 'This is all left over from the riots?' I asked.

'Yeah.'

But it was fifty years ago, I thought to myself. Half a century, and evidence of the riots was still here, untouched. And it hadn't been left for historical reasons or as a memorial; it had just been *left*.

'It's the same shit you see all over the city,' Brannock said, referring to the other ruined neighbourhoods. 'But this stuff is from the '67 riots. Fourteenth Street was hit hard. This was a predominantly black neighbourhood at the time and it was kind of residential, so they went after the white businesses that lined Linwood and Dexter – they're the major roads that run through here. That's what suffered the most.'

Brannock pulled alongside a short row of derelict shops on Linwood Street.

'This is all left from the riots,' he said, tapping a finger on the frost-covered glass. 'You can still see the store signs.'

I looked over at the weather-faded signs above dark cavities that had once been local businesses – a music shop, a liquor store. There was not a single window or door left behind; just empty shells, covered in graffiti, slowly rotting away. Piles of rubble were gathered where once there had been counters, shelving and paying customers. The stores looked as though a car bomb had exploded directly outside. In some, the old wooden floors had given way, revealing cavernous basements, filled with piles of snow-covered litter, smashed bricks and pieces of burnt wood. These relics of Detroit's dark history were a sorry sight.

And yet, I thought, just four years before the 1967 riots, everything had been so different, so progressive, and so hopeful. Martin Luther King, who just two months before, in Birmingham, Alabama, had been meet with batons, police dogs and fire hoses, was greeted in Detroit by marching bands and the Police Commissioner, George Edwards.

Martin Luther King was in the city to lead his Walk to Freedom. The Walk saw well over 100,000 Detroiters, Michiganders and others, white and black, stepping along

Woodward Avenue, arm-in-arm. Commissioner Edwards, a white man from Texas, and a progressive, equal rights advocate, keen to transform the image of the Detroit police, had walked with King at the front of the crowd, and had allocated King his own police bodyguard – the highest-ranking black officer on the department. Edwards had instructed his officers to leave their batons at the station, and King commented on how different his welcome had been in Detroit compared to the South, calling it 'a relief'.

It was immediately after this march, in Detroit's Cobo Arena, that King had first spoken the words 'I have a dream' – a whole two months before these same words would be so famously spoken again from the steps of the Lincoln Memorial in Washington DC.

Although the catalyst for the rioting had been the shutting down of the 'blind pig'

illegal drinking den, the foundations for the troubles had long been in place. The Kerner Commission, set up to investigate the causes of the rioting that had swept the nation, blamed the violence on white racism towards blacks, and black Americans' response to that racism.

Despite once being seen as a refuge from the racist South, in the 1960s Detroit was

still a racially divided city. There had been decades of discrimination, with the favouring of whites over blacks for better job positions and promotional opportunities, along with the ghettoisation of the black population in slums such as Paradise Valley and Black Bottom (named for the soil), where black families lived in cramped, squalid conditions. In a forced segregation, blacks had been kept out of white neighbourhoods by such things as 'deed restrictions', which barred the sale of houses in certain neighbourhoods to blacks. When these restrictions were overruled in court, some black families moving into white neighbourhoods were attacked and soon afterwards, some whites, not wanting to live with black neighbours, moved away.

There was even a six-foot wall built from 8 Mile, running between Mendota Street and Birwood Street, in the north of the city. Known as the Detroit Eight Mile Wall, although it has also been called Detroit's Berlin Wall, and The Wall of Spite, it was built with the intention of separating blacks from whites. It is still there today, although I wonder how many people know of its history and original purpose.

There were also reports of police brutality, often at the hands of the 'Big 4' units – cars containing four police officers that roamed high-crime – and often black – neighbourhoods.

Sooner or later something was going to snap, and this here – the deserted streets and crumbling buildings that Brannock and I were looking at – was the result.

The motor industry, moving plants and jobs away from Detroit, workers' unions and strikes, the Depression, war, corruption and mismanagement had all played a part in Detroit's downfall, but so had racism, the legacy of which is still evident today.

We drove on, and a short distance later we pulled up at another stretch of ruins.

'Even the church is boarded up,' I noted.

Brannock stared at it. 'Yeah, even the church,' he said, before falling silent for a few moments. I waited for him to speak again.

'July seventh, 2007,' he said, eventually. 'It was the fortieth anniversary of the 1967 riots and I was patrolling down here, in this neighbourhood.'

'Did anything happen?' I asked, thinking that maybe the date had been marked in some way.

Brannock continued to stare at the church. 'I'd agreed to work overtime with a buddy of mine,' he began. 'I pulled up on a car right here. It was a baby-blue Grand Marquis. A description of the vehicle had just been put out over the radio as it had been involved in an armed robbery. I went to the driver's side and I fought with the guy over a gun. I ended up shooting him. I killed him right there on the sidewalk.'

Now it was me who fell silent.

'I fought with that guy for my life,' Brannock continued. 'He had taken my partner's gun and we were fighting, real close. I shot him dead. I shot him right in the heart. We were so close to each other that when I shot him, blood flew from his chest and went into my eyes and mouth. The next day, in the newspaper, it said, *Detroit police celebrate the forty-year anniversary of the uprising by killing a young black man*,' he told me, shaking his head in disbelief. 'After that, I had PTSD. I went to the department doctor for that. And just being so up-close and personal with a motherfucker ... It was like I killed him with my own hand. You know what I'm saying? There was that much of a fight that I was fucking exhausted. I went to the hospital myself. So I know what it feels like to have PTSD. You don't know what it feels like until you get it. I was just real paranoid, real worried. Just ...'

Brannock was chewing hard on some gum. He was struggling to find the words to explain just how bad it had been.

'Worried for your own safety, or worried that you were going to shoot someone else?' I asked.

'Everything!' he said. 'Going back to work. Getting in another shooting. Whether I was going to be charged or not; it took the prosecutor's office a couple of months to clear me.' Brannock sat in silence for a while, staring at the church before continuing on. 'Just really stressed. You know that feeling when you wake up and you have something that day that you're really worried about – whether it's flying or travelling or whatever? Well, it felt like that all the time. And everywhere I went I had guns on me.'

'What do you mean?' I asked. 'You thought that people were pointing guns at you?'

'No. I was carrying extras guns. I had a rifle by my bed and one on the dresser. The man I shot was a gang member, so I didn't know if guys were going to come after me.' Brannock chewed his gum, hard. 'I remember going to my parents' house and being by their pool. It was a beautiful day so I went out there to swim and relax. Well, I had my gun at the pool, on a table.'

'Did the PTSD eventually go, over time?'

'Uh-huh. It's like falling out of love, you know? You know that feeling where you're in love with a girl and then you break up and you're kinda heartsick over it? And then it just goes. It just goes.'

We sat in silence some more, before he said, 'And then those girls in the pit. It came back a little bit then too. And when I first got to homicide, I got it a little bit there too. I couldn't believe how much fucking death there was in this city. I had post-traumatic stress disorder from all the death I was seeing. You get to work and straight away you are going to a scene or you are going to the morgue or you're going to a baby death. Every fucking day you are seeing a dead body. It's crazy. And just the amount of violence. In just one weekend we had thirty baby deaths. *In one fucking weekend!*'

We looked over at the boarded-up church a little longer before pulling slowly away, leaving the area and its dark memories behind.

*

Brannock's experiences had been awful but it was refreshing to hear him talk so openly about PTSD. It wasn't that long ago when police officers were expected to 'just get on with it'. Some years ago, as an unarmed police officer in London, I had fought hand-to-hand with a guy armed with a loaded handgun. He stood several inches taller than me and was believed to be a hit-man for a Jamaican gang. Just like Brannock, I had fought with him for my life. Afterwards, a senior officer asked me if I needed to speak to somebody, 'or anything like that'. The look on his face told me that had my answer been 'yes', he would never take me seriously again.

All police officers have dealt with dangerous, distressing incidents; many deal with them on a regular basis. And just because someone has been trained to be a police officer, it doesn't suddenly make him or her immune to what they have to see and deal with in the course of their career.

An average of 130 officers take their own life each year in America. The vast majority are male and most use a gun. Not all of these deaths will be directly related to the officers' job, but some will be.

I have known cops who have contemplated taking – or have attempted to take – their own life. I have personally known officers who have killed themselves. Being a cop can be traumatic, and policing can take its toll. Most people have no idea.

Thankfully, attitudes are changing.

12

American Children

Wednesday, 13 January 2016

Brannock had arranged for me to visit a Detroit high school where adult mentors worked with some of the kids, to help steer them away from crime and gangs. Called 'Dignity', the programme had been considered a success, especially by Brannock, as his unit now had a relationship with some of the kids that hadn't been there before. The mentors, with their own past and reputation, were respected by the kids, which meant that they listened to them or sought them out when they were in trouble or needed advice.

The Dignity programme was more than just basic mentorship, however, and there had been real results, with some boys leaving gang life behind and moving positively forward. It had also given Brannock and the Detroit police a way in with some of the gangs. He and his officers were now closely involved with some of the kids; meeting them after school to get some food or simply to drive them home, keeping them out of trouble and away from harm. It was a programme and a relationship of which Brannock was proud.

Robo decided to come to the school with us, and she jumped into our car. Despite the hazardous conditions, Brannock drove in his usual, unique way. As he switched lanes to get ahead of the slower-moving traffic, the driver of a Mini honked his horn.

'Fucking stupid English car,' Brannock said, ensuring that he caught my eye in the rear-view mirror.

'Actually, they're made in Germany now,' I said. 'They're owned by BMW.'

Brannock fell silent.

'Didn't you say that you're half-German?' I then asked innocently.

Robo burst out laughing.

Brannock put his foot down and sped up. 'Shut up, Mick.'

We weren't going far, just a little deeper into the east side of Detroit, to the 5th Precinct and the East English Village Preparatory Academy. It was a modern building of sand-coloured stone, with a large glass rotunda entrance.

At the start of the week, out of 100 schools in Detroit, less than half had opened. Detroit teachers had called a 'sick out'. They were protesting about the conditions that they and their students had to work in, citing in particular the lack of teachers, and subsequent class sizes, where there could be up to 50 students in a single class. In the current situation, it wasn't uncommon for some classes in Detroit to have no teacher at all, and some city schools had to close due to teacher absences, leaving the students with no place to go.

I had also seen a report which showed that in the 11-year period between 2003 and 2014, nearly 90 Detroit schools had been shut down. The city's finances were stretched and the lack of funding for teachers had become a serious issue. Paid volunteers from a non-profit organisation called Teach for America, which had programmes in a number of low-income communities across the country, were working in Detroit schools, doing what they could to help educate the city's children. Regardless, as far as many of the Detroit teachers were concerned, the situation was now desperate.

Despite the sick out, East English Village Preparatory Academy had managed to remain open. It still had its problems though.

'We had a kid murdered at this school last year,' Brannock told me as we pulled up. 'They had a "Grammys night" – like a talent show – and some Hobsquad members showed up and some Real Warren Kings showed up. There was a fight and one of the Real Warren Kings – Terry Catchings – pulled out a gun and fired into the crowd, shooting this kid called Darryl Smith, who had nothing to do with anything; he was just there picking up his nephew. Catchings bingoed him in the head and killed him.'

*

A uniformed security guard and a pair of search arches greeted us at the school entrance. A poster on the wall read: *I'm not snitching but I am telling.* It was a hopeful attempt to encourage students to speak out about wrongdoing and criminality.

Inside, we walked into a large common area, where there was a scattering of tables and chairs. Kids were everywhere, running around in all directions, shouting and laughing. It looked like prisoners taking over a prison, and other than ourselves, there were no adults to be seen.

A bell rang and I saw a teacher appear at the other end of the room, yelling at the kids to 'get to class'. We followed some of them upstairs and Brannock led me into a small classroom, where the Dignity group met. Standing in the room was one of the largest men I have ever seen in my life. He was black, heavy-set, and must have stood over seven feet tall. He had huge shoulders, a thick neck, big arms and a solid chest. His massive hands looked as though they could crush a Marvel superhero with laughable ease.

'Mick, this is Jermaine Tilmon,' Brannock said, introducing him. 'He's one of the volunteers who works on Dignity. He also works with the Ceasefire programme.'

The big man shook my hand gently, as though deliberately trying not to hurt me with his superior strength, and said, 'Hello, sir.'

Jermaine had an unexpectedly soft voice: it was calm, friendly and respectful all at the same time. He seemed to me like the ultimate gentle giant.

'He's Davontae Sanford's stepdad,' Brannock added.

I looked back at Jermaine. 'Brannock has been telling me about Davontae's case,' I said. 'It must be difficult for you.'

He nodded his head slowly, looking thoughtful. 'It's a waiting game. It is in God's hands. We are hopeful that he will get out soon,' he said softly, sounding almost in prayer, then repeated: 'We are hopeful.'

I mentioned to Jermaine that I had been pleasantly surprised by the relationship that existed between the mentors and the gang officers.

Jermaine smiled, but told me: 'It wasn't always that way. I remember back in the day, 1300 Beaubien (the former Detroit Police headquarters) used to come. They took you back to the basement of 1300 Beaubien, and there'd be a couple of police officers there' (Jermaine lowered his voice and leaned towards me), 'and they beat you up. Beat. You. Up! The cops would tell you, "You'd better not run." Because if you did, you'd get an ass-whopping.'

Then everyone started laughing and joking, reminiscing about how things used to be, back in the 1990s. It was funny, watching Jermaine, Brannock and Robo, as they got all nostalgic for a time when they would have been enemies. But now here they were, jabbering away like old friends. This kind of change gives you hope. It reminds you that most people, underneath it all, and given a chance, are decent and kind and simply want a good life.

'Here's the thing about Detroit, right now,' Jermaine said. 'You got more guys taking out-of-town trips, because the city is literally burnt out. It's burnt out to the core. So, there's really no money here, for the streets. Plus it's its name. The name that Detroit once had outside of the city has changed. People used to fear Detroit, but now they see Detroit as being full of snitches and informants working with the police.'

'So much for the culture of not snitching,' I said.

'It's because some people have no money, so why not get paid for snitching?' Robo said. 'Get paid by the Feds.'

'You see, back in the day, it was like a drug war,' Jermaine said. 'It ain't no drug war right now. Now it's a gang war. Now it's territory, different sets, different neighbourhoods. It's so different from when we came up. It's all social media now. We didn't have social media back then. Then it was straight-up territorial. Now it's straight-up Facebook. Then it was like: "Oh, they rolling down our street? They gonna set up a spot in our neighbourhood? Ah, no, we gotta burn their house down." That's how that was. Now it's online, it's all: "Fuck Hobsquad! We're East Warren, bitch!" And that's how it is.'

*

The door to the classroom opened and four black teenage boys joined us. They had been asked to come in to speak to me. They each took a seat on plastic chairs and sat in a semi-circle. I hadn't been expecting a meeting like this. I had thought I'd be walked around the school, shown some stuff, and maybe bump into some of the kids that Brannock knew. I wasn't anticipating to be sat down in a circle with four boys waiting for me to interrogate them.

Looking at their nervous faces, I wondered how to word my questions. I wanted to go straight in, asking about the craziness of the city and how a person was able to live there. Were they aware of how utterly different their world was, compared to so many others? But how do you soften a question when you are talking about a city such as Detroit? When you are asking about gangs and murder? These boys had grown up here, knowing nothing else. They already understood what a dark place it could be.

After we had all taken a seat, the boys were each introduced to me. The eldest in the group was 17 years old. He had come to the programme after he had been involved in a couple of gang fights in the school corridors. The Principal had wanted to throw him out but had been convinced otherwise.

'That was freshman year,' the boy told me.

'Who was your gang?' I asked.

'Get Money Savages. We was beefing with Right To Defend.'

The youngest of the four boys was just 14 years old. He too had been involved in a gang fight. He had been 'AT'd' (Administrative Transfer) but some of his gang members had pleaded for him to be allowed to return to school. The school agreed, and he and the boy from the gang he had been fighting with were put on the programme.

The third boy, a slim 16-year-old, and the fourth boy – by far the tallest in the group, but also 16 years old – both had a similar story. A gang fight, AT'd but then allowed back.

The boys were each from a different gang but sitting together as they were, they looked like a tight group of friends.

'When you first get put in the programme and you're meeting your enemy in the same room, do you start fighting?' I asked. 'Or do you just accept it and try and become friends?'

'They make you shake hands,' the eldest boy told me. 'But when you don't want to shake their hands they put you face to face, or make you sit next to them. They just keep doing it until you shake hands.'

Everyone laughed gently.

'Have you always lived in Detroit?' I asked.

They each told me that they had.

'And you're all in gangs?'

They each nodded their head.

'Do you call it a gang? Is that the term you use?'

'We call it "fam" (family),' the slim 16-year-old boy said. He sounded bold and confident when he spoke and was the least nervous of the bunch. 'But it depends on what you're doing,' he continued. 'It's different groups out there. Some gangs go ahead and kill people. A family can go a gang way but we choose not to. But if something comes our way, we ain't gonna back down. We're gonna stand up to it.'

'But how do you go from being a kid living in Detroit to suddenly finding yourself as part of a group, robbing and getting into trouble? How do you get there?' I asked.

'What do you mean?' the slim boy asked. 'You mean, how do I live with it?'

'No, I mean, how do you go from being a small kid playing in the street, doing nothing wrong, to suddenly finding yourselves in a group that is committing crime?'

'I was already there,' the eldest boy said. 'We was always fighting. You start by getting beat up in the playground.'

'You had to fight. That's the truth. You had to fight,' the tall boy said, joining in the conversation.

'It really starts with the people you grow up around,' the slim boy said. 'Like me, I grew up around my older brother, and whoever you grow up around, who is older than you, that is how you are going to be. That's all you're gonna know because you grew off from it. And whatever we saw growing up, that's what we know. It's not really gang stuff until people come to your house and try to take over, then it becomes gang fighting and you have to fight back to get back your territory.'

'Did that seem like a normal life, growing up as a kid on these streets, seeing all the things that were going on?' I asked.

'I had a normal life. Going outside and go play,' the older boy said. 'But then it goes crazy.'

'When you grow up around it, it becomes normal,' the slim

boy said. 'It's an everyday basis. It becomes a normal thing when you around it for so many years.'

'But if there's not no reason to fight, I'm just not gonna do nothing,' the youngest in the group said. When he spoke, his shy, unsure voice gave away his young age. 'There ain't no reason just to pick on somebody just because you don't like 'em. They do something, then that's when you pop off.'

'There's always a reason behind the crime that goes on here,' the oldest boy said. 'That's the truth.'

'Everybody in Detroit getting killed, is because of gangs or because of someone owed them something. It's payback, that's the thing,' the tall boy said.

'And what do you rap about?' the older boy asked. 'I'll tell you – death and killin' people, that's what. And when you rap about it and flash it …'

'You gotta kill 'em,' the tall boy said, cutting in.

'When you rap it, you're telling your target, "I've got this, and this dirty. This is how you can come get me." So, of course they gonna come and get you. That's an easy kill. That's like *Call of Duty*,' the older boy said, referring to the warfare computer game. 'If you playing a *Call of Duty* game and you see your man jumping around, you're gonna go over there and kill him. So, if someone's rappin', saying "I did this to your man. I'm on this block", you're gonna get ganged up and go to that block, ready for war and to catch them off-guard. It's easy. And it's not just rapping about it – it's the way you look, the way you *is*.'

'You can get attacked just for the way you look?' I asked.

'My mom keeps telling me, because I keep getting robbed on Seven Mile: "It's the way you dress and how you build yourself. You walking around like you the shit." They see you and say, "Look at this nigga, he think he's the shit, man. Let's watch this nigga for a week and see what he about. And then when we find out about him, we gonna get him." That's how it be. "Oh, look at this nigga. He think he fresh." People don't rob for no reason. You die because you try and impress another nigga that you got money. Because when you come from these streets and you broke and then you get money, you gonna flash it because you never had it before. It's like a fresh meal – I'm gonna chow down on this. You know what I'm sayin'?'

'It's, "I've got cash now and I'm gonna flash it!"' the tall boy confirmed.

'And that's definitely gonna get you killed, because you flashing your money,' the older boy said. 'It's like I'm teasing my dog and after a minute he gonna come get it because you teasing him. That's how it be.'

'Then why flash it?' I asked. 'Just keep it hidden.'

'Because if you never had nothing, how you gonna let people know that you now have it?' the tall boy said.

'Where I grew up, there were no gangs and there wasn't much crime,' I told the boys.

'There wasn't as much crime for you?' the tall boy asked, sounding surprised.

'Not a lot,' I said. 'You're all teenagers and you've all grown up here – have you seen a lot of crime on these streets? Have you seen shootings? Robberies?'

'I've seen fights and shootings,' the youngest boy said softly.

'Like, that's almost a normal day thing,' the tall boy told us.

'When you on the streets, you go through hell in a day,' the older boy said.

'I've been through a lot, dawg,' the tall boy said, sounding as though he were speaking to himself.

'We've been through hell and back,' the older boy said. 'In these streets, it's like a jungle – it's everybody for themselves. You've just got sticks and knives. So, if you get caught slippin', that's the only thing you got to protect yourself.'

'A stick?' I asked.

'A stick is a gun,' the boy told me.

When he said 'stick', I had genuinely thought that he meant an actual stick. I told the boys this and they laughed at my naivety.

'That's the only thing we got to protect ourselves,' the older boy continued. 'Sticks and knives and our family. That's it.'

Hearing all this, I kept thinking, God, this is sad. I mean, what chance do they have? They didn't want this – that was quite clear to me. They were simply trying to survive any way they could, in a desperate, violent city. I felt angry. These were kids, for heaven's sake.

As I listened to the way the older boy was talking, it was clear that he wanted people to know that this was happening to them; that this was what was going on. The kid had a distinct hardness about him that he had learnt from growing up on these streets. He sounded tough, like he was willing to do what was needed to survive, but there was also a tone in his voice that revealed a quiet, almost dignified anger, as though he knew that he and his friends had been abandoned and that there was little he or they could do about it. Instead of safety, help and direction, there were closed schools and gunfire in the streets.

'On the streets you grew up on, can you live a life that doesn't involve sticks and violence and crime?' I asked.

'Yeah, you can, but we not!' the older boy replied immediately.

'Why?'

'If you choose not to have sticks, then that's your problem,' he said. 'We gonna keep sticks because we gonna be prepared for whoever come. You stop using sticks and someone comes up to you, you ain't got nothing to protect yourself and you gonna be naked. We gonna be ready for war. When you saying about having a normal life, that can't happen – because of all the people around you.'

'You can't choose not to arm yourself, and avoid the gangs?' I asked.

The boy leant forward and looked me straight in the eyes. 'When you choose not to protect yourself, you letting someone else come to your house,' he said. 'When you in these streets, niggas be hungry – starving! – and they be having to eat. In the streets, your momma on drugs, your daddy in jail, so you ain't got no older people in your life. Your first thing is to jump on the streets with your friends and get money. And the first thing that comes with it is robbing people – that's your first step as you're trying to come up. So, if I see you without a gun, that's an easy rob, right there. If you choose not to have a gun, then that's on you. It means that we haven't got to worry about getting shot and we get an easy rob. We get to eat.'

'Is it all about wanting money simply because you're hungry and you've got no cash?' I asked.

'Yeah,' he said.

'It's about that but also you haven't had no attention like other peoples,' the tall boy added. 'You come to school looking like a bum in front of everybody. Everybody got moms and dads taking care of them and you don't got nothing. You got to walk to school in the rain. And they be jumping and hurting people – attacking you. And one day you get tired of waking up and seeing the same thing, so you go fight for it. You go grab what you gotta get.'

'Is it the same in school?' I asked. 'Are you still having to fight?'

'Yeah, because you scoping who you gonna eat off of. That's how it is,' the oldest boy said. 'You don't never stop scoping people. I'm in school all day and I'm scoping everybody out, like, "Oh yeah, let me see if he walk home, I'll be able to get him. It'll be easy because he ain't gonna have no gun, coming from school." But I'm gonna stash my gun close to the school and after school, when he walk home, I'll go get it and catch him slipping. That's how it's gonna be.'

'People can't afford an iPhone,' the slim boy said. 'If you got an iPhone and I see you don't carry it with you – you leave it on a desk and walk away – I'm gonna easy finesse you. I'm gonna take your phone.'

'If you say to someone, "I want your chain," and they say, "No", it's still coming off you!' the tall boy said. 'It might be snatched off, a gun might just pop up in your face – anything. It's really unpredictable.'

'But what happens when you come to school the next day?' I asked.

'You're not thinking about that. If you come to school the next day and that person say something to you, then he want beef.'

'What – no one's saying, "I'm going to call the police" or "I'm gonna tell the school that you robbed me"?' I asked, surprised.

The taller boy sat back and folded his arms. 'You tell the school and you will drop. You will be dead,' he said with emphasis.

'And you'll be arrested,' I told him.

'And then we gonna put our money together and bail our bro back out,' the slim boy said. 'That's how it gonna be.'

Three of the boys told me they had been locked up in juvenile detention previously. Only the youngest hadn't.

'What was that like?' I asked them.

'Crazy,' the tall boy said.

'Does it stop you from robbing? Does it change you?' I asked.

'It depends on what person you is,' the older boy said. 'If you got people at home telling you that you can do better, then when you go there, to juvenile, you think: No, this ain't for me.'

'When I first went around, I was going crazy,' the tall boy recalled.

'Crazy how?' I asked.

'I was doing stupid stuff. Then they put me in here in eighth grade, and we just talking. Went to every different programme and I just chilled.'

'So coming here has made a difference?'

'Yeah!'

'That is the truth. I won't even claim I gangbang no more,' the older boy said. 'I call my old gang "my fam", but I don't even hang around them no more.'

'It's just an MIA (Missing in Action) thing,' the tall boy said. 'But your gang still gonna do what they do.'

'They're okay with it? You can be MIA?' I asked.

'Yeah. You just tell them you gotta clear your mind and they okay with that,' he said.

I wondered if the boys had any plans beyond high school, beyond the here-and-now, beyond Detroit. I wondered if it was possible to see a future when you grew up and lived on these streets. And who wouldn't want to escape this? Some of the cops on Brannock's unit had grown up and gone to school in these very neighbourhoods and although they might still be working those same streets, in a way they had managed to get out.

'You are all going to be leaving high school soon. What are your plans?' I asked. 'What are you going to do when you leave?'

'I'm gonna go to college and play football,' the tall boy said.

'My plan is to take *any* college out of Detroit,' the slim boy told me. 'It's crazy though because we all in different gangs, reaching for that one goal, but if we all come together and reach for it together, it'll be easy.'

'What's the goal?' I asked him.

'To get money.'

'And disappear,' the tall boy quickly added.

'Disappear and leave Detroit,' the slim boy agreed. 'That's what everybody want to do. Get money and get off of these streets. If we work together as a group and grab for that one top thing, it's going to be more safer, with less killin' and everything. But people on these streets, they like to think for themselves.'

'Everybody don't follow the same train,' the older boy told me. 'Everybody want to be different.'

'Is that what you all want to do? Get out of Detroit?' I asked.

All four boys nodded their head and said, 'Yeah.'

The older boy continued, 'Everybody go out on the streets to get money to get out of Detroit, but you gotta go through that tunnel to get there.'

'And it's a dark tunnel,' the tall boy muttered.

'I'll hopefully get to college and go,' the older boy said. 'But if it ain't there for me, then I won't.'

'I'm surprised so many go to school,' I said. 'If you're running with a gang on the streets, what makes you get up in the morning and come here? Why not just gangbang?'

'Because I know my brothers are gonna be here, if there are any problems,' the slim boy told me.

'I'm not even worried about my brothers,' the older boy said. 'Honestly, for me it's a personal thing. I know I've got potential. I know I can be something, but it's just the predicament that I've been through and what I'm going through. But if I'm not a dummy and I know how to read and write and comprehend for myself, what can anybody cheat me out of or take me through that I can't possibly already have gone through? Honestly, half of my friends have dropped out of school or left or whatever. But I don't do that. I go to every class. It's just a personal thing but it's up to you.'

The room fell silent for a moment and then the slim boy said, 'Honest truth, if it wasn't for this Dignity group, I would have dropped out, I swear to God. Every day I wake up and I think about dropping out. Man, I'm tired at waking up at 7.30 every morning.'

'What does Dignity do that makes you turn up each day?' I asked him.

'My only thing is, it gets me off the street, because I don't want to kill nobody, but if they try and kill me, I'll shoot first. But I won't just run up on you and start shooting. Like, if me and him go to war,' he pointed at the older boy, 'we both gonna be scared to shoot but he not gonna let me just shoot him; he gonna shoot back. So, when I wake up every morning, I'm trying not to go to that predicament. I don't want nobody blood on my hands. I don't want momma in the house crying. So, I gotta do what I gotta do. Do anything. Do everything! Go to what I got to go to. I wanna try and make it to the NBA (National Basketball Association). I ain't trying to be no street thug nigga who got tattoos everywhere. See, when I get wealthy and get tattoos, I'm gonna get smart tattoos – ones I wanna keep.'

'What do you think caused all these problems for you and your families and your streets?' I asked. 'What's the reason this all happened – the gangs, and the gangbanging?'

The kids all mumbled something but then the older boy said, 'Crack.'

'Crack cocaine?'

'Yeah, crack,' the boy repeated quietly, as if he were afraid that someone might hear him.

Crack. Crack had ruined Detroit and many other cities and communities across the US. It was just as the guy in the Runyon video had said – crack cocaine had landed in the neighbourhoods and utterly wrecked an already fragile society and an already desperate people. Crack, as far as many were concerned, was the catalyst for the decades of horror that followed.

'It's also the population and how people say we is,' the tall boy said. 'If I keep telling you, you just there as the added third (unwanted), one day you gonna think: I really is the shit, bro. I really *is* the added third.' The boy thought for a moment before continuing. 'And there's a different between dirty money and clean money. With clean money you can just sit back in your chair and not worry about nothin'. With dirty money, you got to have your shooters, you gotta be on point every day, have a back-up squad, you gotta have the bond money for when you get locked up. You gotta have all that ready. If you don't, then you gonna get fucked up on these streets.'

The other boys listened in, intently, each nodding their head in agreement. The boy was talking about crime and violence, but as I listened I also heard planning and leadership, and I wondered what these boys could have become if they had grown up in a different place. How much talent was being wasted? How many gifted kids were bleeding to death on the streets of Detroit?

'There are people here who know they are gonna die one day,' he went on. 'They be the people who know they ain't leaving these streets. And when you know you're not going to leave, you act like you not going to leave. You gonna kill anybody who comes to you.'

'Do many of your gang friends end up in prison?' I asked.

'Six of my homeboys got locked up at the same time,' the slim boy said.

'What for?'

'Crazy stuff,' he said, sniggering nervously. 'Couple of months ago, bro got shot. Now they in jail. Crazy. Crazy out in the field.'

He used the word 'field' as though he were a soldier.

'That's how I got locked up,' the older boy said. 'When you got friends, some of your friends you find out that they not really your friends. Some of them friends you got just because they need you – you just that extra person – and so they going to throw away your life with theirs. That's how I went to jail.'

'What did you go to jail for?' I asked.

'Possession of a stolen vehicle.'

'Have you ever been shot?' I asked.

The boy nodded and leant forward, resting his elbows on his knees, getting ready to tell the tale.

'Yeah. This the real story. It was my first time smoking (weed) with my friends, and in Detroit, when you got friends, you got older friends too – niggas are seventeen, eighteen, nineteen. Them the ones who had the guns and they give them to us. We was all broke, so we all chose to go rob someone. So, we robbed this one

213

person and beat him up and started running. And when we robbed him, we didn't know that he close to his house. He ran back home and told his family and then his family started chasing us. So we running from them but when we robbed him, my friend took some candy from him, and we was all tired and hungry so we started eating the candy. I see these people running at us and I say, "Who these niggas here?" But I ain't really thinking they can see us because it's dark. I'm like, "Bro, who's these niggas?" So we all stopped and looked, and they just got to shooting at us.

'I took off running and when I took off running, my friend grabbed my jacket. I told him to keep going but he was like, "Hold on, brother, I'm shot." I was like, "Bro, come on bro, we going." He's like, "No bro, I can't run no more." He started falling, so I had a choice to either keep running or come back for my man. So I choose to go back for him. I be growing up with him and if he get shot, I'm going back for him and we gonna die together. That's how my mind set. So I went back for him and I carried him.'

I was stunned by what I was hearing from this teenager. I couldn't help thinking that soldiers on a battlefield receive medals for this sort of bravery. But this wasn't a battlefield – not in the traditional military sense anyway – and yet here was a kid, coming under gunfire, going back to save his shot friend on a city street in America. I was impressed by his bravery but deeply saddened and troubled at the same time. Yes, he had robbed someone – but consider the circumstances that had placed him in that situation. It's not an excuse for his behaviour but I do believe it's a reason for it.

The boy sighed. 'The man still buzzing at us, and that's how I got grazed, because he still shooting at us. But I was so scared I didn't feel it until I got home. But long story short, we in the back yard looking at the people across a big old field, but they can't see us as we up under the porch, ducking down and my man, he

214

screaming. I'm saying, "Bro, be quiet, bro, or they come over here and they finish us off." And they grown-up niggas and everything, so they would shoot a nigga. They looking to find us for half an hour. So, he bleeding out and keep passing out and I'm crying because I might lose him and I've got his blood all over my face and stuff like that. If he had of died that day, I would have dropped out of school and I would probably be dropping bodies left and right because my mind was set for it.'

'How old were you when that happened?' I asked.

'This was around a year ago. I was fifteen.'

'Where were you shot?' I asked.

'It grazed my shoulder, right here,' he said, pointing to where the bullet had struck him.

The school bell rang in the corridor, and the boys all fell silent.

'Mick, school is out,' Jermaine said softly.

*

Jermaine was one of a number of mentors that Brannock worked with to help steer kids away from gangs and crime. Some of these mentors had criminal pasts, including murder convictions, but all had left their previous lives behind, serving their time, growing up and moving on. They understood the streets and they wanted to help others avoid what they had been through themselves.

A lot of police officers would have balked at the thought of developing such a close relationship with ex-cons and gangbangers. Many cops I knew had a zero-tolerance approach to such people – 'once a criminal, always a criminal', that sort of thing. But of course, some people can and do change, and they deserve a second chance.

Brannock was willing to mix with the very people he policed, rather than looking down his nose, checking the creases on his shirt and walking around holier-than-thou. He had embraced the help he received from Jermaine and all the other mentors. After all, why wouldn't you want to tap into that knowledge and experience?

It was one of the many things I liked about Detroit police officers; for the most part, they were ground-level. They work in a busy, desperate city and they understand how hard life can be for the people who live there. They also recognise that there are a lot of grey areas when it comes to policing.

Brannock and I had talked about what it was like to police a city such as Detroit. He had said to me, 'Let's say you make a traffic stop. You pull over a mom who doesn't have a driver's licence. She has a kid in the car. Now, in the suburbs, your ass is going to jail. But in the city? The lady don't have a driver's licence, she don't have insurance, and she's just trying to get her kid to school. Maybe she ran a red light? Do you really write her a ticket and impound her car and make her and her kid walk away from the scene?

'You can't be out in the suburbs and live "high on the hog" and then come down here and police like an asshole. You have to know the challenges these kids are facing and why they're joining these gangs. Some kids don't have a chance in hell. So, you have to be cognisant of what the fuck is going on around you in the city, and what these people are going through. And at times, what they're going through is pretty horrific.'

In a city like Detroit the cops are kept busy enough without the need to persecute people just for the hell of it. I've seen overzealous policing elsewhere – but never in Detroit.

Brannock was still Brannock though. As we left the school, he said, 'I told Jermaine you were Australian.'

*

216

After speaking to the boys, I was left wondering what it was like for girls in Detroit. Was their life better? Worse?

'Do girls become gang members as well?' I asked.

'Oh yeah. There are female members inside all of the gangs,' Robo told me. 'There was an all-female group, that was an off-shoot of a guy gang.'

Robo explained to me that girls were often used by the gangs to carry drugs and guns, in the belief that there was less chance of them being stopped by the police.

'They'll also work in the kitchens and cook the dope up, or they'll count the money,' Robo told me. 'They work in the strip clubs and push the dope there too. The guys use them and buy them off by promising to get them clothes, or get their nails or hair done. They're giving them things that they think are important right now. But I wouldn't say that the pressure for girls to get into gangs is huge. I don't think they are forced to choose a side as much as the guys are.'

'Why do the girls get involved with these boys to begin with?' I wanted to know.

'Love,' she said. 'Love and attention. They're just looking for a sense of acceptance. Then they'll end up having kids at a young age with multiple gang members, and that sometimes starts feuds or gang wars.'

'What about a girl who isn't in a gang and just wants to go to school and do regular stuff? Are those girls at risk?'

'Yeah. For sure. When I was working in patrol we had something called "the rape detail" up in the Ninth Precinct and on the east side, because girls were being raped on their way to school. Years ago, the public transportation in this city wasn't so great, so a lot of the girls had to walk to school. We would patrol the routes they took. I don't know if they still run a programme like that, but there was a rash of rapes at one time, which is why we were put on that detail.'

It wasn't only girls walking to school who were in danger. Children of all ages were at risk of being abducted, raped, and murdered. Of course, these things can happen in any community and any city, and it would be unfair to claim that these terrible crimes only occurred in Detroit, but I would read numerous reports of young children – 4 and 5 years old, for example – whose tortured, abused bodies had been found dumped in vacant houses. And if a fire had been started to try and destroy any evidence, what was left of those children was often little more than charred remains.

'The sexual abuse and rape that goes on is downplayed big-time,' Robo told me.

'Who downplays it?'

'Society. Law enforcement. I think if a girl gets raped, it's always like, "Why was she there? What was she doing?" It's always a "her fault" thing.'

I found out that in 2009, in a Detroit Police Department storage warehouse, over 11,000 rape kits were discovered, some dating back to the mid-1980s, that had never been sent for testing. These evidential kits, which could have potentially identified a suspect, had simply been put in storage and forgotten about.

Upon discovering these thousands of kits, the county prosecutor, Kym Worthy, ordered that they be tested. To date, more than 800 serial rapists have been identified following this move. Of those serial rapists, more than 50 are known to have raped between 10 and 15 victims. So far, there have been more than 120 convictions won. But how many victims of rape are there who would have remained unmolested, had those kits been tested at the time they were taken? How many rapists were free to continue their actions unhindered for years?

It was also found that victims' accounts were dismissed based on who they were or how they looked: we're talking about addicts, prostitutes or the mentally ill. And this is not the case in Detroit alone; there are believed to be hundreds of thousands of untested rape kits all across the United States. Progress has been made in Detroit: since the rape kit scandal, the state has passed legislation that creates timelines on how the kits are to be handled and dealt with.

'Are rapes and assaults getting under-reported?' I asked.

'Oh yeah. The girls don't trust law enforcement,' Robo said. 'They've been down that road before and it was downplayed, so they're like, "Why should I report it?" They think that no one's going to believe them anyway, including their own family.

'I had a girl recently – she was, like, the star volleyball player. Her mom was a prostitute and was in and out of her life. Her mom's best friend kind of became this girl's mentor and took care of her. Well, that mentor passed away, and after she passed away, that girl stopped going to school, stopped playing volleyball. She was having a really hard time, and she was real depressed. The teachers were worried because she had been a star pupil. So, some of the community mentors, people like Jermaine, reached out to us and asked us to talk to her and find out what was going on. We talked to her but she put a wall up. Then we eventually got through and she started to open up and express herself a little more. However, when her mom came into the room, the girl got real defensive again.

'Finally, the girl broke down. She started crying and screaming. She told us how all her relatives had raped her. Her uncles and her grandparents had been passing her around. And her mom was like, "Well, you didn't get it as bad as I did. I had twenty relatives rape me; you only had ten." But then how do you expect this woman, who is completely broken, to help her daughter, who is also now broken? And if no one gets to her and helps her now, what does her world look like, going forward?'

'What's the answer?' I asked.

'I don't know. I've been thinking about that for twenty years. Maybe the answer is they need to get to these kids earlier. Some of these kids haven't showered in weeks. Some don't even know how to brush their teeth. They need a health education class at school, to teach them things they are not learning at home. My mom and dad taught me these things, but if you don't have a mom and dad at home, then no one's teaching you.

'Then you need to teach them that the proper way to get love and share love is not by violence and it's not by forcing yourself on someone. Some of these kids have been molested at a very young age. When I was at homicide, the desk next to me was sex crimes. It was sick. I didn't know how those guys did it. I could look at dead people all night long, but the sex crimes, and incest, and molestation … it's unreal. Unreal! Kids and cousins are often corralled into one house – usually the most responsible house, where they are all kept together. And then "Johnny" wakes up and his cousin is lying next to him, and he doesn't have anyone to stop him from doing anything. The reason there is so much sexual deviancy is because at a young age they are having sex and it feels good; it feels like love because they don't know any better. Some guys are getting it whenever and wherever they want, and the girls are putting out as early as nine or ten years old. They've caught kids at elementary schools having sex in the playground. For some, there's no morality line.

'Then they'll talk about God. Some guy in a gang will shoot five people and then get killed himself, and they'll all say "Rest in heaven", "Ball in heaven". You think he's going to heaven? He just killed five fucking people! What makes you think he's going to heaven? They get tattoos, *God's children*, *God's angels*.'

'Well, they do say that God loves us all equally,' I offered.

'I know and I understand that. Fine if you are going out there to rob someone to feed the mouths of your younger siblings, but not fine if it's just because you like someone's watch and want it for yourself.'

'So you understand why some of the kids do what they do?'

'I may not always agree with what they do but I can sometimes understand it. And I've heard people – adults – say, "Hell, yeah! I'd have a gun on me too. I wouldn't walk to school without a gun." If your mom's a junkie, and she has five kids and they're all back at home, crying and starving, and you're the oldest boy … The fittest and strongest is going to win.

'I feel empathy for the people that are still here. Before I came on the department I would come to Detroit and work in soup kitchens. But the job's jaded me a little; I think I gave a lot more to the homeless before I came on the job. And it's hard for me, because when I go back to my life, outside of this, outside of work, and I'm going to my daughter's basketball games, I'm there with all these other parents that have no idea of what's going on only ten miles from where they live. And all these people who give money to other countries? Why doesn't someone send a fucking van over to the Number Nine and fucking feed the poor people there, who may also need help?'

*

A few days later, the piece about me appeared in the newspaper, along with the photographs that had been taken at the Hell Zone house. I learnt very quickly that if you're not from Detroit and you decide to have a say about it, you will get some hate. I came in for some criticism in their online comments sections. People were saying that 'Detroit didn't need this kind of negative publicity' and that the city 'had changed'.

They were right about Detroit changing – to a degree. The downtown core, albeit small, had been transformed from a near ghost town, to a mostly pleasant little shopping and eating neighbourhood. Other parts of Detroit too, had actually become trendy, cool places to have a night out, or to get some drinks and great food – Mexicantown, Corktown and Eastern Market, for example.

I truly do believe that Detroit has a brighter future but at the moment we're talking about a concentration of a few okay streets, out of hundreds, and a few small neighbourhoods out of many. So don't try and tell me that the kids who live and survive in the outer areas of Detroit, in the gang-infested lands of the east side, west side, or Southwest Detroit suddenly have it good or that their lives are now better because Lululemon have opened a yoga-fashion store downtown.

To deny that vast areas of Detroit are still deadly dangerous, burnt-out, drug-infested, vicious places, is to deny thousands of Detroiters of their daily reality, of their constant truth. People are living in neighbourhoods where they see – I mean literally see, with their own eyes – their friends and family members die, and where ignored, hungry kids risk getting shot just for walking to and from school or for playing in the street.

Don't get me wrong – some of the progress in Detroit is a very good thing indeed; it will create much-needed jobs, bring in money and then hopefully the benefits will start to push outwards. But businesses don't open up or invest in places because they want to help the poor locals. They are there because they see dollar signs.

Like all things, balance is needed. If Detroit can transform into a thriving city once again whilst simultaneously looking out for *real* Detroiters and the poorest, most disadvantaged residents rather than abandoning them, then it could become an example to cities and communities around the world.

So although I appreciate that people want only the best for Detroit, and that they want people like me to focus on the positives rather than the negatives, I won't pretend everything's pretty and I won't pretend everything's good – especially where children are concerned. As one cop told me, 'They don't get to go downtown.'

(An excellent illustration of these two conflicting sides of Detroit came in September and October 2017. In September the FBI named Detroit as the most violent big city in America. A month later, Detroit came second behind Seville, Spain, in travel publisher *Lonely Planet's* top ten city destinations.)

When a child experiences abuse and neglect, when they live for prolonged periods around violence, or when they see their family suffering economic hardship – all the things that many youngsters in Detroit have to live with each and every day – that child can experience what is known as Toxic Stress. The latter can have devastating and lifelong effects on a child's mental and physical health. It can actually harm brain development, cause stress-related diseases and lead to substance abuse. To expose children to an environment where all the triggers and causes of Toxic Stress are ever-present is to deny entire generations of a future.

Brannock had his own take on it.

'Have you ever seen the movie, *The Matrix*?' he asked. 'It's like that – it's like being disconnected. We go out and we see these suburbanites that work at GM or at IBM, or Apple, and you know, they're out there living their lives and they have no idea what's going on here. And once you become disconnected, that's it.'

He continued, 'I'll go out to eat, I'll talk to people, I'll meet people and they'll ask: "What do you do?" I'll say, "I'm a Detroit police officer." And they'll go, "Oh my God! You're a Detroit police officer? Is it crazy there?"' Brannock shook his head. 'Why aren't you watching the fucking news? Why don't you know that this is going on a mile from you? This is what pisses me off the most. It's these people that live over there in their bubble and they don't know what's going on down here but they still want to come to the city and go watch a Tigers game and all that shit. But they have no idea. They have no idea of some of the insanity that goes on.

'Look at this shit! Look at what's going the fuck on! *You* come police this! *You* dig up these two girls out of this fucking hole, buried in this fucking baseball field. *You* get these two kids that are beaten to death out of this alley. And it doesn't matter – white, black, Mexican, whatever; when you experience this and deal with this fucking craziness and you're picking up these dead kids and shit, yeah, it does affect you. But we do it because it's our fucking job and that's what they pay us to do. I've signed up for this – this is my job. I'm never going to turn my back on it until it's time where I have to call it quits. When I can't do better for the people of this city, when I can't do better for Detroit, then that's when I'm gonna call it quits. I'm here for the officers that have followed me into Gang Intelligence, and for the Detroit citizens that are still here, that are trying. And there are good people here; these guys that are helping us out with Ceasefire, and all the other people in this city that can't get out and go anywhere.

'But it's disheartening. It's a real shame that people don't know what we are going through here. This is all going on a mile from your fucking house, with your white picket fucking fence, right there, with all your flowers.'

*

In September 2016, seven Detroit schoolchildren brought a lawsuit against state officials – including the State Governor, Rick Snyder – for failing to provide opportunities to learn. The lawsuit described awful and chaotic conditions in some Detroit schools, including a lack of basics materials such as pens and pencils, desks and chairs, even toilet paper. Some classrooms had no textbooks whatsoever. Homework couldn't be assigned because there were no books.

No books were bad enough, but sometimes there were no teachers either. It wasn't unknown for students to take a class themselves and attempt to teach the younger kids. It's absolutely heart-breaking. With under-qualified staff and 'unsafe temperatures' (one teacher had set up a fund to buy her freezing students winter coats, hats and gloves), conditions were described as being such that it was 'impossible to teach, impossible to learn' and students were described as essentially being 'warehoused for seven hours a day'.

Add to all this the fact that the Michigan legislature voted to redirect funds and money from school district property taxes, which otherwise could have gone to Detroit public schools, to help subsidise a new sports arena and other such developments downtown. This redirection of hundreds of millions of dollars of school property taxes will continue until 2051.

Responding to the lawsuit brought by the Detroit schoolchildren, the state attorney argued for the lawsuit to be dismissed, as the 14th Amendment of the US Constitution – which says that no state shall 'deprive any person of life, liberty or property' – said nothing about 'literacy'. And this, when in 2015, just 7% of Detroit's 13-14-year-old students were proficient at reading! The attorney also argued that the state wasn't responsible for the Detroit school structure.

Most of the kids in these schools come from deprived, low-income homes and from minority backgrounds. Time and again in Detroit I have been told how these kids have little chance in life; how it is inevitable that they will end up in gangs. But if they're not being taught basic literacy and mathematics, and are left to believe that no one really cares about them, is it any wonder? The kids aren't to blame for their situation, but someone is.

But hey, at least downtown looks nice.

13

Hunting a Killer

Thursday, 14 January 2016

As usual, I arrived in the office at noon, just as Brannock had told me to. And as usual, Brannock wasn't there. Hollywood was in though and was speaking on the phone to his young son about how he hoped to get the weekend off, so that they could spend some time together.

Whispers was also in, and was sat at his desk, watching gang videos online.

Cooter and Joe were in too, but they were just heading out. As they walked out the door, Cooter looked over at me and for no apparent reason whatsoever, said, 'I'm going to have a spot of tea, you bloke.'

Cooter did this every now and then; he'd put on a ridiculous *Downton Abbey* accent and come out with some random English saying or words. Everyone found it hysterical, but none more than Brannock, who would explode into laughter each and every time. I'm not sure which was worse, Cooter's posh English accent or Brannock constantly going on at me about being Australian. It reached a point where whenever they said anything about 'tea and crumpets' or 'kangaroos and billabongs', I would call them 'wankers' – an English expletive that many Americans have heard of but few truly understood. When I explained it to them, they were utterly delighted, and 'wanker' then became the most commonly used profanity in the office. For Brannock, everyone was now a wanker – but especially Robo.

Joe and Cooter were going downtown to speak with prosecutors about one of their own cases. It was a particularly sickening one. The victim was a woman who had been staying at a motel. A group of men had approached her door in the middle of the night and started banging on it, demanding that she open up. She refused, so the men forced their way in by smashing open a window and climbing into the room. They then attacked the woman, hitting her and stamping on her body, beating her to a pulp. They dragged her around the room by her hair, ripping some of it out and later using clumps of it to try to wipe blood from the walls and door. People walked by or watched from other rooms but no one intervened. The woman was then dragged partially out of the room and stomped on some more. She was stamped on so viciously that a shoe-print was left on her throat, and the hyoid bone in her neck was snapped. Afterwards the men simply walked away, leaving her battered body slumped on the ground in a blood-splattered motel room.

The attack had been caught on CCTV and it made for seriously distressing viewing. In the images that had been taken of her battered face and body, she was unrecognisable. The reason for killing her? Mistaken identity. The gang had been looking for someone else but had the wrong room. After the woman had refused to open her door – after all, why would she open it to a bunch of strange men in the middle of the night? – the gang became enraged and attacked her anyway. The only reason the woman had been staying at the motel to begin with was because she had a job interview in the city the following morning. Instead of the interview, her brutalised body ended up in the morgue.

*

Soon after Joe and Cooter had left, Robo walked in carrying a large metal pot.

'Chilli,' she told me. 'I used to have a catering business, so I like to cook for the boys. If I didn't cook food every now and then, all they'd eat is Twinkies. Help yourself.'

Hollywood was already spooning heaps of the steaming food into a Styrofoam bowl. Whispers was hovering nearby and it wouldn't be long until the others arrived, so I got stuck in whilst I could. Eating with cops can be a hazardous business; I knew that from my own experience. If you stood at the back, holding onto your bowl with your politeness and principles, you were going to go hungry. With the nature of their work, cops usually ate when they could – and as much as they could – because they never knew when they might get to eat again. Besides, if there's anything that cops value above all else, it's free food – that and overtime.

Then Hunter walked in. He was starting to say 'hello' when he spotted the steaming pot and immediately grabbed a spoon and dived in.

'I love it when Momma cooks,' he said, grinning widely and laughing. 'She likes to look after her babies.'

A few minutes after taking his bowl of chilli into his office, Hunter walked back out, holding his cell phone in one hand and his spoon in the other. 'Mick, Brannock just called. He's stuck at some meeting downtown and said that you can come out with me, if you like?'

'Sure,' I said. 'If that's okay with you?'

'Of course, man. You're all good.'

Hunter was heading out to Southwest Detroit, to the 4th Precinct. Homicide had received information that the suspect for the firefighter murder had a girlfriend in the neighbourhood: they believed there was a good chance that he would be there.

'There's this street that I want to check out,' Hunter said. 'I want to see who's moving back and forth. Hopefully we will see his girlfriend; then we know where the pussy is at. Doesn't matter how mad he ever gonna get, he's gonna come back and get some pussy.'

Southwest Detroit was a largely Hispanic neighbourhood, which also meant Hispanic gangs. Despite all the years that I had been coming to Detroit, it was an area of the city I hadn't got to know well, so I was interested to see how it compared to other areas, not least the 9th Precinct.

'Our job today is to see what these people are all about,' Hunter told me. 'And we've already done a little research on the suspect. His name's Timmy Soto.'

Hunter pulled a sheet of paper from his equipment bag and showed me a poor quality black-and-white printout of Soto's face.

'He's a white guy?' I asked.

'Yeah, and he has a warrant out for his arrest for a parole violation.'

Soto had a history of violence and criminal behaviour stretching back over 10 years. Judging by the information Hunter had, it appeared that Soto was currently moving around from house to house.

'He lives under the radar, so to speak,' Hunter told me. 'So it's a little more difficult to catch him, because he doesn't have an actual address that he's frequenting all the time.'

One of the reasons Hunter thought there was a good chance that Soto was still visiting and staying at the girlfriend's address was because of the activity on Soto's Bridge Card, which revealed that he had been using it in stores close by. The girlfriend, Nicole O'Neill, had been using her own Bridge Card, which showed that she too, was still active in the neighbourhood.

'She has a warrant from Lincoln Park for damage of property,' Hunter told me. 'But our interest in her is in relation to her association to this dude – Soto.'

Hunter's hope was that we would see O'Neill coming and going from the address we were heading to. He had no intention of picking her up though; he simply wanted to confirm that she was still living there, and then, hopefully, she would lead us to Soto, or else we would eventually see Soto himself, going to her address.

Being a former Narc, Hunter was also keen to see how much other activity was happening at the address.

'Lots of people going in and out would be consistent with my experience with narcotic trafficking,' he said. 'Is she selling pills? Or is someone else selling pills from here? Hopefully we'll see something, bro.'

'What sort of pills?' I asked.

'Xanax, Oxys, prescription pills. There are some pills that have codeine in them. And then there's ecstasy. Ecstasy is a big thing. People go over to Canada and buy the pills in bulk, to bring them back over here. They catch some of them – but can you imagine the numbers that they don't?'

I could. I myself had crossed the border many times over the years and had observed that few cars are searched – not because border officials don't care but because there is so much traffic. If they stopped every car, the entire border system would come to a standstill. The Ambassador Bridge alone handles 40% of all truck traffic that travels between the USA and Canada.

Even though there was nothing to suggest that Soto was currently active in a gang, with so much of the criminal activity in the city being linked to gangs in one way or another, Gang Intel often found themselves helping out other units. Officially, the GIU were meant to dedicate their time to the 9th Precinct, but Brannock wasn't going to turn down requests for help. To him, it was all part of the greater good, all part of making the city safer.

'Where there's drugs, there's guns, because they need to protect their drugs,' Hunter told me. 'Where there're gangs, there is illegal activity. There's prostitution, there's narcotics being sold – pills, heroin, lean. You know, all that type of shit.'

'Do they actually sell lean?'

'Oh definitely! But it's illegal. And what's so funny about lean is, to get your hands on it you have to get a prescription for the pharmacist, for the codeine. And a doctor just wants to be paid, right? So a guy goes to a doctor and says, "Hey man, I'll give you seven hundred dollars, man, just give me a prescription for some codeine." And there you go. You know what I'm saying? It's an on-going fucking problem, man.'

'And the lean gets them high, right?'

'Yeah. And then they go out and shoot and terrorise the fucking community.' Hunter laughed deeply, not because he thought it was funny, but just at the craziness of it all. 'It's a vicious fucking circle, man,' he said. 'It's piece-of-shit, fucking kids, man. Sixteen, seventeen, eighteen-year-olds.'

'Are you from Detroit?' I asked.

'Yep. I started on the west side but my parents didn't like the schools over there so we moved to the east side. My old school is just a few blocks from our patrol base.'

'Why do they call you "Hunter"?' was my next question.

'I came on the job in 1995. In 1997, me and my partner were performing a traffic stop on a vehicle with one occupant – a black male. He failed to stop and it became a pursuit. He pulled up in an alley, bailed and took off on foot. We followed and got out after him. But as he ran, he turned around – I think he had a .40 calibre – and he fired shots at us. Me and my partner had no ability to have a direct shot because there was obstacles and debris in the alley. There were vacant homes and he was going in between the lots. I feared that if I took a shot, I'd miss, hit a house and kill a kid – you know what I'm saying? So ultimately, we ended up losing him. And I was pissed because he had been shooting at me!

'I called my boss and he was like, "Hey, man, if you don't want to go home, stay as long as you want."

'I said, "I don't give a damn. I'll work for free; don't worry about it. I'm getting this guy."

'We got shot at on Wednesday night. So, I hadn't been home, hadn't been to sleep. All day Thursday I hunted and I hunted and I hunted, and then finally I tracked him down to this house on the west side and contacted a raid crew. The crew did a controlled buy on the house and purchased narcotics. I finally took a nap on the Friday and then the raid crew called me and told me that they had the search warrant.

'They asked me, "You want to come with us?"

'I said, "Hell, yeah!"

'I knew that the gentleman had a tattoo across his chest because he didn't have his shirt on when we chased him. I recalled it said *Thug . . .* something. When I got in that house, man, there he was, armed with the gun. And from that point on, my name was "Hunter".'

Hunter was now 50 years old, although he looked 10 years younger. He was a late joiner to the police, having taken up the badge at the age of 27. He was Detroit through and through, I learned. Before signing up with DPD, he had worked as a dye cutter for a printing company, making the finishing details for Cadillac motor vehicles. At just 19 years old, he was making nineteen dollars an hour – good money even today – and more than the current starting salary for a Detroit cop. Having secured a great paying job at such a young age, Hunter hadn't bothered with college but over time he became disheartened with being stuck inside a windowless factory every day. Despite the money, the realisation that this would be the rest of his life was too much. He 'wanted to get some air', so when he saw a TV commercial for the police department, he applied and passed the tests.

'A buddy of mine tried to get me to apply sooner,' Hunter told

me. 'He said, "Hey, man, we can join on the buddy-buddy thing."
I was like, "Ah, fuck that shit, man." So he went and he passed,
and now he's got five years more than me! He became a
Commander and then retired. And I'm still here!' Hunter
chuckled to himself.

'The department is majority black now,' I said. 'Was it mostly
white when you joined?'

'It was. My first five partners were white.'

'Did they treat you differently because you were black?'

'No. They didn't treat me any differently. It was basically, "I'm
in control, so if you want to learn something, shut up and listen."
And that was it. For me, once I crossed over to that world of law
enforcement, I became family. And within that family I've got
white friends that love me to death and I've got black friends that
love me to death. And I love them too. In law enforcement we
have to save one another, we have to have one another's back. We
have to train together. It never came down to race with me.'

A cop in Detroit had previously told me how being white and
female had placed her at the 'bottom of the totem pole' in the
DPD, with black males being at the top. She called it 'reverse
racism'. Another officer had told me how, as a white guy, there
was no point complaining if a black supervisor was 'fucking with
him', because no one would want to hear about it.

When I asked Hunter for his own thoughts about this, he
guessed – correctly – that I had been speaking to older officers.
He didn't agree with what those officers had said and was certain
that, had I spoken to younger officers, I would have heard a
different story.

'What about the city?' I asked. 'I guess it's a different place to
when you were a kid.'

'In a sense, but a lot of things are still the same. It's just that
the people are different.'

'The people?'

'Poverty is more prevalent,' he said. 'Non-education is more prevalent. Illiteracy is more prevalent. Lots of kids don't finish high school or get their diploma. I heard that if you don't finish high school there is a 50% increase in your chance of becoming a criminal. If you have no education, you can't fill out an application to get employment or show a diploma to your potential employer; therefore, you have no job, and if you have no job, you still gotta eat so you have to find victims, to survive. And that's where the problem lays, man. You know, you're eighteen, in a single-parent home, your mother is on drugs, your father left when you was a baby – and he's probably got fifteen other kids. Mom can't take care of you as she's making little or nothing for money, so you have to scrape by. And then there's peer pressure, and that's how a gang gets started, and that becomes your family now. All day long you're stealing and robbing, breaking into houses to look for guns. It's a vicious cycle, man.'

'Does it make you sad, seeing what's happened?'

'A bit. It's gradually gotten worse over time and that's because the poor and middle-class are getting closer and closer. They are kind of eliminating the middle-class. And if you're poor, you have no will-power or drive to get out of being poor, so you become accustomed to it, and on top of that, you're living off General Assistance. So the thinking is: why should I work when you are giving me, giving me, giving me? And you mean to tell me that if I have another kid, you're gonna give me more money? Ah, that's easy; I can fucking pop out kids, no problem. So it's a vicious fucking cycle, man. I don't know where this is going but wherever it's going, it can't be good.' He smiled broadly and started to laugh. 'But who am *I*, man? I'm just a small guy in a pool of craziness!'

As we got closer to the 4th Precinct, Hunter spoke the suspect's address into his phone. A map appeared on the screen showing our location and the route to the street we were after. A recorded female voice called out the directions and we followed them to the location.

'Your destination is on the right.'

'Okay, we're looking for a house over here on the right … and there it is,' Hunter said with a grin.

The house was a dirty white wooden building. Directly outside, parked alongside the kerb in the narrow, tatty-looking street, was a white Honda Odyssey.

Even though the street looked untidy, with peeling paintwork on the houses, cracked kerbs and weeds growing through the pavement, almost every property on the block was still standing. There were no empty plots, and only one burnt-out house, on the entire street. A bit of gang graffiti was visible, but even so, it was minor and a total contrast to other parts of the city.

'This all looks quite clean compared to the Ninth,' I noted.

'Yeah, every house is pretty much occupied here unlike the Ninth Precinct. There you have a block and might only see two houses on it. It's vacant, vacant, vacant, vacant.'

'Why is that? Why is it so different here?'

'Because Number Nine is one of the most dangerous neighbourhoods out there. Basically, you got people who just don't give a fuck in the Ninth. You know, everybody is a criminal and nobody trusts anybody, so everybody's on guard. Plus, a lot of the people there were incarcerated and they all got out of jail at the same time and went right back to doing what they were doing – robbing, shooting, stealing and so forth. Now, a lot of those people are either dead or they've been incarcerated again, and what was left were houses that were burnt down and vacant lots that couldn't be filled. So it's still the same unemployment base and everybody is on General Assistance from the government. And there's an inability to move out because people can't afford to move out. But here, you can see, even if it's just a little bit of money, somebody is working. Somebody is doing something. The Latinos and whites tend to live together. One will come on a visa from Mexico, bring his family, get a job, get the family members a job, and then they all live in the same house to increase the income. One will work and pay for the lights, one will pay for the gas, one will pay for the phone. Then they will save a bit more to get more family members over. And then *they'll* start working. This is a different culture down here.'

Hunter pulled up outside a house, a distance away from where the Odyssey was parked, and put a quick call in to Brannock, to let him know where we were and what we could see.

The target house was quiet but the street was full of activity – another difference to the east side, where everything always seemed deserted. Ahead of us we watched as a woman walked a child towards a small, clean car. The child was carrying a school bag. On the other side of the street, a young couple were strolling hand-in-hand. People were coming and going, with purpose.

'If I walked around this neighbourhood, would I be relatively safe in comparison to say, walking around in the Ninth?' I asked.

'Yes, I think so. You'll be safer in this area because you're a Caucasian male, versus walking around in Number Nine where it's predominantly black. Over there, someone will come up to you and try and sell you something immediately. Like, "What you looking for, bro? What you doing over here? You smoke? Come here, come with me." And they'll try and get you into some vacant house. But you'd have to be a crazy motherfucker to go with them!' Hunter burst out laughing again. 'Over there you have to be really aware, whereas over here you can slip through the cracks. You could fit in better over here. But even so, you still gotta be observant and careful, man, because if you ain't paying attention, they'll kill you over here, just like they will anywhere else. They sure the fuck will!' He laughed again.

We sat in silence for a while, staring out of the windshield towards the house. There had been no movement to or from it at all. Other than the occasional car passing by, the street had started to quieten down as people left for school or work.

'If they're selling pills or dope, you'd think that people would be walking up,' Hunter said. 'But I ain't seen one motherfucker walking up.'

Hunter knew how hard it could be to find these types of people. 'Street people', he called them. Even so, he was convinced that Soto or his girlfriend would turn up, especially as the Bridge Cards had been recently used.

'It's time-consuming, looking for these people,' he said. 'You have to be in the area, driving around, know who you're looking for and then just' (he clicked his fingers) 'get lucky. You need to see the guy sticking his head out a window or sitting on the kerb, smoking – you know, that type of shit. But you gotta sell to make money, and shit, I ain't seen no motherfucker go near that place.'

We sat and watched the house for another hour. There was no one coming or going from it, so there was only one direction for the conversation to go in.

'You hungry?' Hunter asked.

I told him I was. 'And the cold just makes me hungrier,' I added.

'Absolutely. Let's see, where shall we eat? I think we'll stay down here and get some Mexican, huh? Casper's shown me some great places to get food in this neighbourhood.'

'Sounds good.'

I enjoyed hanging out with Hunter – he was polite, inquisitive, easy to be around, and he laughed at practically everything. He had lots of policing experience and lots of time under his belt. His near-constant laughter suggested to me that he had long ago realised that the craziness of Detroit was out of his control. He came to work, did the best job he could and went home. He alone wasn't going to be able to fix the city, so he had reverted to surviving the chaos by laughing at the madness of it all.

'What are you going to do when you retire?' I asked. 'Are you going to get out of this area?'

'Yeah. I wanna go out of state, to Atlanta, Georgia – my sister's there. I'll get me a house – hopefully I can pay cash for it – and I'll fish and just find me a little something to keep me busy and live on the cash till it's gone,' he said, laughing.

'And never come to Detroit ever again?'

'Never, ever, ever!'

'As bad as some of it looks, I genuinely believe that some of these ruined neighbourhoods should be left as they are,' I said. 'Preserved, to remind people in the future, of how it used to be here. It's the history of Detroit.'

'Like a museum?' Hunter asked.

'Something like that, because when this is all cleaned up, people in the future aren't going to believe what it used to be like here.'

'Nobody will, but I don't know if I'll ever see it in my lifetime. You know what I'm saying? We are talking about generations. My kids' kids' kids will probably be able to see and not believe that the city was the way it was, in my time. Because of technology and property enhancements, downtown will probably be what Chicago is today. It will all advance and it will hopefully improve the quality of people that you have. If that happens, then it will be positive.'

'That's why I think they should keep a few streets as they are. So we don't forget how it was.'

But Detroit didn't seem too interested in preserving these aspects of its history – not even the more positive and interesting parts. A few months after my visit, a former Detroit home of Rosa Parks – the civil rights activist, famous for refusing to give up her seat on a bus to a white passenger – which had been left to ruin, was dismantled and taken to Germany. Even the Heidelberg Project – a famous, two-block art installation making use of abandoned houses – has seen many of those buildings destroyed by fire or demolished by the city itself. It seemed a great shame to me to lose these local neighbourhood sights and historic buildings, curious as some may be.

Hunter's comments on how he believed Detroit would become what Chicago is today, was something that I also believed. But becoming like Chicago was also part of the problem. Chicago is a fantastic place to visit – it's full of historic sights, great bars and restaurants, and amazing buildings – but it also has some of the most dangerous neighbourhoods in the entire country.

*

We stopped for a train. It was another long, slow freight train that brought the entire area to a standstill.

'Brannock hates these trains,' I commented.

'Oh yes, he does! He's a special dude,' Hunter said. This time we both laughed.

The final carriage passed and we were on our way again.

'Do you think Detroit has been neglected?' I asked. 'You know, in the way New Orleans was, after Katrina? People said that was about race – it was a black city, so no one cared.'

'We're not the only city,' Hunter said, nodding his head. 'There's Louisiana, St Louis, Baltimore, parts of New York. And believe me, they don't want too many more Obamas! Imagine if we gave all black people and people of colour the ability to educate themselves, learn the fucking shit that they need to learn to get up in there; then you're gonna have the drive to get to congress, to be a state representative and try to lobby and make changes. Shit! The rich white folk don't want to see my black ass up in there talking about how I'm gonna take money out of their pocket! Are you kidding? Why is it like that? I don't know, Mick, that's just the way it is, man. But a lot of white people don't want to see it. Drugs, for example. I know that black people ain't bringing it here, because they can't afford the fucking plane! They don't have the connections with all the fucking cartels and all that kind of shit. So how the fuck the drugs getting here? It's got to be government and whites; somebody's putting money in their pockets.

'And guns! Again, the planes, the connections – I'm talking about crates and crates of firearms. They (blacks) ain't got that shit! So there you go again – put it in the hands of a black person, they put it in the community and then they sell it to the people. It's a vicious, vicious cycle.'

*

As well as the residential neighbourhoods in Southwest Detroit looking different from the east side of Detroit, the commercial areas too, were noticeably busier and more productive. Whereas in the 9th, the only place for people to go seemed to be the neighbourhood party store, here there were restaurants, cafes and other businesses.

We passed one coffee shop close to Mexicantown where I noticed a young hipster type, sitting by the window, working on a laptop – a normal sight in most towns and cities, but something that truly stuck out to me in Detroit, for being so unusual from anything I had seen in the past.

'This really is a different neighbourhood,' I said to Hunter, as I stared out at the bustling streets.

'Really, really different,' he agreed.

I spotted some kids playing in a garden, throwing snowballs at each other.

'It's nice,' I said.

'It's actually a liveable community, man. People actually care a little bit about where they're living,' he said, pulling into the large parking lot at the Mexican restaurant.

After we had collected our burritos and began to head back, Brannock called up to ask how we were getting on. Hunter told him that we had left the street to go and 'get a bag' (get some food). It turned out that, whilst we had been out on the streets, Brannock had been speaking with Detective Sullivan from homicide. Sullivan had received information that an Odyssey might be linked to the firefighter case. In reply, Brannock told Sullivan that we had just seen an Odyssey at the target address.

Things were starting to come together.

Brannock said that the Odyssey we had seen was now to be considered a 'target vehicle'. He wanted us back at the address as quickly as possible to watch for it and told other units to start making their way there, to back us up.

Back at the street, we drove by the house to take a quick look before settling into our original position. But there was a problem – the Odyssey was gone.

'I swear, we leave this location for just a moment ...' I grumbled, then: 'Wait a minute, what's this car?' The Odyssey turned into the street and stopped outside the house just seconds after we had driven past. Timing is everything.

'Okay, here it is,' Hunter said. He got back on the radio. 'Heads up, I've got a return of that target vehicle. It's pulling back up in front of the target location. I'll let you know how many times occupied and who gets out. Stand by ... Okay, I've got rug rats (small kids). Rug rats coming out of the house and getting inside the vehicle.'

A couple of small kids had run down from the house and stepped into the rear of the Odyssey. No one got out.

'I can't see the driver,' Hunter continued. 'I've seen nobody exit. I may do a drive-by just to take a peek inside.'

Hunter started towards the Odyssey but before we reached it, it pulled away again, the rear tyres skidding slightly and kicking up a spray of dirty ice and snow.

'It's away from the kerb,' Hunter told the other units. 'Should I trip with it and see where it's going?'

Brannock came on the radio. 'Yeah, fourteen,' he said. 'Fourteen' is code for okay/copy/understood. 'Go with it.'

'Okay, I'll give directions,' Hunter said, putting his foot down to gain some ground on the Odyssey. 'Hollywood, you've got to catch up with me, because I'm gonna need two vehicles. It's coming up to Springwells. It's got its left hand out (left indicator/signal). Left hand out, to go north.'

As the car drove past numerous side streets, Hunter called them out, so that the other units could hear exactly what our location was. Up ahead, a traffic light, jerking around wildly in the freezing wind, changed to red.

'We're coming up to a ruby,' Hunter called over the radio. Then the light changed to green and we were away again. 'We are heading northbound on Vernor.'

Just then, Casper pulled onto Vernor. He tucked in behind the Odyssey to pick up the follow, allowing Hunter to peel off. Hunter put his foot down and the engine roared as we sprinted away. Listening to Casper's commentary, we were able to parallel him along the next street.

A few blocks further on, Hollywood pulled in behind Casper, allowing Casper to pull off at the next cross street.

As Casper gave his final update before handing over to Hollywood, we realised that the Odyssey was about to cross the road ahead of us. Hunter quickly pulled over, stopping by the kerb. We watched and waited. Moments later the Odyssey appeared at the junction on our left, waiting for the traffic to clear so they could cross.

'Can you make anyone out in it?' Hunter asked.

All I could see was a young-looking girl – possibly a teenager – sitting in the front passenger seat. I couldn't make out the driver, and the windows for the rear seats were blacked out. Then the traffic cleared and the Odyssey drove closer towards us as it crossed into the junction.

'Okay, take a peek inside,' Hunter whispered to me.

I looked across as casually as I could, doing my best not to appear too obvious as I glanced over at the car.

'Woman driver, girl on the front seat,' I said.

Hunter got back onto the radio. 'Okay, we got a good look inside. It's gonna be rug rats and the mom.'

Brannock was now calling up; he was in the area.

Hollywood followed the Odyssey across the junction.

'Hollywood's in her trunk,' Hunter told units over the radio.

Further on, as we took over again, allowing Hollywood to peel off, Hunter realised that we were heading closer towards the interstate.

'Up ahead is the I-94 and our future,' Hunter called to the other units.

Brannock was already up ahead of us, preparing to take over as the follow hit the interstate. But just before the turning, the Odyssey suddenly swung to the right, diving into a short side street. It was one that Soto had once had an address on, and perhaps still did. As we reached the junction, we saw the Odyssey, stopped in the centre of the narrow road, which was lined with beaten-up cars and tatty row houses.

'The girl's out,' I said.

A girl – perhaps in her teens, maybe older – jumped out of the front passenger seat and ran towards one of the houses. The rug rats also stepped out of the car, following behind her. Hunter put it up on the radio.

Brannock then came on the air and gave out the house number that they had listed for Soto. From our position at the end of the street we couldn't tell for sure, but it was likely that that was the same house that the girl and the kids had gone into.

Then the Odyssey was away again, turning towards Brannock.

'Call it from there, Brannock,' Hunter said. 'The vehicle went to your right.'

Brannock got in behind the Odyssey and began the commentary, relaying the locations and cross streets as he followed. Hunter paralleled him, one street over. Listening to Brannock's voice, I could hear that he had become professional and serious. There was no joking around now. This was work, this was important and his tone had completely changed from his usual teasing banter. Just like the others, he was completely switched on to the task at hand.

The route the Odyssey was taking led Brannock to believe that it was heading back to its original street and he asked someone to get ahead and watch for its arrival. Hunter put his foot down and we made our way.

Minutes later the car pulled up outside a corner party store. Brannock kept watch. A short time after that, the car pulled back out, turning into its original street. By now, Hunter had found a spot to park that was far enough to keep us out of their view but close enough to give us a clear look as the car arrived. As the Odyssey pulled up, a second vehicle, a grey Impala, stopped directly behind it. Hunter put it up.

'I need somebody to do a DB (drive-by),' he said.

'I've got you, Hunter,' Hollywood called. 'I've got your six.'

'Yeah, fourteen. I want to see them getting out.'

As I watched, I could see someone stepping out of the Impala. It looked like another young kid. Then the woman driver and a girl got out of the Odyssey and went into the house.

Nearby, unseen, a dog began to bark. I was concerned that it might draw attention to us, but other than the activity outside the target house, there was no one else around and the people we were watching never looked over.

The woman then returned to the Odyssey and just like that, it was away again. Hunter put it up to Brannock, but by then, the

Odyssey had disappeared into the warren of narrow side roads. Brannock, Hollywood and Casper, along with Scrappy, who had now also joined the party, were calling to each other, giving the last known location and searching the area for it.

The Impala was still holding outside the house, so we stayed where we were, watching it.

'Hey, Brannock, if the Impala moves, do you want us to trip with it?' Hunter asked.

'Yeah, why not,' he replied.

By now it was starting to get dark, giving us further cover but making our view less clear. Then the driver climbed out of the Impala. It was a man, but other than that, it was hard to see anything else distinctive about him. Was it Soto? Impossible to say. Then the man walked up to the house and went inside.

Brannock came back on the radio. 'Hunter, take a look at the front of that Impala and see if it has any bullet-holes in it. It's supposed to have two.'

Hunter and I looked at each other. How did Brannock know that the Impala was meant to have bullet-holes? What Hunter and I didn't know was that Detective Sullivan had received information that Soto was believed to be driving an Impala. Not only that, but a couple of months before, Soto had apparently been shot at whilst attending an illegal street race. If this Impala had bullet-holes, there was a very good chance Soto himself would be behind the wheel.

Before we had a chance to check, the man was back out and into the driver's seat. The brake lights came on and we prepared for it to move.

'Hey, Brannock, if someone moves off in that Impala, are we taking it down, or what?' Scrappy asked over the radio.

'Negative, negative,' Brannock replied. 'Just follow it.'

At that very moment, the Impala took off.

'Vehicle's away,' Hunter called. 'It's coming to you, Casp.'

The car turned right, out of the junction. We were just behind it but as we turned, the Impala, like the Odyssey before it, disappeared. Just like that, both vehicles were gone.

Despite losing the cars, the surveillance had been a success. We hadn't definitively found Soto, but we had at least had some movement with the Odyssey, so we now knew that it was being used. As well, there was a good chance that at least one of the female occupants of the car could have been O'Neill. The fact that the car had travelled to one of Soto's known addresses also indicated that there was a chance he was still in town. And of course, there was now the second car that had shown up – the Impala. As intelligence-gathering exercises went, it had been a reasonable haul. Thanks to the surveillance and Detective Sullivan's input, everyone was now sure that we were watching the right place.

'Hunter, do you have the English guy with you?' Brannock asked over the radio.

Hunter chuckled as he repeated Brannock's words. 'The English guy!'

'You'd think he'd know my name by now,' I said.

'He knows it,' Hunter said. 'He's just being Brannock.'

'At least he didn't call me Australian.'

Brannock wanted me to jump in with him, and we met at a nearby parking lot where I switched cars.

Brannock turned to me as I stepped into his 4x4. 'Have you finished writing that book about me yet?' he asked, in faux annoyance.

'Nope,' I said.

'What the fuck have you been doing all day, Mick?'

'You know, surveillance.'

'No dope being sold at that house, from what you saw?'

'No, but something is obviously going on there.'

Brannock drove away from the area and took a nearby ramp to the highway.

'We going somewhere?' I asked.

'Yeah. We're going to see my S.O.I. – my Source of Information,' he told me. 'Some girl I know from the city. She gives me bits and pieces on the gangs sometimes. But she's always hungry. She wants me to pick her up some food from Mexicantown. She loves that food, man.'

Brannock took an exit on the highway and headed towards Mexicantown. An icy wind careered through the empty neighbourhood, and heavy flakes of falling snow billowed around chaotically in the handful of narrow old streets.

'This weather sucks dick,' Brannock said glumly as he pulled up in an empty parking lot behind a Mexican restaurant.

'Perhaps you should move to Florida,' I told him.

'Fuck that, it's too hot.' He pushed at his door, forcing it open against the freezing squall. 'Wait here,' he told me.

He jumped out and shuffled towards the rear entrance of the restaurant. A white guy was standing around the parking lot in a fluorescent 'valet' tabard, which he wore tightly over the top of an extra-thick down jacket. I watched him slapping his gloved hands together in a hopeless attempt to keep warm. Apart from us, there were no other customers.

Brannock returned ten minutes later, carrying a small plastic bag. He opened the door and the ferocious weather charged into the vehicle, stinging my warm face. Brannock handed me the bag without saying a word. The bag was hot, and a smell of strong spice wafted up to my nostrils.

As we moved away from the parking lot, slipping on a thick layer of snow, Brannock mentioned how he couldn't understand why his S.O.I. had wanted to meet in the street she had given him. They had never met there before and as far as he was aware, she had no connection to the location. The street was a fair distance away from Mexicantown and although the roads were practically deserted, even Brannock had no choice but to drive carefully. The fresh dumping of snow, which was still tumbling down, had covered dangerous traps of sheet ice, and several times we skidded forward an alarming distance as Brannock slowed down for stop lights. By the time we reached the street his S.O.I. had given, the hot bag of Mexican food had cooled down to barely warm.

The area we were now in felt claustrophobic and isolated; a forgotten street in an already forgotten neighbourhood. Few houses had numbers on them and those that did were hard to see in the wintry darkness. Brannock drove slowly along the pitch-black street and we both stared out hard, squinting at the front aspects of the small, single-storey houses.

'Why is she meeting us here?' Brannock questioned.

'This could be a set-up,' I said. And I was serious.

'Yeah, that's what I was thinking,' he said, sounding genuinely concerned. 'Fuck this.' He drew his gun from its holster and held it on his lap.

'Arrived,' the satnav said.

Brannock came to a stop and we stared out at the house next to us. The small building was behind a wire fence and everything was dark apart from a single light bulb, glowing weakly above a door at the side.

Unsure why the woman had brought us here, Brannock wasn't keen to step out of the car and approach the house. He picked up his phone and called his S.O.I. She answered almost immediately. This time Brannock put his phone on speaker.

'Hello?' she said, in a slow, dopey-sounding voice.

'Where you at?' Brannock asked.

'I'm at the Coney,' she said, giving the cross street for the Coney Island food joint.

'Coney Island? I thought you were going to be at this address you gave me?'

She mumbled something about needing food, seemingly forgetting that she had already asked Brannock to fetch her something from Mexicantown.

'Well, are you coming here or not?' Brannock asked.

'You may as well come to the Coney Island,' she told him. 'I've already ordered my food.'

'Oh my God, girl! All right, we're coming down there now.' Then he raised his voice. 'DON'T LEAVE THERE!'

The girl giggled gently at Brannock's mock anger and hung up the phone.

'Why did I ever get involved with this fucking girl?' he asked himself.

Brannock actually had real concerns about the flakiness of his source. There were obvious dangers for anyone who became an S.O.I. for the police – get found out and you could end up dead. A source needed to be careful, discreet. They needed to be professional, even. But Brannock was concerned that his S.O.I. wasn't taking her position seriously enough.

'This girl,' he said, shaking his head. 'She's all over the fucking place. She's going to get her ass shot.'

We pulled into a small parking area outside a box-shaped Coney Island fast food place. A black girl in her twenties, wearing a short, cheerleader-type skirt despite the freezing conditions sauntered casually towards the car. Brannock brought down his electric window. Being in a public place, there was no time for any talk. Brannock wasn't here for information, he was simply keeping his S.O.I. fed, and he handed over the bag of Mexican food. The girl took it without saying a word, spun around and walked away. As she did, she looked back at us over her shoulder, smiling suggestively. She gave us a twirl of her body, showing off her backside. She was flirting with us.

'What the fuck?' I asked.

'She's crazy as fuck!' Brannock said, laughing. 'She's too much!'

He brought up the window, cranked up the heat and headed back to the base, shaking his head but still laughing.

14

Nowhere to Run

Friday, 15 January 2016

The following day, I was back out with Brannock. We were driving slowly along Gratiot Avenue, staring out at the roadside devastation. Drive along many American highways and you will often see a scattering of fast-food joints. Gratiot was no different and had a number of its own. But there was one major variance: where once, families and kids came for a burger and a special treat, or hungry travellers stopped for a quick bite before continuing on their journey, these businesses had been transformed into something else entirely.

'The reason I came down here is because this has got to be *the* first drive-thru marijuana dispensary,' Brannock told me.

Apart from a line of white paint near the roof, the drive-thru had been painted completely green.

'Fuck me, it's not exactly subtle,' I said.

'It's obviously like an old Taco Bell or Burger King,' Brannock said.

'It's open twenty-four hours, as well!' I marvelled, reading the words written across its walls.

'Yep. You just pull around and get the strain of marijuana that you want. Is this not absolutely fucking crazy?'

Some years before, in San Diego, California, I had been taken to a 'pot shop' by a cop I was riding with. The building had been unremarkable – just another anonymous, small brick store, with covered windows and no obvious markings or name. If you wanted to buy any of the marijuana products they offered, you first had to get a prescription from a doctor. However, everyone I spoke to told me how easy it was to get one; you only had to tell the doctor that you were having headaches or suffering from anxiety or some other made-up nonsense, and you were written a script that you could then take to the dispensary. It was suggested to me that some doctors took a cut from the marijuana dispensaries: that was why it was so easy to get the prescription in the first place. Here on Gratiot though, was a whole other level – a 24/7, drive-thru, fast-pot place.

Brannock laughed out loud, enjoying my shocked reaction.

'How can that even be allowed?' I asked.

'I do not know!' he said, still laughing.

'Like this city's not fucked up enough?'

'Right! And this is not like the marijuana from back in the day – the brown shit. This is like, hydroponic.'

'Skunk, you mean?'

'Yeah. And they sell hash oils and all kinds of stuff. Pipes and brownies and cookies. So you get that shit and you eat it and now you're high and you're fucking driving around!'

High and driving around with an AK-47, I thought to myself.

In Detroit, I learned, possessing up to an ounce of marijuana was decriminalised in 2015 – even though it is still illegal in the state. An increasing number of states in America are either legalising marijuana or decriminalising it. And one of the biggest providers of legal, medical marijuana in America – as unlikely as it may seem – is a former British police officer. No, not me.

Brannock turned into a side street, heading back towards the base. Nearby, he stopped at a large party store.

'I want to grab a bottle of water,' he told me. 'Plus I know these guys. I wouldn't come here otherwise.'

The party store was a large single-storey concrete building. Like many of the party stores I had seen, there wasn't a single window. The narrow glass door at one corner of the building was dirty and worn, and almost impossible to see through.

Inside the store it was bright, with colourful neon strip-lights lining the walls, and a long row of glass-fronted refrigerators. The shelves and cabinets were stacked with junk food, candy, pop and cheap bottles of wine. Four Middle Eastern men worked behind a long counter, protected by a thick plastic screen that reached from the counter all the way to the ceiling. Behind them, on dozens of shelves, were various bottles of spirits. There were four turntable hatches within the plastic screen and it was at these hatches that the transactions were made. A customer placed their money on the turntable, which the men behind the counter then spun around, so that they could take the money before placing the customer's change and purchase on the turntable and twisting it back to them. At no point were the men behind the counter ever openly exposed to the customer, and there was no way that anyone could jump the counter to assault the men or rob them.

Brannock knew the men and they welcomed him warmly, no doubt pleased to have a cop in their store. They opened a security door to allow us to join them behind the screen and Brannock introduced me.

Although the cigarettes and spirits were behind the screen, most of the products in the store were on open display, on the rows of shelving. With the men locked behind the counter, it would be easy for someone to come in and just take stuff.

'Do many people come in here and steal?' I asked one of the men.

He laughed. 'Yeah! All day,' he said, as though it were the most obvious answer in the world. 'Moms even send their kids in here and tell them to take stuff.'

The other men were serving poor, defeated-looking people, and no words were exchanged between them. Items were placed on the turntables, cash was passed, and then the people left. It looked like a depressing job, stuck behind this thick plastic screen, serving unhappy people, watching kids steal from the shelves and wondering who was going to cause trouble or start shooting at you.

'Is this screen bullet-proof?' I asked.

'It won't stop an AK-47,' one of the men said, matter-of-fact. 'But a normal gun would need to shoot four or five times before it got through.'

'If they did get through, how would you protect yourselves?'

The man opened a small drawer under the counter. There, amongst used envelopes, sets of keys, various plugs, chargers and wires, were two handguns – a Smith & Wesson, and a Glock. Then he pointed behind himself. Resting up against the wall, next to a fire extinguisher, were a large wooden club and a shotgun. It was like a saloon in the Wild West.

'Working in there is like being in prison, except you're the prisoner and the people outside are free,' Brannock told me as we returned to his car.

*

Back at the base, the office was empty. The rest of the team were out, hunting for Soto. Brannock had his handheld police radio standing on his desk, the volume up high, in case anything happened. We could hear various members of the unit speaking to each other on the radio – Hunter, Hollywood, Casper, Whispers.

'*Stay with him! Stay with him!*' someone said urgently.

They were behind one of the suspect cars and it was starting to sound like a chase.

'This has got to be Soto,' Brannock said. 'He's driving like an asshole.'

'*Northbound 75. He's trying to get away from us big-time, now.*'

Then someone began shouting incoherently. It was clear that the units on the streets were having trouble sticking with the suspect car. They were calling out locations and directing each other to surrounding streets, but the car was getting away from them.

'*He's getting off at the Dearborn exit but I can't make it. He's way ahead of us.*'

'*He's probably gonna double back.*'

'They've fucking lost him,' Brannock said.

'*There he is! Get this out on District, we need him stopped!*'

'Oh, they've found him again,' Brannock said, picking up the radio and turning up the volume.

'*How many times is that vehicle occupied again, sir?*' It was a District unit, coming on the air.

'*You've got him!*' Scrappy said, calling out to the District unit. '*He's pulling up to the red light. That's the car that we need stopped, right there. The green Impala.*'

'GREY!' Brannock yelled. 'GREY, YOU FUCKING IDIOT!'

More District units started to call up, their sirens blaring in the background. They were moving in to support the gang officers and the District unit that was already approaching the Impala.

'Okay, let's go,' Brannock said, jumping up from his chair.

I grabbed my stuff and we darted out of the office, running down the concrete stairs and pushing open the heavy metal doors to the parking lot. A rush of freezing, razor-like wind smacked us in the face and I slipped backwards on some ice but managed to stay upright. I leapt into Brannock's Jeep, quickly slamming the door shut as a final whoosh of bitter wind followed me in.

Scrappy was still calling out directions over the radio. The car was on the move again, getting away before the District vehicles had a chance to stop it.

Brannock started the engine and we set off, but we were on

the opposite side of the city, in diabolical winter weather, so making any kind of progress – even with Brannock's driving skills – was going to be difficult without risking a serious accident. It was something that the driver of the Impala was less concerned about, as that person did their best to evade the officers.

'This motherfucker's got nothing to lose,' Brannock said.

Shards of ice and freezing rain battered relentlessly into the windscreen, filling the car with a static-like sound. The streets were practically deserted. Layers of untouched snow carpeted the roads, and flashing traffic-lights swung and twisted violently in the wind, threatening to tear away from their wires. Our car skidded wildly in the snow as Brannock put his foot down, trying to build up some speed.

The Impala had been lost again, and District units were now out searching for it, along with the gang officers. Everyone was calling out the car's description and last known location to one another.

A new District unit now came over the radio. '*If we spot that vehicle, do you want us to stop it?*'

'FUCK! YES!' Brannock exploded, shaking his head. 'He's wanted for homicide! What the fuck is this officer thinking?'

Brannock knew that we were close to catching the firefighter's killer. The urgency in his voice was clear; he didn't want Soto getting away again. By now, the District units on the street were fully aware of the seriousness of the case. They were also aware of the potential danger that the occupants presented.

A District unit came on the radio. '*All units, if you come across that vehicle, do not attempt to stop it. Request other units to assist.*'

'OH MY GOD!' Brannock screamed angrily. 'WHAT THE FUCK?'

'*Do not attempt to stop that vehicle unless you call for another vehicle to assist.*'

Brannock was pissed. He picked up his phone and called Sullivan, the homicide detective who was working the firefighter case. Brannock turned on the in-car speaker, so that he could drive and talk at the same time.

'Hello?'

'Hey, we just fucking lost him,' Brannock said. 'He's in that grey Impala.'

'Yeah, I know; I've been hearing this shit,' Sullivan said. 'That Seven-O (sergeant) unit needs to take his fucking diaper off and drive.'

'Right. And Soto's going to go back to one of his houses. Motherfucker! Right. Bye.' His annoyance now vented, Brannock ended the call.

A dispatcher came on the radio, giving out police runs to units not involved in the hunt for the murderers. Brannock's agitation increased.

'Why the fuck are they giving out police runs?' he said. 'They've got a motherfucking murderer running through the precinct and they're giving out police runs and shit!'

Brannock had a theory about where Soto could be. He was believed to have been involved in a recent car-jacking, and the vehicle had been dumped around the area of Michigan Avenue and Martin Road. Brannock figured that Soto must have had a safe house to go to in that area.

'He's not going to dump a car too far away, especially with how cold it's been,' Brannock said. 'So let's take a look over there.'

'If he's got the Impala, why is he car-jacking cars?' I asked.

'I don't know,' Brannock shrugged. But his tone of voice was saying, *Why not?*

Units were speaking over the radio, putting up numerous possible sightings of the Impala. Various colours were called out – green, grey, silver.

'It was dark grey, right?' I asked.

'Yeah, like a charcoal grey,' Brannock said.

Just then, a grey Impala passed us on the opposite side of the avenue we were driving along.

'Er … that might be it!' Brannock said.

He spun the car around and drove after it. The Impala turned into one of the streets that Soto was known to frequent. It was looking good.

Brannock tried to cut into the radio traffic but everyone was talking over each other and it was impossible to get on. In the end it didn't matter. As we caught up with the Impala, we could see that the grey colour wasn't dark enough for Soto's car. Then we saw the number-plate. That was different too.

'Fuck!' Brannock said.

'What are the chances of that?' I asked. 'Right car, correct street.'

As it turned out, the chances were pretty good. All of a sudden, the previously empty streets seemed to be full of Impalas. Everywhere we looked, either driving through the storm, parked along kerbs or held at traffic-lights, there was Impala after Impala. I had gone from having never heard of an Impala before, to becoming something of an expert.

The noise of the freezing rain hitting the windscreen increased, forcing Brannock to turn the volume up on his radio. Officers were still talking over each other, putting up various Impalas that they had seen or passed.

Then there was a moment of silence and Brannock finally managed to get on the radio. 'Hey, you guys need to watch the air. Watch the air,' he told them. Turning to me, he said, 'They always want to talk on the fucking radio!'

The weather had become worse. Thick sheets of sleet were moving in heavy waves along the wide avenues. Anything not firmly attached to something else was swinging and swaying uncontrollably in the wind.

'There's no way these people are going to be staying out in this weather,' I said.

Brannock didn't answer. This was a normal winter in Detroit, so there was every chance they would be staying out.

We headed towards Michigan Avenue, close to the area where Soto was believed to have dumped the stolen car.

'We had him yesterday, in that Impala,' Brannock said, sounding annoyed. 'And now we're chasing that fucker around in the rain.'

'What's so different?' I asked. 'How come we can arrest him today but not yesterday?'

'They've got a statement from the safecracker,' he told me.

After Madrigal had been killed, the safe that had been stolen from his home had been taken to an acquaintance of Soto's – a man called Angel Miranda-Moll. Miranda-Moll had broken the safe open and around a thousand dollars was taken from within it. He was then given a gun for his troubles and told to dispose of the safe. But Miranda-Moll later saw the firefighter's murder reported on the news. Realising that the vehicle Soto had driven to his house was probably the same one taken from the murder scene, together with the safe, Miranda-Moll decided that he wanted nothing more to do with it. He took the safe apart, dumping the nuts and screws in an alley, and spray-painted the main body of the safe before dumping it in a vacant building.

By now, homicide was putting the pieces together. They paid Miranda-Moll a visit. He led them to the safe and provided them with a statement, thereby becoming a prosecution witness. With his testimony, homicide could now move in on Soto and others who were involved in the murder.

There were other developments also. The child's Pistons cap that had been found at the murder scene was believed to belong to O'Neill's young son. After the murder, the boy had been sent to Tennessee to live with his father. Detective Sullivan had gone to Tennessee and taken a DNA swab from the boy. It matched a sample taken from the Pistons cap. The evidence was building and the net was closing.

Brannock pulled off Michigan Avenue and turned into Martin, Southwest Detroit. We cruised slowly along the street, searching for the Impala amongst the lines of tightly parked cars. Before long, Brannock spotted a dark grey Impala, parked a little further ahead. He moved towards it and asked me to call out the plate number. Once again, it wasn't our car. We continued on, searching the surrounding area, moving from one street to the next: systematically, slowly, determined.

We pulled into Dayton – a narrow one-way street with a number of cars parked on either side of the road. Most of the lots along the street were occupied by tatty, worn houses, but there were still a number of cleared, empty plots. We drove along the street, through low trenches of snow and slush, peering at the lines of parked cars. Then Brannock spotted another dark grey Impala, parked opposite a boarded-up house towards the end of the street. The Impala was so closely backed up against a pick-up truck that it was impossible to check the plate until we were right up on it. Brannock came to a near halt and I looked through a sliver of space between the truck and the Impala and called out the number-plate.

'That's it!' Brannock said. 'That's our Impala!'

He immediately got on the radio to inform the other units. 'I'm gonna set up stationary here, as close as I can, but everyone move to this area, Dayton and Central. The vehicle is facing eastbound,' he told them.

Brannock found a space between some cars outside an abandoned house and parked up. Our search had now turned into a stake-out.

Hunter came on the radio. 'Brannock, I'm just west of you. I'm in an alley, facing north. You copy?'

259

'Get as close as you can,' Brannock told him. He was feeling confident about finding Soto but he didn't want to risk losing him again. He wanted the area surrounded and all possible escape routes covered. 'Once everyone gets here, I need to know positions. I'm on the target vehicle but I need one north, one south, one east, one west.'

The Impala was parked outside a vaco, so it was impossible to tell which house Soto was inside. In an effort to try and pin down where he might be, we tried to figure out which houses were occupied and which ones were vacant. Some were obviously inhabited – lights on, movement in and out – but we knew that houses that looked empty or abandoned could still have people living in them.

Behind us there were now three cars, stopped in the middle of the street, each with their headlights on and engines running. The headlights were caught in my wing-mirror, blinding me.

'What's with these cars stopped in the street?' I asked.

Brannock had also noticed them. 'I don't know,' he said, sounding wary, 'but keep an eye on that shit.'

Our own engine was also running; it needed to be, to stop us from freezing but also because the interior lights would all come on if the engine was turned off, briefly but with time to completely illuminate us inside the car, for all to see. The cars that were stopped behind us may have been innocent, but being in this neighbourhood, doing what we were doing, they were also a concern. With the engine running, our dashboard was lit up with a variety of coloured lights. They too created an unwanted and potentially dangerous glow.

'Do you have a scarf or a hat I can use?' Brannock asked.

'I have a hat.'

'Give me your hat.'

I reached over to the back seat and grabbed my red woollen hat, which had *Canada* embroidered across the front.

Brannock, knowing full well that my wife is Canadian, instantly saw an opportunity to try and push my buttons. 'What the fuck is this shit?' he asked. 'Canada?'

'Do you want it or not?'

'That's not even a real country,' he scoffed.

He snatched the hat and shoved it against the dashboard, covering the lights and immediately dimming down the give-away glow.

Brannock got back on the radio. 'Someone get onto District and tell them to keep their marked units out of this area, but to be close enough to come in if we call them.'

I checked my mirror and took another look at the three cars behind us, which were now each beginning to move off. They passed slowly by but paid us no attention.

We sat in silence, listening to the others calling out their locations over the radio, as violent gusts of wind punched our car and blew up wafts of loose snow and dead leaves. I stared over at a house a few doors down, opposite from where we were parked. The porch light was on and I wondered if Soto was inside. Was he watching us? Were others watching us? We were two men, sitting in a large black 4x4, with the engine running. Even with the dash lights covered, we would have stuck out.

Brannock must have been having similar thoughts. 'Let's lean back a little bit,' he said, and we dropped our seats back so that we weren't sitting up so straight and obvious.

A set of headlights lit up the road behind us. A white van was driving cautiously along the street, through the snow. We both slipped down a little further in our seats as the van came level. It passed us but then stopped a couple of car lengths away, pulling into a space just ahead of the Impala. Brannock picked up his radio.

'Heads up, guys, I've got a white Sprinter van pulling up to our target vehicle. Standby.'

A man stepped out of the van and walked up a set of broken wooden steps onto the open porch at the front of a vacant-looking house. The building appeared severely fire-damaged and was missing all of its windows. A large sheet of blue tarpaulin, partly attached to the roof, was blowing around furiously in the wind. The man pulled out a flashlight, pointing it at the front of the house and around the porch.

'What the hell is he doing?' I asked.

'I have no idea,' Brannock said.

Then the man opened the door of the house and walked in. At the same time, the porch light on the house next door – the house I had been looking at – went off. The front door to this property then opened and someone stepped out. Being on the passenger side, I had a better view of what was happening.

'Is anybody coming out?' Brannock asked.

'Someone's at the door but it's too dark to make them out.'

Then the door shut again and the porch light switched back on.

'Do you think they've spotted us?' I asked.

'I don't know,' Brannock said.

Scrappy was talking over the radio, giving other units directions to the area and advice on where to plot-up.

Another car – a black Jeep Cherokee – now drove slowly along the road behind us, and its headlights illuminated the inside of our vehicle. For such a minor back street, there was an awful lot of activity and we began to feel increasingly edgy. The Jeep crept closer until it was almost level with our own vehicle. Once again, we dipped down in our seats.

The car passed by but then came to a halt, stopping outside the house with the porch light. The door of the house opened once more. This time, two people stepped out – both women. They were then followed by a man, but in the darkness it was impossible to make out if any of the people were those that we were looking for. All three quickly ran down the front steps and got into the Jeep.

Brannock picked up his radio. 'I've got three out of a house, loading up into a black Jeep Cherokee. We might want to stop this vehicle,' he told the other units.

The Jeep took off, turning north onto Central Avenue. A moment later, Hunter came over the radio to say that he had eyes on the vehicle. After Central, the Jeep turned onto Radcliffe, and Hunter slipped in behind, following.

There was now more movement, this time coming from a couple of houses behind us. People were jumping into waiting cars, which moved off, passing us by a few moments later.

'What did the guy look like in that car that just passed?' Brannock asked.

'White guy,' I said. 'Had a slight limp when he came out of the house. Looked like he was in his twenties or thirties. How old is Soto?'

'Twenties,' Brannock said.

Before we had a chance to put the car up, officers started to speak excitedly over the radio.

Hunter was saying something about 'needing handcuffs'.

'Just get him out of the damn car!' someone else said.

Another officer was asking, 'Do you have S1?' (S1 – Suspect 1.)

Brannock and I looked over at each other, confused. *What the hell was happening out there?*

Hunter came back on the radio and was again asking for 'cuffs'. In the background we could hear a number of voices – men and women – speaking quickly and loudly.

'Give me the air,' Hunter said calmly, trying to get some air to talk on the radio. 'We have S1. I say again, we have S1. Thank you.'

Brannock looked at me. 'They got him!'

Soto had been in the Jeep Cherokee after all.

'They tried to sneak the fuck out of here, didn't they,' Brannock said.

Even though they had Soto, Brannock wanted to stay where we were. The Impala would need impounding at some point and leaving would give anybody still inside the house a chance to dispose of any items or evidence that may have been in there.

As we sat watching, Brannock took a call from Detective Sullivan. He was adamant that no one should mention the homicide to any of the suspects, at this point. Instead, Soto was only to be told that he was wanted for the car-jacking and a parole violation.

Then the radio came back to life. Hollywood, who was with the Jeep, was calling up Brannock.

'Sergeant, we have the female.'

'Is it S2?' Brannock asked. S2 was Suspect 2 – Nicole O'Neill.

'Yeah, fourteen.'

'Bingo. Bingo. Great job, guys!' Brannock said.

Hollywood came back on to tell us that a teenage girl, who had also been in the Jeep, had been found with a bag of pills stuffed down her bra. The pills were believed to be Xanax. Soto had told them that he had given the pills to the girl to hide, just before the police had stopped them.

'Well, it's another charge for him,' Brannock told Hollywood.

Then Brannock picked up his phone. He had a mischievous grin on his face. 'Let's call the Assistant Chief,' he said to me.

'Dolunt?' I asked.

'Yeah,' he said, putting the phone on loudspeaker.

Dolunt answered immediately. 'Hello?'

'Hey, AC, it's Brannock. I'm here with this proper wanker you sent me from England.'

'Now *he's* a wanker?' Dolunt asked. 'Oh Brannock, you're killing me.'

'He's a *proper* wanker,' Brannock told him.

'Oh God! I'm afraid of what Mick has learnt from you!'

'Well, I can tell you this,' Brannock said. 'This will make you happy. Me and Mick are watching a house on Dayton, in Southwest. We just watched a guy come out of the house – the guy who killed the firefighter. We just got him in custody. Him and the girl. Timothy Soto is his name.'

'You got him in custody?'

'Yep, just now.'

'Do we have enough PC on him?' (PC – Probable Cause.)

'We're charging him with a parole violation first off,' Brannock said. 'And he did a car-jacking, so we got him on those two charges. He also had Xany pills. So we got a VCSA charge on him, too.' (VCSA – Violation of the Controlled Substances Act.)

'This is all great news,' Dolunt said. 'But is Mick ever going to be the same again, after this?'

'No,' I told him. 'But I've learnt a few new things!'

'Oh God! I don't want to know what you've learnt,' he said. 'I put you with a great crew though.'

He certainly had.

'And I nearly got him shot too,' Brannock told Dolunt proudly.

'Oh my God!' Dolunt said, and he hung up the phone.

Almost immediately afterwards, Brannock's phone rang. It was Robo.

'Who was shot?' Robo asked.

'Where?' Brannock said.

'A task-force agent was shot at the Southfield Marriott,' she said.

'I have no idea,' Brannock told her. 'But we got this guy.'

'You got him?'

'We're still on it but we have him. He ran from us, there was a car chase, we lost him and then me and Mick spotted his car over here. Then he comes out of the house with his girl, gets into a

Cherokee and takes off. The guys stop him and they got them both with some dope.'

'Nice!' she said. 'Anyway, I'm glad you guys are all right; I heard that some undercover task-force officer was shot, in a parking lot.'

'Nothing to do with us,' Brannock assured her.

The incident Robo had been talking about was a human-trafficking operation, just to the north of the city, which was being conducted at the same time that we had been out on Soto. An officer had been shot and a suspect killed.

Our own surveillance operation had been a success, but the way Brannock's unit had gone about it seemed very organic to me. It was refreshing to see a unit that 'just went with it' but I knew there were many other police units that wouldn't have been so casual in their methods. I mentioned it to Brannock.

'But how else can it be done?' he asked.

'There would be more planning,' I told him. 'Risk assessments for officer safety, and all that sort of stuff.'

'Oh, fuck that!' Brannock snorted. 'Everybody that does surveillance, they all think that these motherfuckers pay attention. With a lot of this shit, you just park up and blend the fuck in. Besides, this today was too fast-moving. We have to be fluid. There wouldn't be time for all that. We just had to get on with it otherwise we'd lose him again.'

I liked Brannock's approach, even if it did feel a little dicey at times. There is a lot to be said for acting on impulse – not 'winging it' exactly, but simply getting on with the job at hand. And even though we had been parked up, with the engine running, practically outside the house, Soto and the women had stepped out, without a care. One of the women had even skipped joyfully to the waiting Jeep.

*

Brannock was starting to get restless again. He wanted to hit the house. We had been sitting outside the property for almost an hour and we still didn't know who else was inside or what they might be planning. As far as we knew, Soto might even have put in a call, to warn them about the police.

Brannock called over the radio to see if anyone was available to come by and join us. A couple of officers called up to explain that they were still dealing with the occupants of the Jeep but assured us they would call up when they were free.

I settled back into my seat, believing that we were going to wait until other officers were able to join us, but Brannock had other ideas.

He called over on the radio, once more. 'I need my guys to make this house over here, except for whoever is with the prisoners. Come on.' Then he opened his door. As he stepped out of the car, all I heard him say was, 'These fucking clowns …' The rest, if there was any more, was immediately snatched away by the freezing wind that was barrelling through the murky street.

I looked over at him. He had his gun drawn and was marching towards the house. *Fuck*. I leapt out of the car and ran after him. He was already at the top of the steps by the time I had chased him across the road, the small flashlight attached to the front of his handgun illuminating the porch. He banged his fist against the front door.

At that moment, Scrappy suddenly appeared, leaping up the steps to join us. Seconds later, four US Border Patrol cars arrived, stopping a few buildings down from the house we were hitting. The Border Patrol officers, dressed in olive-green uniforms, stepped out of their vehicles, carrying AR-15s, and quickly created a perimeter around the front of the house. Then the front door opened a few inches. Brannock was standing up against it, his gun pointing down, towards the ground. Scrappy was standing on the opposite side, his body bladed against the building, so that he presented less of a target. He too had his handgun out.

As the door opened a fraction more, a woman's face appeared. She was in her mid to late twenties, thin and scantily dressed in a loose-fitting pair of shorts and a baggy vest. Brannock said something to her and as she opened the door fully, he and Scrappy stepped into the house. I followed them inside.

Sitting on a green leather couch was a 5-year-old boy, watching funny animal videos on the TV. He ignored us, as though having strange, armed men entering his house was an everyday occurrence. Sniffing at our feet nervously was a brown pit-bull puppy. The house felt overly warm, tidy and clean. Stacks of DVDs were piled up around the living room, and in the kitchen opposite, the door-less cupboards were neatly stacked with tins of food.

Brannock and Scrappy still had their guns drawn as they stepped through the room, opening a storage space that contained old toys, and looking up a set of stairs that led to the upper floor.

'There's nobody else here,' the woman said, trying to reassure them.

'When was the last time that someone was here?' Scrappy asked.

'About half an hour ago,' she replied.

Brannock continued to search through the house. The little boy laughed at the animal videos on the TV.

'You got any weapons in the house?' Scrappy asked the woman.

'No.'

'No shotguns or anything?'

'No.'

Brannock poked his head back around the door, from the kitchen. 'Does she have any guns here?'

'She says no,' Scrappy told him.

Brannock asked her again anyway. 'Are there any guns in here?'

'No.'

'Who do you live here with?'

'My boyfriend.'

'Whose black Jeep was that?'

The woman didn't reply.

'How do you know Timmy Soto?'

The woman shuffled uncomfortably by the couch. The kid, still watching the TV, was laughing and yawning at the same time. The pit-bull puppy wobbled up to me, with his pencil-thin, trembling tail held nervously between his legs. I leant down and tickled his ear.

The boy looked over. 'He only bites bad people,' he said.

'Cops are good people,' I told him.

'Except the bad cops,' he said. 'I don't like the bad cops. I only like the good cops.'

'We're the good cops,' I assured him. 'What's his name?'

'Peanut.'

I tickled Peanut's ear some more.

Brannock stepped back into the living room, his gun now holstered. The house was clear. Peanut scampered towards him and Brannock leant down, continuing where I had left off. 'You wanna come home with me, don't you?' Brannock said to Peanut. Peanut's tail was now flapping about excitedly.

With the search complete, we left the house and returned to the car, which had already become an icebox. Brannock turned the heaters on and we headed to where the others had Soto detained.

The Jeep had been stopped on Lonyo and Radcliffe – one block north of us. As we drove along Lonyo Avenue, we could see the red, yellow and blue strobe lights of half a dozen police vehicles, up ahead.

Lonyo was a relatively short avenue that travelled south and north, and it still boasted a number of decent-looking, large family homes. At its north end, however, where we were, the houses thinned out to empty plots, until you reached a railway track that cut across the avenue immediately north of the turning with Radcliffe. This was where the black Jeep and Soto had been stopped.

Mixed in amongst a dozen or so Border officers, I could see Casper and Hunter. Standing at the front of a police cruiser, with her hands cuffed behind her back, was one of the women that we had seen getting into the Jeep, back at Dayton. Soto was still sat inside the Jeep, also handcuffed, and was being spoken to by Hollywood.

As we crossed the street and approached the others, a light rain begun to fall. Brannock told Hunter that he wanted the woman – Nicole O'Neill – to be mouth-swabbed for DNA. They would then 'cut her loose'. As for Soto, he was to be arrested for the car-jacking and the parole violation. The arrest for the homicide would come later.

Watching his officers deal with the people at the scene, Brannock seemed satisfied. Despite all the shenanigans, the operation had been a success; the man who had killed Detroit firefighter David Madrigal had finally been caught.

As we drove away from the area, Brannock pointed to a car going in the opposite direction. 'Look! Another grey Impala!' he said.

15

Heat Wave

Tuesday, 12 July 2016

I was back in Detroit, six months after I had left. Six months since Soto had been arrested. Six months since I had last been called an Australian.

Much had changed in that time, not least the weather. The arctic winter had become a scorching summer, and the humidity sapped away at my soul. It was the sort of heat that pounded you down to half the speed of a sloth and punished you with a crushing headache if you stayed out in the sun for longer than a minute. Blasts of air-conditioning wherever you could get it, and the constant intake of bottled water, were essential.

Regardless of the seasons, crime is always there but the weather can have a dramatic effect on how much. Gang activity and shootings happened all year round in Detroit, but there was usually a significant increase during the spring and summer months. Come the good weather and lighter evenings, people became more active and more confrontational. They also spent more time outside, and that made them easier targets.

Since I had left Detroit in January, there had been almost 130 homicides in the city – three on the very day I returned in July – and just as the crime reporter George Hunter had warned me, many had gone unreported. But there were a few that had made the press and they had made it for very specific and tragic reasons: they all involved children or babies.

In March, a 3-year-old girl was killed in a shooting on Detroit's west side. Shots had been fired from the street into a small house. The shooter had then forced entry into the building and continued to fire. Two men were shot and wounded. They both survived. The 3-year-old girl, who was also in the house, was shot twice and died.

Three weeks later, also on Detroit's west side, as children played in the street, some men, who had already driven by to recce the location, came by again – but this time they opened fire. One man, who had been in the street, was shot in the thigh. He survived. A six-month-old baby girl named Miracle, who had been sitting in her stroller, was shot in the chest. She died.

One week passed. A man was teaching his 4-year-old son how to ride a bike when another man stepped out of a car, aimed his gun at the 4-year-old and shot him. He then turned the gun on the little boy's father and shot him too. The boy survived, his father was killed.

A month after that, over on the east side and following a fight in the street, a suspect was handed a gun, which he fired towards a car. A 2-year-old girl who had been sitting in the car, was struck in the head by one of the bullets. Still alive, she was rushed to hospital in a critical condition. Two days later she was declared brain dead, and two days after that, her life support was switched off.

A fortnight later, and just a few days before I returned to Detroit, another 2-year-old was shot, on the city's east side. The child was sitting in a car when a man, who had been asked to leave a party following an argument, had opened fire, hitting the child in the back.

One case that Brannock's officers had assisted in, involved the death of a 13-year-old boy – Deontae Mitchell. A man had gone to a party store on East Warren, in Detroit's 5th Precinct, close to East English Village, and had accidentally dropped around $70 in cash outside the store. Two kids, who had been riding around on their bikes, found the money. One of the kids – Deontae – had picked the money up and taken it.

The man, realising he had dropped his money, returned to the party store and started to threaten people, asking where it was. Someone told him that one of the kids had taken it. The man then went outside and chased after Deontae, grabbing him by the arm and dragging him into his car, abducting him. For two days the police were searching for the boy. He was eventually found, lying in tall grass, in a vacant lot in the 7th Precinct, just to the west of where he had been kidnapped.

Deontae had been beaten, tortured and strangled to death.

If you didn't read the news or if you lived outside of Detroit and Michigan, you would probably never have heard about these deaths. But child deaths happen all the time, and not just in Detroit.

There are some heroic people and groups out there who do campaign against these crimes and speak up for those dead children – and of course, there is the anti-gun lobby – yet many remain silent. Where is the outrage? Where are the marches? Why are so many politicians and activists silent? Why aren't people demonstrating for *this* cause?

The death of these children is an absolute disgrace. It is America's great shame.

*

There was a new sign on the door to the Gang Unit's office: *Abandon hope, all ye who enter here.*

The office was air-conditioned and pleasantly cool. Whispers was sat in his usual spot, typing a report. He looked over and grinned. Opposite him was Kap, the young female officer from the raid. Kap was now a full-time member of Gang Intel and was working as Whispers' partner.

'Remember the last time you were here, Mick?' Whispers asked. 'I was head down, quietly getting my work done?' That was exactly how I remembered him. 'Well, now I have to stop every half-hour to give a compliment or to make sure that I didn't say anything I shouldn't have,' he told me, smiling.

Kap threw a screwed-up piece of paper at his head.

I grabbed a coffee and sat down with them, to catch up on the past few months.

'Mick, let me show you this,' Whispers said, typing something on his computer.

I looked over. On the screen, Whispers had brought up a web page from an organisation called 'New Era Detroit'. They claimed to have been formed 'to bring back Black unity within growing Black communities' and to 'empower and encourage Black residents to build, buy and invest … in the communities they live in.'

As an organisation, they could be assertive. They had previously blocked traffic, and had protested at gas stations and party stores, where the owners had allegedly abused or threatened members of their community. They talked about 'taking back our streets', but also organised Mother's Day BBQs and street patrols to protect school kids and the elderly. When they marched and protested, it was with clenched fists held in the air, echoing back to the time of Black Power movements of the 1960s and 1970s; members of New Era Detroit sometimes chanted 'Black Power' during their protests, and some members carry the red, black and green pan-African flag.

But there was one thing in particular that had brought New Era Detroit a wave of attention, and it was this thing that Whispers wanted me to see. New Era Detroit had created a 'street code'.

They had published it on their website as well as handed out a flyer version in the neighbourhoods. The street code listed a '10-point mandate' – a list of voluntary rules to follow to prevent you from becoming 'public enemy number 1' within the community. Using their own spellings and capitalisation, these included:

'NO Drive Bys', because 'too many Black Babies are being killed from random drive-bys.'

'Concerts and Parties are Neutral Territories … handle your beefs at your own risk and in your own space.' And 'All beefs must be handled away from school grounds, churches and businesses.'

'No slinging (drug dealing) to the children or pregnant women! Thats GENOCIDE ON OUR PEOPLE!'

'Do not shoot victims of robbery. There is nothing more cowardly than robbing someone, getting what you want out of them then shooting them after …'

The point of the mandate was to make the streets 'honourable' and 'respected', as though being robbed but not being shot would make the victim think, 'I really respect that robber for stealing from me but not shooting me; he's a man of honour.'

But perhaps New Era Detroit – and there are other 'New Era' chapters elsewhere in America – are just being realistic about crime and are trying to do something to bring the high number of killings and deaths down. Putting out a statement saying, 'no more crime, no more shooting and no more gangs', would be laughed at and ignored. But by trying to bring in a 'street code' (some may call it a criminal code) they were acknowledging and accepting that crime was going to happen anyway, and at least they were trying to do something to control part of it. If their code resulted in fewer deaths, they could argue, wouldn't that be a good thing?

And what about those kids I spoke to in East English Village, who had told me how they had resorted to robbery just to *eat*? Robo and Brannock had both expressed empathy with their situation.

Robberies were going to happen regardless of a code, and sometimes victims were killed for no other reason than 'because'. So in this respect, was the code such a bad thing, if it was actually followed? Or are we, by accepting New Era's 'street code', legitimising and normalising the activities of the criminals and gangs? What if kids started to think that it was okay to rob and shoot, so long as it was all done within the 'code', created for them by the adults?

'Yes, I shot him, but I did it in a private place, so that must be okay.'

'Yes, I deal drugs, but only to middle-aged men, so that's okay.'

'Yes, I robbed him of all his money, but I didn't kill him afterwards.'

Whispers was unimpressed with New Era Detroit and considered them to be just another gang. The media attention they had gained had given them 'some juice', he told me. 'So now they are looked at like a community organisation,' he said.

When speaking to Fox News, Chief Craig called New Era Detroit 'well meaning' but went on to say, 'The code addresses the safe zones or neutral zones where we don't shoot. Well, what about just no shooting, period?'

*

Brannock marched into the office. 'Ah, the proper wanker has returned from England,' he said. 'Did you ride over here on your kangaroo?'

I smiled. All was back to normal. Sort of. Since my previous visit, Brannock had lost his nice, private office and had been relegated to a much smaller one. It was about a quarter the size of his old office and it made his huge TV computer screen look even more gigantic and ridiculous.

'What happened?' I asked.

'Since you were last here, Ceasefire has spread into the west side of Detroit,' he told me. 'So there have been a few changes.'

With Ceasefire pushing out west, Gang Intel had also grown, and there was now a separate office dealing with that side of the city. Casper had been moved over to that team, as the area they policed was largely Hispanic, and he could put his Spanish to good use. The department had also decided that Gang Intel needed a lieutenant to oversee things, now that the unit was that much bigger – hence Brannock's new digs.

The arrival of a lieutenant had brought a new feel to the office, as the presence of a supervisor often did. It seemed a bit quieter, dryer, more regulated. The office now had a morning roll-call at 11 a.m., and although there was still some flexibility for the hardworking officers, it just didn't seem as easy-going as it once had. Hunter had told me previously how he believed having a lieutenant in the office would smother Brannock's creativity. I wondered if he would now be proved right.

There were a few other changes, as well. AJ, for instance, had left the unit and transferred to the 9th Precinct. A number of other officers were on furlough (leave), including Robo, which also accounted for why the office was a little quieter. This was not because Robo was particularly loud, but because Brannock was temporarily without his sparring partner.

Reef was still off sick but he had responded well to his treatment in Texas, and was now back at home with his family, recovering. In time, he would become well enough to return to work.

Hollywood had ended up having some problems, after I had left. There had been an incident where a Surenos gang member had been shot dead by police. Hollywood had spent a number of years working in Southwest Detroit, and as he was so well known by the Hispanic gangs, he had been put up as the cop who had killed the gang member. The truth was, Hollywood had been at home that day and had nothing to do with it. Regardless, he had been 'green-lighted', meaning it was authorised for the gang to kill him on the spot. Two gang members from Central America came to Detroit to carry out the hit on Hollywood but they were caught before they had the opportunity.

Brannock, in his usual, caring way, had pinned a sign on the door to Hollywood's office. Written in Spanish, the sign – complete with an arrow pointing into the room – when translated read: *Surenos, Hollywood can be found in here.*

Hollywood was blasé about the whole affair, however.

'Am I in constant fear? No,' he told me, when I asked him about it. 'I'm not going to live my life like that. God forbid if it does happen, if they killed me – and this is going to sound cheesy – I'm good with God. That's how I look at it.'

There had been some developments out on the streets too. Davontae Sanford had been released from prison after serving eight years for a quadruple murder he didn't commit. The efforts of his family, lawyers and supporters to clear his name had finally paid off. Vincent Smothers' admissions to the killings, along with other evidence including the confession by the Detroit Homicide Commander James Tolbert that *he* had drawn the plan of the Runyon house and not Davontae, resulted in Wayne Circuit Judge Brian Sullivan finally releasing Davontae.

Following Tolbert's admission, the Michigan State Police had submitted a warrant to the Wayne County prosecutor's office but despite the evidence, the prosecutor Kym Worth, who had originally called for the Runyon case to be re-investigated by the state police, decided against charging him with perjury.

The armed guy who had come up to Brannock, Robo and myself on Lenox had been given something called HYTA – Holmes Youthful Trainee Act. Effectively, it meant that he had pled guilty, and in return was given probation, with the offence kept out of public record so as not to hinder any future career prospects, as he wouldn't need to reveal that he had a criminal conviction. HYTA is a programme open to 17-24-year-olds, although not everyone was happy about it. A number of cops complained that the system was abused and that some offenders were given HYTA over and over again.

Along with Timmy Soto and Nicole O'Neill, a third suspect in the case of firefighter David Madrigal's murder had been arrested: 19-year-old Christian Rasnick was accused of being with Soto and O'Neill when they had gone to rob Madrigal at his home. All three were charged with the homicide, but after preliminary hearings, the judge – despite calling all three 'scum' – threw out the homicide charges against O'Neill and Rasnick. Soto alone was to face trial for the murder, which was scheduled for later in the year.

The Ceasefire programme suffered a setback after one of its kids had murdered his uncle. Brannock had attended the scene in the 9th Precinct – and had found the uncle's body in the hallway of his apartment block. The story was that the uncle had slapped the boy's mom, so in retaliation, the boy had got a gun and shot him dead.

Despite all this, Ceasefire, along with the work put in by the Gang Intelligence Unit, had delivered real results. Shootings were down by over 50% in the areas where they had been operating. This was by far the largest drop in any of the areas; the next highest had seen a drop of only 4%. Spreading the programme out to the west made perfect sense.

Brannock himself put the reduction in shootings 100% down to the work of Ceasefire. He explained how, rather than just responding to incidents, they had become more focused, actively targeting the gangs' 'shooters'.

'There's only a handful of guys that pull the trigger,' Brannock told me. 'They're the shooters in the group. Once you start eliminating those guys, the crime starts to drop, because the rest of them are thugs, but not shooters.'

'Are the shooters allocated that role, or are they just the ones that are bad enough to do it?' I asked.

'Just the ones that are bad enough to do it,' he said. 'Some are asked to step up though, and they may be willing to do it, but they are actually soft, one-on-one.'

He told me about a Ceasefire kid who had been part of Hobsquad. As the gang's shooters were being removed by the Ceasefire programme, the gang's younger members were told to start 'pulling their weight' – to go out and rob and shoot. The kid Brannock was talking about didn't want any part in it and called one of the Ceasefire mentors for help.

'He was just a groupie,' Brannock told me. 'He wasn't going to be *that* guy who pulled the trigger. He was an internet gangster. A social media gangster.'

Brannock told me that Ceasefire was 'thinning the herd' through 'focused enforcement' on the gangs, and that it was having a real effect.

I thought about the work that Jermaine Tilmon and the other mentors working with Ceasefire had been doing. These men – these desperately needed father figures – had managed to reach out to many of the kids who were involved in gangs or just trying to survive in the neighbourhoods. They had steered many away from crime and gang-life, and possibly prison and even death.

Best of all though – at least in how I saw it – was that the mentors were working together with the Detroit police and the cops of Gang Intel. It needed both parties – police officers and former criminals – to be willing to move beyond their own histories and their own prejudices, so that they were able to work together for the greater good. Their two-pronged approach – the mentors tapping into the kids, helping them to break away from their former lives, together with the pro-active work and reactive investigations of the officers – made for a pretty good system. At serious crime scenes, whilst the cops were handling the things that they needed to deal with, such as suspects, evidence, etc., the mentors could be on hand, mixing with the community, calming tensions and supporting those who were grieving.

A few days later I would see this working relationship put to use once again, but during the most tragic of incidents.

*

Brannock was keen to get back out on the streets so that we could compare the differences between the summer and the winter. Scrappy and Hollywood decided to come with us. In the yard I looked for Brannock's black Jeep Cherokee but couldn't see it. Instead we walked towards a silver Dodge Charger. This was another change. Brannock had lost his 4x4.

'I'd gone over the lease mileage limit, so they sent it back,' he told me. 'Now I have to drive this Charger.'

'This was my fucking car,' Scrappy grumbled.

'Yeah? Well, now it's my fucking car,' Brannock told him, switching the air-con as high as it would go.

As we got ready to move, another officer pulled into the base, driving a Ford Mustang.

'Now that's a real *American* car, right there,' Brannock said, turning to me with a teasing grin.

'Yeah, fuck your little rice-burning bullshit English cars!' Scrappy said. 'That's real Detroit America!'

'That's American muscle right there, son,' Brannock added.

'Yeah, because American cars have such a good reputation around the world,' I replied, having a friendly dig back at them.

'You know nothing about that style of vehicle,' Brannock said. 'That's red, white and blue right there. Screamin' Eagles!'

'Do you even know what that is?' Scrappy asked Brannock.

'What?' Brannock asked.

281

'Screaming Eagles,' Scrappy said.

'Yeah, isn't it the fighter jets?'

'No, you fucking idiot! It's 101st Airborne.'

'That's what I said!'

'No, you didn't; you said fighter jets. 101st Airborne are paratroopers, you fucking idiot!'

'Same thing!'

'You're a special kind of stupid,' Hollywood told him.

Brannock grinned, and we pulled away from the yard.

Almost as soon as we left the base, Brannock pointed out a telephone pole on East Davison Street. 'That's a new post,' he told me. 'A couple of months after you left, Robo drove her car into the old one. She destroyed the post and destroyed her car.'

'What happened? Did she skid on the ice?' I asked.

'No, someone swerved in front of her and as she moved out of the way, she hit the post.'

'Is she okay?'

'Yes. Unfortunately.'

Ahead of us, red lights were flashing and barriers were dropping down across the street. The freight train was coming. I could practically feel Brannock's blood pressure rising.

'This fucking train!' Brannock screamed. 'I'm gonna shoot this fucking train!'

I smiled to myself. Some things were definitely still the same.

*

The residential streets of Detroit were completely transformed from what I had seen during the winter. With the heat of the summer, trees, grass, plants and shrubs had exploded in an orgy of super-sized growth. Houses that were once naked and exposed to the ice and wind were now swallowed up and enveloped by the deep-green wilderness. Many of the vacos were completely hidden behind crazy tangles of branches, leaves and tall grass, and the plots looked like enormous, house-sized bushes.

If the water had been left on in the vacos – or had been left leaking – small, plot-sized swamps would appear. Entire streets looked like rows of messy woodland and it was impossible to make out any houses until you were level with them. Many of the roads were also lost, hidden under layers of grass and weeds that had sprouted through the countless cracks in the tarmac.

'Welcome to the forest,' Brannock said.

As we turned a corner, an old black man was mowing his small lawn at the front of his tidy little bungalow. Everything else around him was overgrown, out-of-control and wild. It was the oddest sight – a lone square of civilisation in an otherwise untamed environment. Around another corner, a dazzling rainbow arched across a neighbourhood crossroad; someone had illegally opened a fire hydrant, and tall jets of water were reaching into the air as kids splashed with delight in the deep, cooling pools of water it had created.

'I once heard a guy in the neighbourhood call this a "ghetto carwash",' Brannock told me. He turned the wipers on and we rolled slowly through the spurting water.

Further along the street, I watched as a bunch of kids rushed towards an ice-cream truck. The truck was playing a warped rendition of 'She'll Be Coming 'Round the Mountain' over a busted speaker. It was like no ice-cream truck I had ever seen before in my life. The vehicle was tatty and severely run-down, with fading, poorly painted cartoon characters dotted around its rusting body. The windows were mostly cracked or smashed and each had metal grills covering them. It was like an ice-cream truck from a nightmare. The sort of thing Banksy might come up with.

Around another corner, Brannock slowed to stare at a tree stump. The naked stump, like the vacant house it was in front of, was ruined and barely standing. It looked like a shattered tree on the battlefields of the Somme. Dead, diseased or damaged trees are common in Detroit, and the city has actually been busy removing and replacing literally thousands of them.

We continued on until Brannock came to a stop outside a small brick house. Sat out on the front porch were a middle-aged black couple and three young kids, who I guessed were their grandchildren. Lying on the grass, staring up at us, was a dirty but muscular, foaming-at-the-mouth, mean-as-fuck-looking dog. This was the reason Brannock had stopped.

'Is that dog full-blooded?' Brannock asked the woman.

'Yes, she is,' she replied.

I turned to Scrappy. 'What sort of dog is that?' I asked.

'That's a Presa Canario. It's a type of Mastiff,' he told me.

'She's pretty,' Brannock called out to the woman.

Now, if there's one thing that fucking dog wasn't, it was pretty. Then, to my horror, Brannock started to whistle at the dog, calling it over to the car. The dog slowly lifted its giant head from the grass, and a gallon of foamy drool slipped down from its huge open jaws. Then it hauled itself up and edged towards us.

'Bloody hell! Would you at least put the windows up!' I said. All of the windows in the car were fully down.

Brannock leant his hand out and started to rub the top of the dog's enormous head. 'Hey! Hey, what's up, buddy?' he said, in a soft, soppy voice. 'Oh hey, you're pretty!'

'Why are you stroking it?' I asked, horrified.

'It's filthy,' Hollywood added.

'It looks fucking rabid,' I told him.

'It's a dog!' Brannock said.

'It looks like a killer,' I said.

'I've got a gun. I'll Glock that motherfucker to death,' Brannock said. 'Besides, that dog is no killer. You've got to know your dogs if you work in the 'hood. If the dog's wagging its tail, and he's looking at you like he wants to give you a blowjob, that means you can pet 'em.'

Bored of Brannock's petting, the dog sauntered off back to its owners.

'That dog looked insane,' I said.

'No, it wasn't. That dog was fucking beautiful,' Brannock said.

'It wasn't exactly a Basset hound, was it?'

'You're a fucking sissy,' Brannock told me.

As we pulled away from the house, he brought all of the windows back up and switched on the air-con.

Two blocks further on, Brannock spotted another dog and he slowed the car down.

'That looks like a pit bull,' I said. 'Don't you bring the windows …'

But it was already too late. The windows were all down and Brannock was whistling at the dog.

'That dog is giving me crazy eyes!' I said.

'His tongue is hanging out,' Brannock said.

'Yeah, but his tail ain't wagging.'

Brannock brought the windows back up, called me 'a little bitch', and drove away.

As we lost ourselves in the warrens and corridors of dense greenery, I began to spot the occasional young black man walking slowly along the broken streets. Some watched us nonchalantly, too hot to be bothered by our presence. Sometimes a man would raise a hand or a couple of fingers – a sign that if we wanted to buy drugs, he could help, although there was always a chance that they would rob you, or worse.

'They don't like to rob too many people though,' Brannock said. 'It's bad for business.'

Over the police radio, calls were coming out for various incidents around the city. Most sounded serious, and in many other towns and cities, they would have warranted a turning up of the radio volume, along with a concerned or interested look, but Brannock, Scrappy and Hollywood didn't seem in the least bit troubled.

'*Regent and Rossini, four persons with weapons,*' the dispatcher called over the radio. '*Regent and Rossini, persons with weapons. Female caller states there is a car with four males inside, one hanging out the back window holding a gun.*'

Brannock leaned forward and turned the volume down. 'Mick, have you finished writing that book about me yet?' he asked.

'Not yet,' I told him.

'I'll buy a copy of your book, Mick,' Hollywood said.

'I ain't buying shit,' Brannock said. 'I don't have to; I live this shit every day.'

We drove slowly through the long narrow streets, which were practically melting in the sweltering heat. Some of the streets, thick with foliage and tangled trees, had just a single vacant house left standing on them. Yet we were just a few blocks to the west of East English Village, with its large, beautifully restored homes that some out-of-towners were buying and moving to.

In some of the more populated backstreets we saw uniformed officers with booster cars, 'shaking guys down', searching them for drugs. People were out on the streets, hustling, selling dope and trying to make some money.

We drove towards a white SUV which had pulled up at the side of a road. The car was large and clean and had Georgia plates – a long way from Michigan. We rolled slowly by and turned to look at the driver. He was a white man in his forties, sporting a well-trimmed goatee beard and a pair of wraparound shades. Sitting next to him was a young black woman, perhaps just out of her teens.

'The girls show people where to get the heroin,' Brannock said. 'Then they give them a blowjob or whatever the deal is, in exchange for some of the drugs. They're probably shooting heroin now, that's why they're both looking down.'

'*Units, we need your help here. Shots in progress, shots fired,*' the dispatcher called over the radio. '*Caller said a shot went through her bedroom window.*'

As uniform units were dealing with the calls, there was little for us to do, and the conversation in the car turned to food, and for some reason, English and German sausages.

'I don't like Bratwurst,' Brannock said.

'Is sausage a big part of the English diet?' Scrappy asked. 'Bangers and Mash?'

'It is,' I said.

'I like French Fries,' Hollywood said. 'Or as I like to call them: American Fries. Freedom Fries.'

Brannock burst out laughing. 'Freedom Fries!' he shrieked. 'Screamin' fuckin' eagles!'

As we continued to drive around, we began to see young women – white and black – strolling along the centre of the narrow streets. They all wore ill-fitting, tight, revealing clothes. The track-marks and infected lumps from countless injections of heroin showed up clearly on their arms, chests, body and legs. They were malnourished, and appeared wasted on drugs; stumbling and lurching like zombies along the baking, forested streets, with no real consciousness of where they were or what they were doing.

'Pull alongside this girl,' Scrappy told Brannock, as we approached a skinny white woman. She wore a grubby yellow cotton vest and a tiny pair of pink flannel shorts. Her eyes were covered with cheap, oversized plastic sunglasses. She was staggering down the middle of the street, the sun beating down on her abused, broken body.

Scrappy brought down his window. 'Hey, what's up, girl?' he asked.

She smiled awkwardly and I noticed that the bottom part of her face, around her chin and mouth, was heavily scarred, like she had been burnt in a fire. She didn't say anything but just stared at us, swaying a little.

'You okay out here?' Scrappy asked.

'Yeah,' she said slowly.

'How did you get like this?' Scrappy asked. His question was one of gentle concern rather than judgement.

'Just how it is,' she said. 'I got off the drugs for about a year but I ended up back here.' She shrugged her bony shoulders and continued on her way, looking for someone who wanted a $10 blowjob, so that she could get her next fix.

A couple of overweight black guys – the only other people on the street – had stopped to watch us talking to the woman, perhaps looking to see if we were after some dope. As the woman walked away, the men turned and continued along their own path.

We drove on. A few people were sat on the front steps of houses or slumped in tatty chairs and old couches, on half-collapsed porches, following us with their eyes as we cruised through the streets in our air-conditioned Dodge. A brick house with boarded-up windows had a hand-painted sign outside: *For sale $8,000 or nearest offer.* Even at that price, it seemed too much. There were only three other houses on the entire street and just one of them looked occupied.

'I don't know what happened down here but this area just got decimated,' Brannock said, as we drove along the streets. 'Scrappy, what happened down here?'

'A bomb,' Scrappy said. Although he was joking, his answer fitted the outlook.

Along another street we saw a house with only three standing walls and a roof that had completely fallen in. It looked as though there had been a huge explosion. Outside the pile of rubble, there was a sign: *For sale. Serious offers only.*

'Honey, we're home!' Brannock said.

'Here you go, Mick,' Scrappy said. 'Here's that property you wanted. Your own little piece of Detroit.'

'I'll claim it for the Queen,' I said.

Over the radio, another call came out, this time to a shooting on the west side. A young man had been shot but he had survived and run to a party store for help, on Joy Road. The shooting appeared to be gang-related, so we made our way there.

Two police units were parked outside the entrance to the party store – a windowless corner building on Joy and Vaughan. The shooting victim had already been taken away to hospital, so we drove down a couple of blocks to Stout Street, to look at the vaco where the shooting had taken place. The vaco was the usual dirty-white bungalow with a missing door and a bunch of smashed windows.

The shooting had taken place in the back yard and we looked about for spent shell casings. We found a number of them hidden amongst the tall grass, but they were rusted and old – previous shots, fired for previous reasons. Then, sitting on an old piece of wooden board, we saw a large, shiny brass casing. Scrappy lifted it with the end of a pen, to ensure he didn't contaminate it with his fingerprints.

'That's a big-ass case,' Brannock said, leaning in for a closer look.

'It's a forty-four,' Scrappy said. He checked the details online, on his phone. 'It's a round for a Magnum but it can be fired from a Desert Eagle, which would explain why it's been ejected from the gun.' A Magnum, being a revolver, wouldn't have ejected the case.

A west side gang detective walked over.

'What's the story?' Brannock asked.

The detective suggested we move into the shade of a tall tree, where he told us what he knew. The victim of the shooting was a man in his mid-twenties. He had come to the location to pay another man some money that he owed him. When he arrived, there were a bunch of men there to meet him. The detective believed the men were a Joy Road gang. They accused the young guy of previously breaking into a house and stealing a gun. Then one of the men opened fire, shooting at him. One round grazed him but another round went into his arm, before exiting and hitting one of his nipples, taking part of it off. The victim fled, running to the party store, where he had asked for help.

A black lady in her late sixties, with grey hair and a loose-fitting pink vest top, approached us.

'Hello, ma'am,' the detective said. 'Do you have some information for us?'

'No, I just wanted to see what y'all doing.'

'So you walked all the way down here and you don't have no information for us?' he said playfully.

'Somebody was just shot here, ma'am,' Scrappy told her. 'Did you hear anything?'

'I hear gunshots around here every night!' she said.

'But what about today?'

'There were maybe four shots fired. They was very loud but I didn't see nothing,' she said, and she wandered back along the street, towards her house.

Another woman shuffled past us. 'Joy Road should be called Misery Road,' she said, her voice emotionless.

As the shooting had happened on the west side, the newly-formed west side Gang Intel Unit took the case. Scrappy and Hollywood wanted to remain at the scene, to talk with the other detectives, so I left with Brannock, who had plans to drive over to the nearby neighbourhood of Brightmoor. He had worked the area in the mid-1990s and he was keen to find out what had become of it.

He was shocked by what he saw.

16

Brightmoor

'Jesus!' Brannock said, as we drove along a street called Chapel. 'What happened to this place?'

'Detroit happened,' I said. It was a corny, predictable line, but absolutely correct.

The long narrow streets were almost completely hidden in the fields of tall grass and forests of untamed trees. Silence hung in the air. It was like driving along farm tracks. You would never guess that this area had once consisted of vibrant neighbourhoods, where families had lived and kids had grown up.

'This was all houses once!' Brannock said. 'I mean, this is crazy to me. You do believe me, don't you? There really were houses here – you can still see some of the driveways.'

I believed him. Every now and then I would spot a small uncovered patch of broken concrete or a long-redundant fire hydrant – the only evidence that houses had once lined these streets.

As we cruised along one of the roads, I noticed a hand-painted wooden sign, nailed to a post. *Dumpers will be shot* it warned.

'Dumpers?' I asked.

'People dumping their trash and shit,' Brannock said.

Would it make any difference if they did? I thought.

Over the police radio, there was a call to 'shots in progress'.

'This is Winston Street. I had a double-homicide at this house over here a few years back,' Brannock told me. 'Two white boys.'

He slowed the car down and stopped outside a grimy, cream-coloured wooden bungalow on another street where nature had taken over. The house was rundown and uncared-for, and there were clear signs of fire damage.

Brannock stared over at the house for a moment. Then he told me what had happened.

'These were some black guys that were staying at this house; they were selling dope out of it. One of the white boys went to school with one of the black kids that stayed here. The black kid owed the white kid some money, but he didn't want to pay him. So the black kids got the white kids in this house and tied them to some chairs and beat them. Then they took them in a van from here and drove them to Central District, close to downtown. Then they killed them. They beat them and then they shot them.'

Brannock pulled out his phone and located the images he had taken at the scene where the boys were found. I looked at their bloody corpses. Next to one of the bodies was some brain matter.

'They shot them in the head?' I asked.

'Yeah.'

Brannock scrolled through the images.

'Afterwards, the black guys painted the inside of the house,' he told me. 'And they burned the carpet in the backyard. There's a huge backyard. It had a pool and a deck at one time. It looked like a real nice house. Want to take a look?'

We stepped out of the car and walked over to the house, went through an open gate and into the backyard. It looked like a building site or a dump. There was a huge pile of burnt wood, broken plaster and old insulation material. Some of the windows at the back were boarded up but the patio doors were wide open.

'Because they had beaten them in the house, there was blood on the carpet, so they took it all out and set fire to it here, in the backyard. When we got here, the carpet was still on fire,'

Brannock told me. 'The guys ran out the back as we pulled up to execute the search warrant.'

'How did you find out about them?' I asked.

'Someone snitched on them.'

We stepped through the open patio door. The inside of the house was severely fire damaged. The walls were black and some walls were missing altogether. In some of the rooms the ceiling had collapsed, and there was plaster and insulation scattered around the bare wooden floors. There was no furniture and no sign that anyone had ever lived here apart from a barely visible, fire-blackened, stencilled word – *Welcome* – on the wall in the small entrance hall.

We stood in the front room.

'This is where they tied them to the chairs and beat them,' Brannock told me. 'So like I said, they stripped out all the carpet and then they painted the room, because there was blood-splatter all over the walls. When we got in here, the paint was wet to the touch. But at the top, where the wall meets the ceiling, you could still see the blood. There was also a sheet that had blood on it and we ended up taking that for evidence. They didn't have enough time to finish cleaning it up before we got here.'

'Who set fire to the house?' I asked.

'After the investigation, someone just came in and burnt it up.'

No one knew who had committed the arson. Some suspected the victims' families but it could just as well have been local residents, people connected to the murderers, or even bored kids. It truly was a house of horrors and it felt eerie, standing in the spot where the boys had been beaten before being dragged away to their deaths.

'You've seen and dealt with a lot of horrible shit,' I said to Brannock as we walked back to the car. 'Do you think it's affected you? Are you different to how you used to be, before you got on the job?'

Brannock scratched his head and thought about this question for a moment, before saying, 'There was something always wrong with me!'

Continuing along the empty streets, we saw a wall that was covered in gang graffiti. Brannock slowed down to take a look, as it was important to know who was making their mark in the area. Some of the graffiti had been crossed out – literally with an X sprayed over the gang names. It was a dangerous thing to do. Gangs took it as a serious, personal insult and a challenge to their reputation. Crossing out another gang's graffiti was the type of thing that got people killed, so seeing who was crossing out whom was another way of finding out which gangs were beefing with each other.

Sprayed on the wall in black and blue paint was a collection of words and numbers that would have been indecipherable to most people: *60s*, *CRIP*, *CIXTIES RUN it* (there was an up arrow sprayed within the letter *C*, and the *S* was made into a dollar sign); *7654* and *BGC*. The words *SIXTY*, *CIXTIES* and *60s* had all been crossed out.

Brannock explained to me what we were looking at.

'BGC is probably Brightmoor Gang Crips. See, it says 60s? That's probably an LA gang that came over here – they're called the Rollin' 60s. The Crips, in LA, they go by their block, so if you live in the 2000 block of Crenshaw, you're a Rollin' 20s. This guy that came over here was a Rollin' 60s Crip. And then see how it says Cixties, with a C and an up arrow? That's "Crips up".'

I stepped out to take some pictures and then started to stroll along the street, as Brannock followed slowly behind in the car. It felt good to walk, even if I did have an air-conditioned car with an armed guard to protect me.

I stopped to take a picture of an abandoned house that sat completely alone on a long, straight street. The small wooden building was covered in Joy Road gang graffiti. Brannock stopped the car and got out to join me.

'See, they're tagging "Joy Road" in Brightmoor, when they aren't even supposed to be up here,' Brannock said. 'So that's kind of fucked up.'

As I focused the camera I heard Brannock calling out to me in a whisper. 'Mick! Mick! Look!'

I spun around and looked over to where he was pointing. Twenty yards away, emerging from the woods and onto a field of grass, were two deer the colour of sand. They were both young bucks, their short antlers clearly visible. I had heard stories about deer returning to parts of Detroit but had never seen any until now. It was incredible. The deer paid us little attention and instead began to pull at branches and leaves, eating from the abundant vegetation. We watched them for five minutes, carefully moving forward to see how close we could get, but we pushed our luck and the deer disappeared into the dense scrub.

We climbed back in the car and continued on. At a small crossroad, hidden amongst the vegetation, I spotted a tiny white house – more a shack, really. It looked utterly derelict. On the porch were two heavily soiled, rotting pink armchairs. The floor of the porch had worn away to bare wood. The shack was like something from another century and looked as though it hadn't been lived in for decades. As we began to pass it by, I noticed a white man in his fifties opening the rickety front door and stepping out, onto the porch. He took a seat on one of the pink armchairs.

'Want to speak to him?' Brannock asked.

I did.

We pulled up outside the house and gave the man a friendly wave, to try and allay any fears he might have about two strangers approaching him. As we stepped up to the porch, Brannock showed his badge and identified himself as police.

The man was wearing soiled track pants and a torn T-shirt. On his feet he wore a pair of plastic sandals. He smelt as though he hadn't washed for a couple of weeks. But he had the most mesmerising, bright blue eyes. Amid all the desolation, they sparkled like jewels.

We explained who we were and the man seemed happy to talk to us. He told us that he had lived in Brightmoor all of his life – for fifty years. He had been in this house for sixteen of those years.

'I was a police officer at the Sixth Precinct back in '96,' Brannock told the man. 'This was all houses when I worked here. Now there are no houses over here at all!'

'Yep, they was burning the houses down like crazy here for a while,' the man said. 'I must have called 911 twenty times in the past two years, for burning houses and electrical problems – big flashes of light! I'm not getting near anything electrical. I touched 220 when I was a kid. I'm scared of electricity.'

As we had been driving through the neighbourhood, we had noticed that some of the abandoned houses had been boarded up and that the boards had been painted with colourful designs and words of hope. There were rainbows, suns, the planet Earth, hearts and stars, with the messages *Be Happy, Be Still My Soul, We Are the World*. The man explained that the city had done it in an effort to make the area look nicer.

'At least it's something,' Brannock offered.

'It looks better,' the man agreed. 'They asked me if the boards helped and I figure that people are too lazy to break into the properties now and burn them down.'

'And I take it that everything of worth has already been stolen? All the copper and stuff?' Brannock asked.

'Yeah, there were people stripping the hell out of them for a while.'

'What's it like living here now?' I asked.

'You know, you get good and bad wherever you go, but for the last couple of months I've been keeping my butt home,' the man said. 'There's too much attitude in the summer, so I try and stay away from the trouble. I watch the news every morning and there's somebody always getting shot. Some guy tried to rob me once but I told him I didn't have nothing to give. He had a gun and he nearly shot my friend because my friend had a cane and when he told us to raise our hands, my friend raised his cane! But I emptied my pockets and all I had were two halves of a cigarette and an empty cigar box. I begged him not to shoot us. I learnt around here, mostly, if you mind your own business and stay out of the wrong places, you don't do too bad. You just gotta watch yourself.'

He told us that he spent almost all his time on the west side of Detroit but had once had to go to hospital in East Detroit, for a colonoscopy. He had walked there and back, and had slept on the grass, on empty plots of land. On the east side, people had tried to rob him twice, but he warned the robbers that he would 'turn all cannibal' on them if they tried anything; after telling us this, he added that he hadn't eaten for four days. Acting crazy had saved him, and on both occasions the would-be robbers had decided to walk away.

'Do you work?' I asked.

'No, I'm not working,' he told me. 'I had six hundred and sixty pounds drop on my head, back in 2003. Mostly I just do shit around here.'

He told us that even with so few properties left, the gangs, who had been responsible for much of the devastation in the first place, still plagued the area.

His life was one I could barely imagine. Every day he got up and looked out of his rotting shack at a vanishing neighbourhood. There was little here other than deer and ghosts.

Before we left, I lifted my camera and asked the man if I could take his picture.

'No,' he said. Then he began to laugh out loud. 'I don't look photogenic any more! If I could get you a picture of me when I was younger … But I don't want none of my girlfriends associating me with this neighbourhood.'

As we returned to our car, the trees began to rustle loudly and a warm wind started to blow through Brightmoor. Trash and dirt lifted off the streets, dancing and twisting high into the air. The sky was turning platinum-grey and sheet lightning flashed above our heads.

'People are literally living in the woods,' I said. 'It must be like living in the Appalachian Mountains.'

'But this is a major metropolitan city!' Brannock added. Despite the years he had spent working the dangerous streets of Detroit, the city could still shock him.

Over the police radio there was a call to some boys setting fire to piles of paper. '*Caller says they are the same boys that had previously set the school on fire*,' the dispatcher said. '*Units to respond.*'

'This area was hit hard during the years we had Devil's Night,' Brannock said. He slowed the car to look at the remnants of a brick house. 'The only thing standing there is the fucking chimney!'

And it was. Other than the chimneystack, the 'house' was literally a pile of bricks.

We drove along Beaverland Street. There were a handful of ruins hidden amongst chaotic knots of vegetation, but mostly the street was lined with tidy family homes, with cut grass, and cars parked on clean driveways. There was even a community garden that had been planted in an otherwise derelict plot, where vegetables were growing abundantly in neat rows. These wonderful little community gardens and 'urban farms' had been springing up in various locations across the city for a few years now. There were literally hundreds of them and they were becoming increasingly popular. No one seemed to mind these local initiatives – at least not whilst the value and price of land was still so low.

'We once stopped an FBI agent on this street, who was doing surveillance on us,' Brannock said, as we continued along Beaverland.

'On you?' I asked, surprised. 'Why was he doing surveillance on you?'

'When I first got here, to the Number Six, they indicted eight officers for corruption, for stealing from the dope man and all that,' he told me. 'So, we had seen this guy following us and we stopped him. But he didn't want to identify himself as an officer or FBI agent. He was trying to hide it. But he knew that we were finding out who he was, and when we were getting him out of the car, he was scared as fuck!'

'What did he think you were going to do? Drag him out of the car and shoot him?'

'That's what I think he thought,' Brannock said. 'He thought we were going to do serious harm to him.'

Brannock drove away, heading across the busy I-96 expressway towards some built-up neighbourhoods, just to the south.

'Much of Brightmoor is gone,' he said. 'So, this is where everybody has moved to. The anchor here is the new high school. This is the new territory that some of the gangs could start to fight over, especially as this is also where the kids from RTM – Related Thru Money – all hang out.'

He stopped outside the school – Cody High – on Greenview Road, in a residential neighbourhood close to Joy Road. The school was a fairly modern-looking, three-storey brick building. Brannock described it as once being a sought-after school, but then tapped his window, pointing to some burnt-out vacos opposite.

'You would never have dreamed that this area would be like this,' he said.

The houses that lined the street opposite the school were mostly bungalows, and many still looked occupied, well-cared-for and decent, but amongst them was the occasional Detroit ruin. It would be a sad sight, I imagined, staring out of your classroom window at these wrecks.

Brannock pointed to a set of three stone steps at the side of the school building.

'I remember these steps,' he said. 'As you know, I had been in trouble for fucking cars up when I first got on the job. I was just doing stupid shit. I even got a car stuck between two poles, one time, whilst I was chasing a guy. So anyway, my sergeant gave me a newer scout car to drive, and he was like, "Do not fuck this car up!" So, I'm coming down Cathedral, and I see this kid up there by the school. It's late, he looks like he's bladed his body and I thought that he probably had a pistol on him. So, I drove up to the front of the school and he took off running, this way. He's running down here and it's dark, so I have no idea that those fucking steps are there. I jumped the scout car off those steps, although it didn't jump, obviously, like in the fucking movies, but instead it just landed and crushed the whole trunk. I started jumping up and down in the trunk, trying to push it all back together, and all I could think about was that my fucking boss was going to kill me.'

*

Other officers from Gang Intel had been staking out an address over on the east side. The address was linked to the recent shooting of a woman who worked in a nursing home in the 9th Precinct. Leaving work one evening, the woman had been approached by a man armed with a gun. He shot her twice – once in the stomach and once in the arm – but she survived and managed to get away. The gang officers had finished their stakeout and had left the area but Brannock wanted to take a look for himself, so we drove back over to the 9th Precinct.

The house was deep within the neighbourhood. By now, night had fallen and the streets were pitch black, with no lighting. It was claustrophobically dark and the heat of the day still lingered. We were now well away from all commercial businesses and there was just the occasional dim light coming from a house porch, here and there. Shadowy figures sauntered down the middle of the roads. Some were holding flashlights to see where they were going, as invisible crickets chirped in the undergrowth.

The house we were looking for was on the corner of a neighbourhood crossroad. Brannock drove quietly along the street. The eyes of wandering dogs, or other animals, glowed when the headlights of our car reflected in them.

'This is the house,' he told me.

I looked over to my right. Gathered outside a small wooden house were approximately twenty men and a handful of women. They shuffled about in the darkness, talking, drinking, dancing a little. As our car reached the junction of the crossroad, most of the people stopped what they were doing and looked over at us. A few of the men started walking towards the road. Brannock almost came to a stop but then slowly – very slowly – began to creep the car forward. We both stared out at the men, searching their faces to see if we could spot the man who had shot the nurse. In the darkness, the only faces we could see were those that had come close enough to us to be illuminated by the car headlights.

We rolled past them and continued along the narrow, suffocating road. Brannock brought up the speed slightly, but we were still moving at a slow pace; the eerie darkness made it necessary but I suspected Brannock also wanted to hear what was happening all around us, in the streets. Over the chaotic orchestra of the crickets, we could hear distant shouts, laughter and violent rap music. Brannock turned the block. Then he turned again. We were going to take another look at the busy corner we had just passed.

I began to feel a pang of nervousness. These streets had few cars driving along them. We had already made ourselves known and this had drawn a lot of attention. The streets were absolutely pitch black. Anything could happen and we wouldn't see it coming. And there would be no witnesses. Other than us – two guys in plainclothes, one of whom was unarmed – there were no other police in the area. I felt exposed and vulnerable.

As we rolled up to the junction for the second time, more men moved forward. One, wearing a heavy-looking pair of sunglasses, despite the fact we were in near total darkness, stepped off the kerb and into the road. As we rolled by, he bent down, looking into the car, with a serious, angry stare.

In these neighbourhoods, any unknown vehicle paying close attention to gangbangers and gang houses would have been of concern. The men didn't know who we were. We could be the police – two white guys in a Dodge Charger – but we could also be another gang, coming to look for trouble. It felt to me that slipping past the house a second time was inviting trouble. Even if they did think we were the police, it was no guarantee that we wouldn't be shot at.

I shuffled in my seat and felt myself slipping down a little as we drove by. A sense of relief swept over me as we moved past, away from the houses and the men.

'Let's go by again,' Brannock said.

'Fuck! *What?* Again?'

'Yeah, I want another look to see if I can spot that guy who shot the nurse.'

'They could start shooting at us!'

'Well, duck down!' Brannock said.

'This car isn't going to stop the rounds, and besides, I'm on the side that will get shot.'

'Good, then they won't shoot me!'

As we approached the corner, I felt certain that our luck was about to run out. I was convinced that I was about to be killed. But then, as we reached the crossroad, we could see that everyone had disappeared.

'Looks like we must have spooked them the second time we came by,' Bannock said.

My relief was audible.

As we drove away from the neighbourhood, he added, 'I would never do what you're doing. You must be a crazy motherfucker to come out here without a gun.'

At that moment, I was inclined to agree with him.

17

American Ruin

Friday, 15 July 2016

It was a scorching Friday afternoon and Brannock decided to celebrate the end of the working week by heading downtown to get some lunch. He wanted to take me to Lafayette's, one of the oldest and best-known Coney Island joints in the city.

As we sat eating our Coneys – hotdogs covered in chilli meat sauce – a call came out over Brannock's radio. There had been a shooting on Coram Street, a Seven Mile Bloods area in the 9th Precinct. It was just a few blocks away from where we had been the previous evening, searching for the man who had shot the nurse. As we listened to the details, a District unit started to shout over the radio, saying that they were chasing suspects on Chalmers – a street close to Coram.

'This could be related to the Coram shooting,' Brannock said, turning up the volume. Other customers continued to tuck into their Coney Dogs and paid no attention to the urgent yelling that was coming from the radio. 'We'd better head over there.'

We screamed up Gratiot towards the 9th Precinct and quickly spotted a District unit parked at the side of a road. One officer was sat inside the vehicle and a second was standing on the street. In the rear of the police car were two black men. This was the unit that had put up the chase. The stern-looking but handcuffed men in the rear of the car were the runners.

Brannock brought down his window. 'Was this chase linked to that shooting over on Coram?' he asked.

'Yeah,' the cop on the street said. 'When we turned up, people were pointing at a red car. We went after it and it just took off. It's possible that they've thrown the gun as we chased after them.'

'We'll go take a look,' Brannock told him.

We drove slowly along the route the car had taken, but with the grass so tall it would have been pure luck if we had found the gun. So instead, we made our way to Coram, to the scene of the shooting itself. It was pandemonium.

Half-a-dozen scout cars were parked at random angles across the street – three at either end of the Coram Road murder scene. Yellow police tape had been stretched across the road also, but no one seemed to be taking any notice of it. Young men and teenage girls were charging about, back and forth, screaming, shouting, crying. Older groups of women stood gathered on front porches, watching what was happening. Detroit police officers and homicide detectives were scattered around the scene, searching for any evidence that might have been dropped on the cracked tarmac, or else trying to gather and control the hordes of angry youths.

'Jesus!' Brannock said as we pulled up.

'This doesn't look good,' I said.

As we stepped out of the car, and into the crushing heat, Brannock grabbed hold of a uniformed officer and asked her what had happened. The officer explained that two young men had been play-fighting in the street but another man had then shown up and shot one of the men dead.

Young men and women were arguing with each other, like two rival families. Suddenly they all lunged forward, as if to start fighting. A couple of cops rushed over, putting themselves in between the two warring groups.

Just to the left of the fight, there was a patch of scruffy

wasteland – an old house plot. It was here that the man had been shot. He had already been rushed to hospital, but it was too late. He had died. Now all that was left were the two large groups, overcome with grief and anger.

Closer to where Brannock and I were standing, a teenage girl was walking in small circles under a large maple tree. She was pulling at her hair with her clenched fists. 'MY BROTHER! MY BROTHER!' she cried, before letting out a piercing scream. The fighting groups paid no attention to her and continued to argue.

To our right, just on the outside of the crime-scene tape, an older black lady was stood on her porch. She was smiling and laughing loudly, and she danced a little as she watched the mayhem before her. It was surreal.

A bare-chested man in his early twenties stomped towards the crying girl. The guy was shouting and screaming out obscenities, thumping himself in the chest. The girl slapped him hard, across the face.

'HE DEAD BECAUSE OF YO MOTHERFUCKERS!' she screamed at him.

A couple of nearby cops ran over to separate the pair.

'AIN'T NO NIGGA DEAD 'CAUSE OF ME!' he shouted back at her angrily. 'FUCK YOU!'

The girl lunged forward, trying to hit him some more but was held back by a female cop. Whispers and Hollywood, who had been standing nearby, then ran over to hold back the man.

'WASSUP? WASSUP? WASSUP? WASSUP? WASSUP?' he shouted at them as they pushed him back, away from the girl. 'THE FUCK Y'ALL WANNA DO? NIGGA, I'LL FIGHT EVERYBODY DOWN THERE!'

The girl and man staggered back towards the main groups, taking their argument with them. All around, various young men were quarrelling with cops, trying to push past them, trying to get through the crime-scene tape, ignoring their instructions.

'Take that uniform off and come to da 'hood without your gun, nigga!' one man spat at a cop who had stopped him from crossing into the crime scene.

A woman walked over. She dragged the guy away, telling him, 'We don't need this right now, okay?'

As he was walked away, he turned to look at the cop and said, 'Y'all should have been here instead of letting my nigga die! I wish I would get killed by the law; there wouldn't be no peaceful protest!'

The cops were at the receiving end of everyone's anger, frustration and sorrow. This was a real murder, in a real neighbourhood, in broad daylight. It was as far away from one of those slow-paced, moody TV police dramas that you could get.

As the two rival groups continued to argue and scream at each other, a tatty car drove towards the police tape. The woman driver spoke to one of the cops, who lifted up the tape so that she could drive through. I watched as she drove right alongside the arguing gangs and parked her car by the kerb. The lady then got out, opened the back door and lifted a small girl from the back seat and without a word, walked into one of the houses that appeared to be linked to one of the groups.

Then, within the groups, there was new uproar. Someone must have said something that caused both sets of people to explode. They charged at each other, brawling in the middle of the street. Every single cop around them, including Brannock and others from the Gang Intel Unit, jumped into the melee, pulling people off from one another.

A *Fox News* helicopter was now hovering above the scene, the heavy sound of the rotor blades muffling the screams and shouting.

A small band of cops once again stood between the two fighting groups. People from each side walked off, towards two houses that were four or five doors away from each other.

A woman on one of the porches was shouting at the women on the other. 'ALL YOUR KIDS LIVIN'!' she screamed out angrily. 'ALL YOUR KIDS LIVIN'!'

The young man who had been killed was her son. The women she was shouting at were apparently the family of the killer.

Up ahead I could see the bare-chested guy being handcuffed and placed into the rear of a police car.

'This is going to blow up,' Brannock said. 'This is a hotspot. I want to get this shit calmed down, otherwise there is going to be more from this.'

'Like one killing isn't enough,' Hollywood said, shaking his head.

Hunter and Casper arrived. They had gone straight to the hospital after the call had come out, and they gave us the low-down on what had happened.

It appeared that the killing had been some kind of family affair. There were two houses, where the people in each were apparently related – though it was unclear exactly how. The man who had been shot had been visiting relatives at one of the houses and had started to play-fight and 'slap box' with a young man – possibly a relation – from the other house. The play-fight was stopped after it had turned serious.

The shooter then turned up in the red car with some friends. Someone had said that the shooter was related to the second man in some way and he had got into an argument with the first man, over the fight. It was also suggested that the shooter had recently been released from prison. Someone then handed the shooter a gun. From looking at the scene, it appeared that the first man, on seeing the gun, had made a run for it, but the shooter had caught up with him a few yards further down the road. As the man ran onto an overgrown, empty plot of land next door to his family's home, the shooter fired the gun and shot him dead.

'He just shoots him with everybody out here watching,' Brannock said.

Along with everyone else in the street, the young man's mother had also been watching, and had witnessed her own son's murder. She told one of the cops that after the shots had been fired, she had seen her son's head drop backwards and she knew at that moment that he was dead.

The shooter then got back into the red car with his friends and they made off. A scout car (the one that Brannock and I had first seen) had been close by and had given chase. One of the men from the red car had then run off but was found hiding in some undergrowth, nearby. The driver had also been caught. All that was missing was the gun, which the officers from the scout car believed had been dumped during the chase.

On the ground, the casing for a .40 calibre round had been found. Hunter speculated that the shooting had started in the street and that the victim had managed to run as far as the empty plot before being hit.

At the hospital the doctors had found two gunshot wounds in the man's back, so it looked as though he had still been trying to get away as he was gunned down.

'All over slap boxing,' Casper said. 'Shit.'

Hunter too was taking in what had happened. 'Damn,' I heard him say under his breath.

The man who had been shot was 20-year-old Cedric Smith. Many of the officers in Gang Intel had known him. He had been part of the Ceasefire programme. Some officers had previously taken him out to eat or had collected him from school to drop him home, to ensure he stayed away from any trouble. It made his death that much more personal for them all.

Gradually things began to calm down. People were still wandering around and speaking loudly – 'putting on a show' was how Hollywood described it – but the fighting and arguing had stopped.

The girl who had been crying earlier, now seemed fine. She

had taken a call on her iPhone and she was literally laughing and joking with the person at the other end. 'Niggas acting crazy, crazy!' she was telling them excitedly.

Mentors from the Ceasefire programme arrived, including Jermaine Tilmon – Davontae Sanford's gentle-giant stepfather. I was glad to see him; his presence was somehow calming. He and the others approached the groups and began to speak with or listen to them. One teenage girl threw her arms around Jermaine, hugging him tightly as she sobbed. He placed his huge hands gently around her shoulders, comforting her as best he could.

As we got ready to leave, I took one last look at Jermaine and the other mentors. Whatever their past – or perhaps because of it – they were an ideal bridge between the police and the community, working to bring peace to the neighbourhoods. They were unsung and unknown outside of this sad, terrible world of Detroit gangs but they continued on, not for recognition or money but because they actually cared and because they wanted to do something to try and make things better. They brought hope where there would be none otherwise. Between them, they had helped thousands of kids – some who had left gangs and gained employment, and others who had finished school and then continued on to college.

For many others it was simpler than that: these men were the role models they had never had but whom they so desperately needed. These men, out here on the street, comforting the kids, were true heroes.

*

As we walked back towards Brannock's car, a small girl who couldn't have been more than 2 years old was yanking at the yellow police tape. She giggled excitedly as she ran around with a torn strip, pulling it behind her in the sun, like a piece of ribbon, oblivious to what it had been there for and what it had meant.

'You knew this kid that was killed?' I asked Brannock.

'Uh-huh. I've taken him home from school a couple of times. He was one of the kids that was real outspoken. He was always joking around – like the class clown. But he was a good kid.'

'And the guy that killed him, he's recently come out of prison?'

'Yep. Apparently.'

'So he'll be going back to prison.'

'For the rest of his life.'

Brannock started the engine. As he prepared to move off, an alert popped up on his phone. Activists had organised a 'Day of Rage' across a number of US cities, including Detroit, to protest against 'police violence and brutality'. Just one week before, during an earlier protest against alleged police brutality, five Dallas police officers had been shot dead and nine others injured by a black gunman who had wanted to 'kill white people, especially white police officers'. The police officers had been gunned down and murdered whilst protecting the very people who were protesting against them.

The Day of Rage protest was scheduled for later that evening. As I looked over at the girl running around with the crime-scene tape, it occurred to me that there were other things people should be protesting about. There were lots of killings and most of them had nothing to do with the police. I thought about the children and babies who had been shot over the past few months. Nobody was marching for them. Why?

*

We left the scene at Coram and went to get something to eat. Hollywood knew a good Lebanese restaurant just across the border from Detroit, in the nearby city of Dearborn.

As we made our way there, a District unit came over the radio.

They were behind a vehicle that was being driven by a man wanted for a parole violation.

Dispatch came on the air. 'Be advised, suspect is known for being armed.'

Then the District unit was in a pursuit. The car had taken off and was headed towards Grosse Point Park. Moments later, a Grosse Point Park PD and a Michigan State Police vehicle were also involved in chasing the car.

'This is turning into quite the day,' Hollywood said.

'Tonight's going to be "that night",' Brannock said. 'As soon as it gets dark, just watch. It's already started.'

The radio was buzzing. All the calls seemed to be for either 'shots fired' or 'shooting in progress', and later that evening there would be another killing in Detroit – at Joy Road, just a few blocks down from where we had been earlier that week.

'Jermaine was really upset about Cedric,' Brannock said, turning to Hollywood.

'It must be terrible,' Hollywood said. 'You get to know these kids, you help them, you see them turning their lives around and they end up getting killed anyway.'

We looked out at the steamy decay in a tired silence. For Gang Intel, another busy season of shootings and murder had begun.

*

There is a tragic postscript to this story. In the early hours of 3 November 2016, Jermaine Tilmon was shot dead. He was unarmed and had his hands in the air. Despite this, his killer, who apparently had beef with Jermaine going back many years, shot him anyway. Jermaine Tilmon was a humble, gentle man. I was deeply saddened when I found out about his death.

I told myself that this is what happens when a city like Detroit becomes part of your life; you lose people. Probably everybody who had a stake in these neighbourhoods had lost someone they cared about. Whether it was a family member, a friend or a colleague, sooner or later someone you knew would be killed.

Though I had barely known him, Jermaine Tilmon had made a huge impact on me. He was the type of man that you could meet once and come away feeling that you had made a friend for life. He didn't deserve to die the way he did and his death was a massive loss for everybody who knew him – and also for those who didn't. He was a good man and yet there were no large, loud protests about his killing; just a small, dignified candlelight vigil held by his family and friends.

Speramus Meliora.

We hope for better things.

Afterwards …

Since writing this book, there have been significant developments in America around the issues of guns and gun control. Following a mass shooting that resulted in the deaths of 14 students and 3 staff members at Marjory Stoneman Douglas High School in Parkland, Florida, in February 2018, new, vocal young leaders have emerged. Hundreds of thousands of students have held 'walkouts' from school, and they are forming a significant block against the National Rifle Association (NRA) as well as against senators and businesses that support the NRA. And their efforts are having an effect.

There has been criticism of these youngsters, including some by those who see them as a serious threat to their Second Amendment rights 'to keep and bear arms'. They have been accused of being paid-for 'crisis actors' and have received abuse and even death threats. And a different type of criticism has come from some who question why it has taken the incident in Parkland for people to really take notice of what many children and families in poor cities and neighbourhoods have been dealing with for decades.

The Parkland survivors have started a movement called March for Our Lives. Other groups too, have emerged or else have seen their support grow, such as Everytown for Gun Safety, and Never Again.

The NRA saw its own increase in support, with a tripling of monetary donations in the month following the Parkland shooting.

A few weeks after the attack, it was estimated that up to 800,000 people marched on Washington DC, calling for tighter gun controls, with hundreds of other marches held elsewhere in America and around the world. In 2018, retired Lieutenant Colonel Oliver North was made president of the NRA. During an interview with The Washington Times, North described the gun control activism following the Parkland shooting as 'civil terrorism' and compared the criticism and attacks on the NRA to 'Jim Crow', a time when blacks were segregated and thousands were lynched and murdered.

*

Although it took 50 years to get going, the changes in Detroit are now happening at such a rapid speed that, since the events related in this book, much has been transformed in the city. New hotels, apartment buildings and restaurants are all opening up downtown. In September 2017, Little Caesars Arena opened in midtown Detroit and hosts both the Detroit Red Wings NHL ice hockey team and the Detroit Pistons NBA basketball team. A new velodrome has been built and there's also been talk of securing a Major League Soccer franchise, which would likely need its own stadium.

Over the years, Detroit has made 7 bids for the summer Olympic games and lost out each time – an Olympic 'record' all of its own. Although the city still has a way to go, it wouldn't surprise me if some time in the future, Detroit's Olympic dreams are finally realised. I truly hope they are.

To add to this wave of renewed positivity, in 2018 there was a net increase in property values in Detroit. The average home is now worth somewhere around $40,000.

And for the first time in four decades, the City of Detroit regained full control of its government operations, having finally emerged from state oversight.

*

Here is some more good news. In 2017, violent crime dropped significantly, with around 5,000 fewer crimes than the previous year. The murder rate also dropped, from 302 homicides in 2016 to 267 in 2017. Chief Craig cited Project Green Light – where businesses display a green light to indicate that the premises are being monitored live by the police via CCTV – and Operation Ceasefire as being big factors in the decrease.

*

As for the police officers in this book, Assistant Chief of Police Steve Dolunt retired from the department in 2017 after giving the city 31 years service. I, and many others, consider his departure a great loss, not only for the Detroit Police Department but also the city itself. Dolunt is without doubt one of the finest – and funniest – senior officers I have ever met.

Hollywood, Casper, Scrappy, Kap and Reef remain with Gang Intel, whilst others have either left the unit or left the department altogether. Brannock now runs a special ops unit from the 10th Precinct. Robo teaches new recruits at the Detroit Police Academy. Cooter has transferred to the Detroit Police Mounted Division. Whispers has been promoted to sergeant and works from the 5th Precinct. Joe has retired from the police completely. Hunter has also retired, and despite plans to move to Atlanta, he now works as a university campus cop in Michigan.

Regarding the criminals in this book, Nicole O'Neill and Christian Rasnick had their murder charge for the killing of firefighter David Madrigal dropped earlier in the year. However, in August 2016 another judge reinstated the murder charge against them. Timmy Soto, Nicole O'Neill and Christian Rasnick were then each convicted for their parts in the killing. Soto pleaded guilty to felony murder and felony firearm and was sentenced to 40 to 80 years in prison. Christian Rasnick pleaded guilty to second-degree murder and was handed a sentence of between 10 and 30 years. O'Neill also pleaded guilty to second-degree murder and was sentenced to between 20 and 50 years in prison.

Whilst being interrogated by homicide detectives, Soto claimed that Madrigal, whom he knew, had invited him to his house for a drink. Whilst there, Madrigal had touched O'Neill inappropriately, which had upset Soto. As Madrigal dozed off, Soto had picked up a weight and struck him.

Rasnick had a slightly different version of events, however, stating that Soto and O'Neill had picked him up with the intention of robbing Madrigal. Part of the plan was for O'Neill to flirt with Madrigal. Whilst at the house, Madrigal had fallen asleep and Soto encouraged Rasnick to strike him. Rasnick didn't want to hit a sleeping man, so Soto had struck Madrigal with the weight, instead.

The man who had shot dead Cedric Smith on Coram Street was 29-year-old Travis Wilson. Wilson was convicted of second-degree murder and received a sentence of 35 to 60 years imprisonment.

A 36-year-old man named Floyd Nix was convicted in October 2017 for the murder of Jermaine Tilmon. Nix was sentenced to between 25 and 60 years for second-degree murder and related offences.

Ten months after Jermaine Tilmon was murdered, his stepson, Davontae Sanford, was shot at the Martin Luther King Apartments. The bullet struck Sanford in the leg but he survived and managed to escape his attackers.

In January 2018, Davontae was awarded over $400,000 by the State of Michigan for his wrongful conviction of the Runyon Street murders. At the time of writing, he had a lawsuit pending against the Detroit Police.

In March 2018, Sanford made headlines again, after he was arrested in Arizona, where he had apparently moved in a bid to start a new life. Police there stated that Sanford and others had been shooting an AR-15 at nearby houses, causing adults and children to run for their lives. Sanford claims that he was shooting a legally held weapon into the direction of local mountains and not at houses or people. In October 2018, Sanford pleaded guilty to 'reckless discharge of a firearm'.

In 2017 it was reported that Vincent Smothers, who had confessed to the Runyon murders, had confessed to yet another killing. Thelonious Searcy had been handed a life sentence for the 2004 murder of Jamal Segars. Upon hearing about Searcy's sentence, Smothers wrote to him, confessing that he had committed the murder. The matter is still ongoing and Thelonious Searcy remains in prison.

*

In 2018 Detroit launched a nationwide campaign to attract visitors to the city. The campaign came with a new slogan: *Detroit: It's Go Time.*

Notes on American Ruin

As I mentioned earlier in the book, in 2016 the police shot around 2,000 people in America, of which just under half died. Compared to some other states, Michigan saw relatively few deaths at the hands of the police – even when population size was taken into account. In Michigan, in 2016, 13 people were killed. California, which has a population size four times that of Michigan's, saw the highest number, with 138.

In recent years, police shootings and other behaviour have come in for much scrutiny. The video of Rodney King being beaten by a group of LA police officers in 1991 resulted in rioting that led to the deaths of 55 people – and that was in the days before the Internet. With camera phones and social media, it now feels as though there is a potential 'Rodney King' video being uploaded almost daily, and the court of public opinion is quick to judge officers' actions. In the age of immediate information, people want immediate justice.

In response to criticism and allegations of wrongdoing, law enforcement is changing. Body-worn cameras are being rolled out by an increasing number of police departments. This is something that will benefit the public as well as the police. Genuine misconduct by officers can be identified whilst false allegations against them are easily dismissed. Some departments are also sending officers on de-confliction courses. As well as enhanced training for officers, there is also training for members of the public and community leaders, who are shown how officers prepare for dangerous situations, and to help them understand the split-second decisions that officers sometimes have to make.

With around 300 million guns in the United States (no-one is sure of the exact figure), it is estimated that one-third of the world's firearms are in the hands of Americans. Data from the non-profit corporation Gun Violence Archive shows that there were nearly 59,000 incidents of 'gun violence' in America in 2016, which included almost 700 children between the ages of 0-11 and over 3,100 12-17 year olds, killed or injured by guns. By the end of 2017 this figure for shot children would be topped by a further 150, and is a number that has been increasing each year.

By the end of 2016, over 17,000 people had been murdered in America, mostly by firearms. Although an increase from the previous few years, the figure is still considered low compared to the peaks of the 1980's and 1990's, when rates were in the low to mid 20,000s. And as well as those killed by intentional acts of violence, many also die through acts of suicide or firearm accidents.

But for every person that dies, many more survive, often with life changing injuries. Well over 4,000 people were shot in Chicago in 2016, for example, but just 1 in 6 died. One hospital I visited in Chicago a few years ago saw so much gun trauma I was told that the military sent their own medics there for training.

In 2016, the number of recorded homicides in Detroit saw an increase from the previous year. In 2015 there had been 295 homicides. In 2016, the city had seen 302 homicides. The FBI's own data showed that violent crime in Detroit rose by over 15% in 2016, when compared to 2015, with 13,705 violent crimes in all – a rate of 20 per 1,000 of the population. It was the highest rate of any major city and brought Detroit to the top of the nation's leader-board for violent crimes. Chief Craig disputed the FBI's figures, however, stating that the fed's were using an out-dated computer system. So whereas the FBI had recorded an increase, Detroit's own data showed a 5% *decrease* in violent crime.

However, in 2017, there was a marked drop in homicides. With 267, Detroit saw its lowest homicides figures since 1966, when there had been 214. 267 is still a large number for a city with a declining population, and it should be remembered that in 1966 Detroit had around twice the population it does now. So, when looked at per capita, the 2017 rate was around 40 homicides per 100,000 of the population against nearly 14 per 100,000 in 1966.

In 2016, when I was in Detroit researching this book, over 300 American law enforcement officers were shot. 143 officers died in the line of duty – 63 of who were shot dead. This number includes Detroit Sergeant Kenneth Steil, who was killed whilst pursuing a carjacking suspect in the 9th Precinct, and Collin Rose, a police sergeant with the Wayne State University who was shot dead in Detroit during a traffic stop (the man accused of his killing went on to shoot and wound two Detroit police officers attempting to apprehend him a few months later). Two further Detroit police officers also died on duty in 2016: Sergeant Kevin Miller, from a heart attack, and Police Officer Myron Jarrett, who was struck by a vehicle driven by a man high on crack cocaine.

In the space of just eight months, between September 2016 and April 2017, eight police officers in Detroit were shot or killed.

The National Law Enforcement Memorial in Washington DC is inscribed with the names of more than 21,500 officers who have died in the line of duty. It grows longer each year.

In 2017, Professor Philip Alston, United Nations Special Rapporteur on extreme poverty and human rights, was invited by the federal government to look at the issues of poverty in America.

Forty million Americans, including over 13 million children, were living in poverty, with around 18 million living in 'deep poverty'. Of those poor children, 36% were Hispanic. White children came second at 31%. Black children were at 24%, whilst indigenous children were at 1%. However, when the figures were looked at for just toddlers and infants, the numbers changed, with black children at 42%, Native American children at 37%, Hispanic children at 32% and white children at 14%.

The United States ranked 35th highest out of 37 countries when it came to poverty and inequality.

Professor Alston also found that the legal and criminal justice systems were being used not for the promotion of justice but as a way of generating revenue. He described it as a system that kept the poor in poverty.

His detailed report on poverty in America covers many areas and is well worth seeking out. It is available online, for anyone to read.

Professor Alston's report wasn't all doom and gloom, however. He pointed out many positives when it came to officials, volunteers and community organisations determined to tackle the nation's social problems.

I have seen much of the same in Detroit, where there are many inspiring people and worthy schemes. Many locals come together and volunteer to make their city and their neighbourhoods better places to live. "Block clubs", where residents clean up the streets and repair damage buildings. Church groups and non-profit organisations that fix-up buildings to rehouse homeless families. Even military veterans from other parts of the country, coming into the city to repair, rebuild and tidy. Scraps of land and cleared plots are turned into urban farms, where people grow fresh and healthy food. Locals – who may be poor themselves – have been known to take in the homeless and give them a hot meal and a warm place to stay on a cold night.

Many Detroiters aren't waiting for others to come and help them, and are instead doing it for themselves and for each other, all whilst crime and gunfire is erupting around them.

Acknowledgements

Writing a book like this would have been impossible without the assistance, trust and friendship of many people. I would like to start by thanking Steve Dolunt, whom I have known for as long as I have been coming to Detroit, and who has always been there to assist me in any way he could over the years. I will never be able to thank him enough and I wish him all the very best in his retirement.

Ed Brannock deserves enormous thanks too. Despite his understandable scepticism about my presence, he eventually found it in himself to accept that Dolunt was of a much higher rank than he, and that he therefore had no choice but to allow me full and unhindered access to himself and his unit. I like to think that we became friends. He may feel differently, however. Brannock, thank you so much for your friendship, your patience, your professionalism, your kindness and all of your help and assistance. This book wouldn't be what it is without you. It would contain far less swearing, for a start.

To Brannock's exceptional, first-rate crew – Robo, Hunter, Hollywood, Whispers, Casper, Joe, Cooter, Scrappy, AJ, Kap, Reef, Hype, Bowser and others who, for whatever reason didn't make it into the final cut of the book, thank you so much for the welcome you gave me. I was very quickly made to feel like one of the team and that is testimony to your openness and acceptance. Again, this book would not be what it is without you. You made my time in Detroit far more interesting and far more fun that I could ever have hoped for. Thank you all.

I would like to thank Chief Craig and the Detroit Police Department for welcoming me once again and for allowing me to examine so closely the great work that the department's brave, dedicated officers do each and every day. I am well aware of how privileged I have been. The relationship and history I have with the department and its officers is something I cherish.

Thank you to Sergeant Eren Stephens, who was there to meet me and look out for me on my very first visit to Detroit all those years ago, and who helped me see Detroit for the great city that it truly is.

Thank you to Jerry Bell for so enthusiastically opening up to me and allowing me to record your story. You have been a great contact and friend for many years, and hopefully for many more to come. Stay safe, brother.

Thank you to Rob and Tara Koch for once again giving me a place to stay in your lovely home. You are generous and kind and have always made me feel welcomed.

To all those people I spoke to in Detroit, including those who contacted me to tell me stories about their city and their lives, I thank you. Despite all the years I have been coming to the city, I am always learning something new.

To George Hunter at the *Detroit News*, thank you for your time and for sharing your knowledge about crime in the city.

Thank you to Mark Bryant at Gun Violence Archive – an extremely valuable and fascinating online resource.

Thank you to my agent Humfrey Hunter who, knowing how important Detroit is to me, encouraged me to write this book, and has been the most amazing supporter of my work.

It can be difficult to hold back when you become so close to your own work, so I must say thank you to my editor Joan Deitch, for her fantastic work at controlling my sometimes untamed ramblings.

Hello to Nathan, Jake, Evie and Dexter, and to Ethan – *meilleur jamais filleul*.

Thanks also need to be extended to my friend Ben Holland,

who has been a champion of my writing for a number of years, and my friend Jane Bussmann for support and advice.

Most of all, I would like to thank my ever-patient, incredibly understanding wife, Lisa, who has stuck by me and supported me at all times, and even enjoyed a Coney Dog with me once, in Detroit. Lisa, I love you and I am extremely fortunate to have you in my life. This book is for you.

Suggested Further Reading

Detroit:
The Last Days of Detroit – by Mark Binelli
Detroit: An American Autopsy – by Charlie LeDuff
The Detroit Riot of 1967 – by Hubert G. Locke
Once in a Great City: A Detroit Story – by David Maraniss
Detroit: A Biography – by Scott Martelle
Detroit – Wildsam Field Guides

Law/Crime:
Rise of the Warrior Cop – by Radley Balko
Locking Up Our Own: Crime and Punishment in Black America
– by James Forman, Jr.
We Are the Cops: The Real Lives of America's Police – by Michael
Matthews
Color of Law – by Richard Rothstein
Another Day in the Death of America – by Gary Younge

Online Articles:
The Hit Man's Tale – by Nadya Labi / *The New Yorker*
Death by Instagram – by Robert Snell / *The Detroit News*
Drop Dead, Detroit! – by Paige Williams / *The New Yorker*

Printed in Great Britain
by Amazon